The United States and Canada

THE AMERICAN FOREIGN POLICY LIBRARY

CRANE BRINTON, EDITOR

Gerald M. Craig

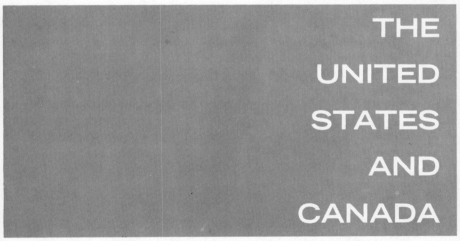

THE

UNITED

STATES

AND

CANADA

HARVARD UNIVERSITY PRESS, Cambridge, Massachusetts

1968

Editor's Note

The American Foreign Policy Library was founded some quarter of a century ago by Sumner Welles and Donald C. McKay. Mr. Welles, in the Department of State, and Professor McKay, on leave from Harvard and serving with Research and Analysis, Office of Strategic Services, had been convinced by their wartime experience of the real need for a series of studies that would be neither journalism nor professional scholarship addressed to experts in international affairs. The books were to be written by experts, not for other experts but for citizens really concerned to form enlightened opinions on matters of foreign policy. The series was, as far as possible, to be kept up to date by frequent revisions and additions. The present editor has endeavored to continue on the course set by the founders.

Gordon M. Craig's *The United States and Canada* fills a gap in the series which has too long evaded the efforts of the editors to fill it. With no nation are our relations closer than those of all kinds, from trade and travel to the arts and sciences, which we have long maintained with Canada. Professor Craig has in the following pages so successfully spelled out the nature of the problems involved in those relations that he leaves his editor little to say that is not at bottom mere repetition. He has, of course, also fulfilled one of the essentials the editors have insisted on from the beginning: he has provided the reader with a well-nourished geographical and historical account of how Canada has developed out of the earliest European contacts with what Voltaire, in one of his less prescient passages, called *quelques arpents de neige*, a few acres of snow. In view of the very great ignorance of Canadian history among Americans — we should have another appellation, like Frank Lloyd Wright's "Usonians," because, after all, Canadians also live in North

America—in view of this ignorance, Professor Craig's book should be all the more welcome.

The main difficulty of relations between the United States and Canada, which are really relations between individual Americans and individual Canadians, is that we Americans assume there are no difficulties. We simply take Canada for granted. This book makes the point well: there *are* difficulties, though not of the magnitude of those profound and far-reaching antagonisms that have grown up between the United States and the Soviet Union or between the United States and China; indeed, if you don't mind the cliché, they are no more than family difficulties. But family difficulties can be hard to clear up, especially if they are not really faced.

This is not an alarmist book. Professor Craig does not believe that trouble is brewing along those famous three thousand miles of border without a fort. He is a Canadian who specializes in United States history and has lived and studied in this country. His own country he knows well. It is a great pleasure to welcome this book in the centennial year of Canada's national union.

Peacham, Vermont   CRANE BRINTON
August 1967

Acknowledgments

I wish to thank three of my colleagues at the University of Toronto, C. P. Stacey, G. R. Cook and R. C. Brown, for reading and criticizing the manuscript. They saved me from many errors, but of course are not responsible for those that remain. I wish also to thank the University of Toronto and the Canada Council for helping me to find time and money to work on this book.

                                                    G. M. C.

Contents

The United States and Canada

I
INTRODUCTORY: SHARING A CONTINENT

1 Northern Miracle?

Canadians sometimes say that their country is a miracle of survival. Occasionally they also wonder whether the miracle will last. From the beginning of their history they have lived next door to one of the most vigorous, expansive, and powerful societies that the world has ever known, one that has pushed out its authority across a continent and one that has exerted a magnetic pull upon the minds of millions of people, even in distant places. These southern neighbors have always been at least ten times as numerous as Canadians, with corresponding economic and military weight. Nor have Canadians had a unified and positive sense of national identity with which to confront the attractions of the American Way of Life. Canadians keep worrying whether they really are different from Americans, while they go on being separate.

Moreover, the Canadian miracle is dual: a miracle within a miracle. Not only has Canada endured and grown, but within the larger entity French Canadians have survived as a distinctive group (some would say nation). This small people, numbering not many more than five million and unaided for over two hundred years by any significant recruitment through immigration, now faces three times as many English-speaking Canadians and forty times as many English-speaking North Americans. Yet they have retained their language as well as customs and institutions that clearly distinguish them from all other residents of the continent. Today they worry about whether they can resist the pressures that they feel all around them, and they are more determined than ever not only to go on surviving but to make "the French fact" in North America a positive and flourishing reality.

It is immediately clear, then, that Canadians and Americans look out upon the world with very different perspectives, despite close friendship and similar ways of life. The differences begin with contrasting historical outlooks; Americans can view their history with only the most infrequent references to Canada, but the United States is constantly to the fore in the telling of

Canadian history. No two countries are so intimately bound together, but still they look at each other from opposite ends of the telescope.

This contrast sometimes leads to irritation on the Canadian end. That few Americans have any accurate knowledge of Canadian geography, government, or society is almost an article of faith north of the border. It is generally agreed that there is usually a vague sentiment of benevolent good will toward Canada, but this feeling often seems to be close enough to condescension to produce more resentment than satisfaction. Canadians find it difficult to realize that as long as they are stable, cooperative, and rather unobtrusive neighbors, they will seldom come to the notice of Americans, who will continue to think more about trouble spots and areas of crisis. And perhaps Canadians fail to realize that there may be some real advantages in being unnoticed by so close and so powerful a neighbor.

For their part, Americans have often been genuinely upset or mystified to come suddenly upon evidences of resentment or even hostility in a people who for the most part seem to be so much like themselves. When this happens, as it often does, Americans may be tempted to think that Canadians are being perverse, or that something has suddenly gone wrong, or that troublemakers are at work. With so many problems around the world, Americans should at least be able to count on the good will and understanding of the people on the other side of the four thousand miles of undefended boundary!

Nor is it altogether easy for an American to bring Canada into focus. One can readily grasp differences that arise out of language or political tradition or religion or economic conflict or military ambition. But to his north the American finds another American country of roughly the same geographical extent but much smaller in population, wealth, and power. It stands for no distinctive social system, its people are not easily identified when they travel abroad, and only in fairly recent years have they attained full political independence. For the most part they speak English with the same kind of accent that the majority of Americans have. To be sure, a third of them have French as a mother tongue, but Americans are used to a heterogeneous ethnic scene. This northern country is a federal state, with shapeless, nonideological political parties and with legal institutions that have developed from the same origins as those in the United States. Economic practices and orthodoxies are shared, as are a whole range of religious and social institutions.

Awareness of this northern neighbor, when there is any, may prompt an American to no more than mild interest. Perhaps Canada is a rather pale reflection of the American republic, a little more sedate, a little less enterprising, which for some curious but not very important reason did not share fully in the great adventure of pursuing the American dream. Perhaps the Canadian blood was a bit too thin for so bold a task. Perhaps the northern people, oddly assorted rejects of history, were merely passed by, left on the shelf. Perhaps, finally, they will yet want to claim fuller membership in the American community. However hard he has focused, the American's view of Canada, apart from some clearly visible details, has tended to be rather opaque. What is there to see?

First, given the vast role of the United States in world affairs, an American will want to see where Canada stands in relation to his own country's defense and foreign policies. He finds that the two countries have been united in the defense of the continent by the Permanent Joint Board on Defense of 1940 and the North American Air Defense Command of 1957 as well as by many other agreements and enterprises. He learns that they became formal allies during the Second World War and that they renewed their alliance through the North Atlantic Treaty Organization of 1949. The record shows that Canada fought with the United States in the Korean War of the early 1950's and that her leaders have often gone out of their way to defend American foreign policy at the United Nations and in foreign countries. Yet an inquiring American will also discover that the tone of Canadian newspapers and of public discussion generally is more often critical than friendly with respect to the conduct of the United States on the world scene. In many areas where the United States is heavily committed, Canada offers no military assistance and often only the most tepid diplomatic support. The northern neighbor may seem to be a less reliable and less faithful ally than several more distant countries.

In trade and economic relations, however, we see a clearer and surer pattern. Here it is easiest for the American to grasp the importance of Canada to his own country, for it can be done by absorbing a few simple yet gigantic facts. In this field the interaction between the two nations has reached an unprecedented magnitude. They exchange the world's greatest volume of bilateral trade. Canadian natural resources and sources of energy have also begun to figure prominently in American economic calculations. Americans have more capital invested in Canada than in any other foreign country, with the result that strategic sectors of the northern economy are controlled or heavily influenced from the United States. (Conversely, per capita Canadian investment in the American economy is even larger.) Canadian railroads, highways, air lines, and pipelines are intimately linked with their American counterparts: in the realm of transportation and communications the border is crossed by a traffic of enormous size and complexity. The majority of Canada's unionized workers belong to organizations that have their international headquarters in the United States. There is literally no equivalent anywhere in the world, no economic and financial interrelationship between two national states that is so vast and so intricate. But the United States itself is so large and its interests now so ramified that it can carry on this continental activity with little awareness that a border is being crossed. By contrast, to Canadians it is the most important fact of economic life, but in it perils and prosperity are inextricably mixed.

Finally, an American may try to see his northern neighbor as a political and social entity, apart from considerations of foreign policy and economics. It is in this sphere that his vision is likely to be most clouded. Canada is obviously in the hemisphere, stretching across more than four thousand miles of it, yet unlike all other American states it never made an open break with its imperial mother country. Today it remains a member of the Commonwealth and does not belong to the Organization of American States. It is a monarchy in a hemisphere of republics, and many of the old ceremonial forms are carefully preserved.

In addition, the American finds that there are two kinds of Canadians. One group speaks an English which for the most part is indistinguishable (except perhaps to a speech expert) from that heard in the northern states along the border. Of British and western European origins (like Americans), English-speaking Canadians have attitudes and customs which do little to distinguish them from residents of Buffalo, Bismarck, or Bellingham. Yet it is in this group that there is the strongest opposition to the elimination of "colonial" symbols. On the other hand there are the French Canadians, who have attitudes and institutions not found elsewhere in North America and who often express their opposition to "Americanization." Yet it is this group which most strongly supports the adoption of constitutional practices and symbols that grow out of life on this continent. Clearly, Canada is an American country with a number of differences.

Again, then, we come up against the problem of perspective. The peoples of the two countries are so close to each other, their affairs are so intermingled, that it is hard for them to stand back for a clear look. Every year millions of people cross the border in each direction, with a minimum of formality and for a multitude of purposes: recreation, business, education, to search for jobs, to go to conventions, or to settle permanently. It is a vastly larger human movement than between any other two countries elsewhere on the globe. Whether their stays are short or long, Canadians and Americans usually find themselves easily at home in the other country and are rarely visible as strangers or outsiders. It is a commonplace of Canadian-American occasions and intercourse that the two peoples are not "foreigners" to each other, but instead neighbors and friends who enjoy the same games, TV programs, and tastes in foods.

It is perhaps the beginning of wisdom in Canadian-American affairs to realize that "hands across the border" talk falls very differently upon Canadian ears from American lips than does the same discourse in the reverse direction. Very often, Americans, from presidents down, have been moved to say that they did not think of Canadians as foreigners, or that the problems of the two countries were like those of a large family or one's hometown. Such well-intentioned remarks, even when coming from the most popular and respected of American spokesmen, make Canadians feel uneasy. And when a speaker's good will becomes so expansive that he wonders why there needs to be a border at all between peoples so much alike, a Canadian listener becomes downright apprehensive. He begins to wonder whether the speaker is confusing his country with another state or group of states in the Union.

In turn, such a reaction suggests an unnecessary testiness on the part of Canadians or at least an excessive concentration upon the possible consequences arising out of their proximity to the United States. Admittedly, it is hard for Canadians to escape from this preoccupation. They are but a narrow band of people strung out irregularly for some four thousand miles, most of them living very close to the American border. They might well echo the old Mexican saying: "So far from God, so near to the United States"; indeed, they are even nearer than the Mexicans, because they adjoin many heavily populated states and, for the most part, lack the defense of a different language. This immensely vigorous society is their only neighbor; they must travel thousands of miles to make contact with any other country. Small wonder, perhaps, that Canadians spend so much time worrying about the protection of their "national identity" from American influence.

Yet many Canadians are coming to see that such a preoccupation is unhealthy and unnecessary, even perhaps rather mean-spirited. It leaves out of account the exhilarating and productive gains, touching all phases of Canadian life, that have always come and still come from contact with a free, lively, and wealthy society. Unnecessary because it sees American influence where it should see the more general trends of modern life. And unhealthy because it takes attention away from the need to make an attack on Canadian problems and leads all too easily to the view that these problems cannot be solved because they originate south of the border.

There are signs of a better balance. American interest in Canada will always be sporadic and fragmented; indeed, Americans, caught up in their own vibrant life, are not noted for their readiness to devote sustained attention to any other society for its own sake. To many Americans Canada will continue to be an "unknown country," where the fishing is said to be good and the Mounties wear red coats. But Canadian studies now have a secure place in several American universities, and there are a growing number of people in government, business, and other fields who have a detailed, even expert, knowledge of Canada. And among the general public, always on the move, there are probably many hundreds of thousands who have traveled more extensively in Canada than have most Canadians. On the other side, as a valuable dividend, the recent stresses and strains upon the fabric of Canadian unity have made Canadians more interested in their own country than they have been for a long time. It has become strikingly, even brutally, clear that there are Canadian problems that only Canadians can solve. Canadians will never cease from keeping a close watch on American events and personalities, but it has come as a revelation to many of them that absorbing matters closer to home demand careful attention and imaginative treatment if the Canadian "miracle" is to endure. And if Canadians find constructive solutions to their problems, they will find that there is interest enough in what they are doing, in the United States as well as elsewhere.

II

NEIGHBOR

TO

THE

NORTH

2 The Land

First, we should begin with the water, both salt and fresh, which has always so vitally affected Canadian development from the time of the earliest explorations to the present day. Like the United States (with the inclusion of Alaska) Canada fronts on three oceans, has a lengthy fresh-water boundary, and is cut through by innumerable rivers, long and short; it has, moreover, many more lakes than are to be found below the border.

Canada is a transcontinental nation of immense geographical extent (exceeded in size only by the Soviet Union), yet an astonishingly large amount of it has direct water communication with the world beyond. It is more maritime than either the Soviet Union or China, and waterways pierce it even more than they do the United States. Few Canadians live very far from lakes or flowing streams, and in the far north there are vast bodies of water that only a handful of Canadians have seen.

Spread widely across the northern half of the continent, where meridians narrow on the way to the pole, Canada reaches out toward both Asia and Europe. Along with Alaska, its north-Pacific reaches are so near to Asia as to furnish a route whereby came many thousands of years ago the hemisphere's aboriginal population, eventually to spread down toward the other pole. And on the Atlantic side, island-hopping via Iceland and Greenland made possible Scandinavian contact with North America long before Columbus made his famous voyage.

The Atlantic approach, which provided both Canada and the United States with their effective beginnings more than a century after that voyage by Columbus, reveals how differently the two countries have fared at the hands of geography. The United States has a coherent Atlantic coast that stretches from New England to Florida. It is sharply indented, to be sure, but back of it lies an extensive coastal plain, with millions of acres of excellent agricultural land. On that plain, between the coast and the Appalachian mountains, the first Americans, long before the American Revolution, built a strong and sure base from which they later went out to conquer the continent to the west. The establishment of that powerful base in the seventeenth and eighteenth centuries is the first important fact of American history, and on it later growth depended. Canada, on the other hand, has a highly dissected Atlantic coast, without the productive plain, which does not reach above southern New England. Its Atlantic coastline is even longer than the American, but most of it is insular or peninsular, without an accessible hinterland, and the one long stretch along the mainland of the continent is made up of Labrador, the very synonym for uninhabitable barrenness. Canada's Atlantic regions look out to sea; they do not provide a base from which to move into the interior. Such a move means bypassing rather than traversing the coastal areas.

The early explorers soon found that the northern approaches to the continent readily led them much farther into its interior than did those to the south. Over four hundred years ago Jacques Cartier found the St. Lawrence, "the River of Canada," and when he reached the head of navigation, at the present city of Montreal, he was more than a thousand miles from the continent's eastern landfall in Newfoundland. His successors in the seventeenth century followed the river into the Great Lakes or up the Ottawa and soon were more thousands of miles into the interior, on their way to the Rocky Mountains, at a time when, to the south, the Appalachians had barely been explored, let alone crossed. Before the end of the eighteenth century Alexander Mackenzie had followed the northern water systems until he had reached the Arctic Ocean along the river that bears his name and had then turned west to become the first man to make an overland crossing of the continent.

And there was still another entry into the interior of the continent that long had an even stronger hold upon men's imaginations. The search for a way around North America, for the "Northwest Passage," was underway before permanent European settlements had been made north of Mexico. Waters bearing the names of Frobisher, Davis, and Baffin mark stages of this heartbreaking quest, preceding that most desolating of disappointments: Henry Hudson's discovery that the great bay was an inland sea. But if the bay did not lead to Asia, it did provide a short route to the far northwest, which the Hudson's Bay Company was using before the end of the seventeenth century. Moreover, the dream of a Northwest Passage never died. It claimed Sir John Franklin's life in the 1840's, and it was not until the beginning of the twentieth century that Roald Amundsen achieved the nearly four-hundred-year-old goal of using the Arctic to go from the Atlantic to the Pacific. Specially equipped ships of the Canadian government and American nuclear submarines have followed in the wake of the explorers. Canada is increasingly conscious of its Arctic frontage.

Finally, Canada shares with the United States a view upon the Pacific, albeit one that is somewhat restricted by the state of Alaska. These approaches were also probed by early explorers. Indeed, James Cook in the eighteenth century made a futile search for a northeast passage, and shortly afterward George Vancouver made the claim that would later give Canada her window on the western ocean. Canada is less broadly based on the Pacific than is the United States. Most activities funnel into or out of the port of Vancouver in contrast to the vast American Pacific empire stretching from Puget Sound to San Diego. But each year the central regions of Canada look a little more toward the Pacific than they used to do, and that coastal region has only begun to realize its possibilities.

Having traced Canada's watery perimeter, we should look at the most noted—or notorious—feature of its natural setting, its climate. One sure piece of knowledge everyone has about Canada: it is a northern country. Not only are winters long and cold over most parts of Canada, but the combined effects of western mountains, cold air from the Arctic, and warm air from the Gulf of Mexico make for frequent and sometimes violent changes of weather. Precipitation is uneven. The west coast receives very heavy rainfalls, as do, to a lesser extent, the Atlantic and adjacent regions. On the other hand the far north receives little precipitation, and the intermountain valleys of British Columbia and the western prairies are dry to arid. Much of the winter precipitation is in the form of snow, which can disrupt communications and lead to costly bills for removal, although its cover can be beneficial to farmers, forest workers, and winter-sports promoters. In general, the northern climate imposes a heavy economic price in clothing, heating, construction, and transportation. Canadians sometimes console themselves by saying that the constant struggle with the elements strengthens character, but their words probably carry little conviction.

Less well known perhaps is the fact that most of the country, away from the coasts, also has very hot summers. Even far to the north where the summers are short, the days are long. Agriculture, for example, is more often restricted by inadequate soil and precipitation than by lack of summer heat.

Next, we should look at the main physiographic regions, with the purpose, first, of ascertaining whether geography throws any light on the existence of Canada as a separate and independent country in North America. This phenomenon is, of course, the accomplishment of men, but did they work with or against natural tendencies? Clearly against, it would seem. A glance at a relief map of the continent suggests that its geographical divisions run north and south rather than east and west. By this reckoning Canada appears as an artificial joining together of disparate regions, each of which, except for the unpopulated far north, is an extension of a related American region, to which it is closer than it is to its adjoining Canadian region.

Thus, the Atlantic Provinces are seen as the northeastern end of the Appalachians, looking to Boston rather than to Montreal and barred from direct contact with central Canada by the northward-jutting state of Maine. Inland, along the upper St. Lawrence and the lower Great Lakes, lies a seven-hundred-mile-long plain trending southwest until it is almost nestled among several eastern and midwestern states. One has only to cross a river to reach Buffalo or Detroit. But to the west, Winnipeg, the nearest city of Canada's next well-populated region, is a thousand miles and more away. From Winnipeg to Calgary the prairies extend for 800 miles, clearly part of the great interior plain reaching north from the Gulf of Mexico. Lastly, British Columbia is entirely within the Cordillerans that stretch from Alaska to the tip of South America, and Vancouver is closer to Seattle and other cities of the Pacific Coast states than to any large Canadian cities. Obviously, geography is not a strong friend of Canada's unity: the four main settled regions are separated by long stretches of difficult terrain, whereas each has good communications with nearby American centers.

But the vertical is not the only way to look at Canadian geography; there are forces that have made for separation from the adjoining American regions as well as for junction. The Atlantic Provinces, insular and peninsular, as we have seen, are more maritime even than New England, and over the years their relations with those states have been more competitive than cooperative. If they are at one remove from the rest of Canada so too are they separated from the American mainland. And when we look at the rest of the country we are again struck by the crucial importance of the waterways. The St. Lawrence–Great Lakes system leads into the west and eventually into the northwest. At the head of this system Montreal from an early period directed a vast commercial empire reaching to the prairies, then along the east-west-oriented rivers of that region, and finally to the Pacific. This fur-trading empire prefigured the Canadian nation that could be built when the east and west were joined by ties (railroad ties) stronger than those made by the voyageur in his birchbark canoe. In short, from the beginning Canadians have discerned east-west tendencies in North American geography and have constantly worked to build upon them.

The regions are now linked by highly sophisticated transport and communications systems, yet they will never merge and overlap to the extent that many sectional lines in the United States have. For instance, distinctions between the New England, Middle, and Central states no longer have the sharpness that they once had; indeed the process of integration wins new victories every year. As we shall see later, cultural or ethnic reasons explain why this is not likely to happen in Canada, but there are geographic reasons too, the main one being the existence of the Precambrian Shield, the dominant formation of the Canadian landscape, shared only slightly with the United States.

Geologically, the Precambrian Shield is the oldest exposed portion of the North American continent. It is a worn but very rugged upland, averaging about 1,200–1,400 feet above sea level but with hills of 4,000–5,000 feet in several places. Much of the soil was long ago scoured away by glacial action extending over many thousands of years. The soil was deposited south of the Great Lakes to provide the United States with the most valuable export it has ever received from Canada. This immense erosion left behind a harsh and stark terrain, nearly everywhere unsuited to farming and incapable of supporting a population of any considerable size. Building railroads across this jumble of rocks and this maze of swamps and lakes was an enormously formidable task, and today it is highly expensive to span it with highways.

The gigantic size of the Shield is hard to grasp and comprehend. It takes up about half the total area of Canada, stretching in a great arc around Hudson Bay. Starting at one end in the western Arctic islands, it covers about two thirds of the Northwest Territories beyond the sixtieth parallel of north latitude. It touches northeastern Alberta, spreads over nearly half of northern Saskatchewan and much more than half of northern and eastern Manitoba. Eastward from Lake Winnipeg, it dips down into Minnesota, and then continues north of Lake Superior and Lake Huron until it crosses the St. Lawrence River into New York state, just east of Lake Ontario. Thus it covers most of the province of Ontario, a province considerably larger than Texas. But the greatest expanse of the Shield is still to come, for the province of Quebec is more than twice the size of Texas and the

Shield extends over nearly all of it. Finally, it envelops Labrador before it reaches far into the northeast, at Baffin Island and the islands beyond. Altogether, it comprises almost two million square miles of rocks, lakes, and Christmas trees, set for the most part in a harsh northern climate.

In the past the Shield was usually thought of as a vast obstacle to the growth of Canada—often dramatic in its visual grandeur, but not a place where people could live in any numbers. To a large extent this view is still sound; population remains small and is not likely to grow markedly. Yet the enormous forest and mineral wealth of the Shield has for many years sustained large sectors of the Canadian economy. The Shield lacks the fuel minerals (coal, oil, and gas), but it does have great water-power resources, both potential and developed. Much of the Shield is also valuable for recreation and is likely to become more so as the continent becomes more crowded.

But the Shield and the North are not synonymous. Beyond it there are further vast regions where settlement is sparse or nonexistent, and always will be. Geologically distinct from the Shield are the desolate reaches of the Hudson Bay Lowlands stretching in a broad band across northern Ontario and Manitoba. Far to the north, beyond the Shield, there are lowlands along the Mackenzie, Canada's longest river (the second longest on the continent), and in the Arctic islands. Finally, there are the plateaus and mountains of the northern Cordilleran region, between southern British Columbia and Alaska, and the most northern mountains of all, the Innuitians, west of northern Greenland. These lowlands and highlands are for the most part economically less interesting than the Shield and if possible even less suited to human habitation.

These regions and the Shield make up most of the geographical area of Canada. Even then we should note that there are still other regions that are incapable of supporting any considerable population. Into this category falls much of the northeastern Appalachian highlands, including Newfoundland, Cape Breton

Island, the Gaspé Peninsula, and parts of New Brunswick. More than three hundred years after the first coming of the white man, these are still sparsely settled areas, whose people have a standard of living well below the North American level. At the other end of the country are the northern plains of Alberta and the Cordilleran country of British Columbia, also thinly peopled but richer in resources. These facts, brute facts, have to be remembered when one hears talk that one day Canada will support a vastly enlarged population. If it does, it will be a predominantly urban population, as is the case at present, and most of the country, well over ninety percent of its area, will remain nearly empty of people. It is true that vast sections of desert, mountain, and high plains country in the United States are also empty, or sparsely settled, but the unsettled parts of Canada are of a different magnitude. Of bogland alone, Canada has a half million square miles.

What then is left? There are four regions, next to the American border but widely separated from each other, where considerable numbers of human beings can live and prosper. From east to west: certain coastal portions of the Atlantic Provinces, the lowland plain stretching on either side of the St. Lawrence and north of Lakes Ontario and Erie from the city of Quebec to the Detroit River, the great plains between the Shield and the Rockies, and, finally, the southwestern corner of British Columbia. Clumps of population are to be found elsewhere, especially in the interior valleys of British Columbia and in several parts of the lower north of Ontario and Quebec, but the great majority of Canada's people live in the four regions of main settlement. Half of them live along the upper St. Lawrence and the lower Great Lakes.

The longest settled but also the least prosperous region is the Atlantic Provinces, containing about two million people. Out to sea though they are, they do not, except along the Bay of Fundy and the southern parts of the Atlantic coast, have a truly maritime climate. The Labrador current helps to produce cool summers, and the Gulf of St. Lawrence is filled with ice in the winter. But more limiting than climate is the scantiness of good farming land. Newfoundland has almost none, New Brunswick agriculture is mainly confined to the St. John River valley and the northwest corner of the province, and Nova Scotia has excellent but limited quantities of growing land along the Bay of Fundy and the Northumberland Strait. The small province of Prince Edward Island has the largest percentage of arable land. In consequence, like the New Englanders to the south, the people of these provinces have always gained a large part of their livelihood from the sea. But most important to these provinces are their forests and mines. About eighty-five percent of New Brunswick is productive forest land and much of Newfoundland and Nova Scotia is also thickly wooded. The pulp and paper industry, sawmills, and various kinds of wood-processing are basic to the economy of these provinces. In mining, the exploitation of Labrador's high-grade iron ores is the most dramatic recent development, but Newfoundland iron ore and Nova Scotia coal and gypsum continue to be important.

Thus these provinces depend heavily upon primary production and upon distant (and sometimes capricious) markets. Population is scattered along the coasts and after more than three hundred years of settlement has not reached very far into the interior, especially in Newfoundland and New Brunswick. There is one fairly large urban center, around the port of Halifax, and two lesser ones at Saint John, New Brunswick, and St. John's, Newfoundland. The region lacks the rounded development that its New England neighbor has achieved and is often inclined to blame the Canadian tariff for its relatively slow growth. But problems of climate and soil and its somewhat remote location are also fundamental. Like New England, its finest products have always been its people, who have found places of eminence and influence wherever they have gone across the continent.

The next region, the St. Lawrence–Great Lakes plain, is the most favored in the entire country, from an economic point of view, and contains about ten million people. This concentration of population and wealth derives from a number of remarkable advantages, of which geographic position is of prime importance. Via the St. Lawrence the area enjoys direct water communication with European and other world ports, while the Great Lakes funnel into it a large trade from the interior of the continent. The plain lies just south of the forest and mineral riches of the Shield and is close to the large population centers of the northeastern and north central states. Energy needs are met by coal imports from these states, by oil and gas pipelines from the west, by oil tankers from abroad, and by vast water-power resources. A network of water, rail, and road communications has made this region the center from which the economy of Canada is in large part directed.

From the beginning of its settlement this plain has been able to build on a strong agricultural base. Although the Shield presses down from the north, there is good farming land along the river and the lakes, broadening out to a considerable width in the southwestern peninsula of Ontario. Warm summer growing weather, adequate rainfall, and easy access to large markets make for varied, specialized, and profitable farming. But agriculture is now outweighed by other activities. Steel-making at Hamilton, automobile plants at Windsor and on either side of Toronto, and textile and petrochemical firms at Montreal are some of the leading features of a growing complex of heavy and light industry. About three fifths of the population is urban and suburban, spreading out from the great metropolitan centers of Montreal and Toronto, the foci of the country's financial and business life. Already highly developed, this region continues its rapid and diversified growth.

Canada has nothing similar to the American Middle West: between the St. Lawrence–Great Lakes plain and the next region of settlement lies a thousand-mile stretch of the Shield. Hence, there is no equivalent in Canadian development to that steady westward movement from the Appalachians to the Rockies which dominated American growth for most of the nineteenth century. In all that period, Canada had no receding frontier in the American sense. Before the Canadian West could come into its own, a mighty effort to traverse the Shield had to be made, and not until almost the beginning of the twentieth century was it made.

This "last, best West," containing over three million people, is usually thought of as the Prairie Provinces (Manitoba, Saskatchewan, and Alberta), but the term is of limited accuracy because much less than half the area of these provinces has a prairie landscape. The Shield is on the east and north, and the Rockies are on the west. Nevertheless, the Prairies are a magnificent agricultural empire, comprising by far the greatest extent of arable land to be found in Canada. This fertile soil grows spring wheat of the highest quality, which was for a long time Canada's leading export and is still fundamental to its economy. Yet it has never been an easy land to live in. Its harsh continental climate brings hot summers, but also early frosts. The Rockies block rain-bearing clouds, with the result that arid conditions frequently prevail, especially in southern Saskatchewan and Alberta. As on the American plains, farmers often have to face blizzards, dust storms, erosion, and flooding rivers, and markets are distant and sometimes unreliable. Nevertheless, the rewards of a good crop can be high, and the optimistic westerners are not easily discouraged. Increased scientific knowledge and government policy have removed some of the hazards from prairie wheat farming.

These provinces no longer depend so heavily upon wheat as they once did, although this crop still dominates the outlook of the people of Saskatchewan. Manitoba has always had a large amount of mixed farming, with emphasis upon livestock, and the adoption of irrigation procedures has brought diversified agriculture to the arid lands of southern Alberta and southern Saskatchewan. The most dramatic development has been the exploitation of mineral resources. Coal has long been mined, but since the later 1940's it has yielded in importance to the oil and natural gas with which Alberta in particular is richly endowed. Copper, zinc, and nickel mining in the Shield north of Manitoba's lakes is an established enterprise, and, more recently, potash mining in southern Saskatchewan has become of major significance. Thus it is no longer correct to think of this region as predominantly agricultural. The convergence of transportation routes and the development of food-processing industries have established Winnipeg as a major metropolitan center, and Edmonton and Calgary, in the midst of oil and gas producing areas, have grown phenomenally. Over half the population of the three provinces is urban, although of course many of these people depend upon the agricultural activity around them.

The last of these four regions of main settlement, separated from the Prairies by several hundred miles of Cordilleran mountains, is the most concentrated of all. British Columbia, Canada's third largest province, is much larger than Texas, but more than two thirds of its population, that is, more than a million people, live in the southwestern corner, in or near Vancouver. This corner, along with the southern end of Vancouver Island, has an authentic maritime climate, with heavy rainfall and a long frost-free season. The year-round port of Vancouver is Canada's second largest, and the city also contains a rapidly growing industrial complex, a center from which the province's forest, fishing, and agricultural resources are processed. The south-central area, close to the American border, contains well-established base-metal mines, and at Kitimat, to the north on the coast, are great aluminum smelting facilities, both of them making use of the province's rich hydropower capacity.

These, then, are the four widely separated regions of Canada where soil, climate, resources and geographic location have brought together considerable numbers of people. From these regions men exploit the sea on the east and the west and the Shield to the north. From them radiate the long lines of communication that hold the country together and tie it into the continental economy that has its center of gravity to the south. Hitherto, the great effort of Canadian development has been directed toward the improvement of east-west routes. With the growing importance of northern resources on the one hand and the American market on the other, one can also expect to find these regions increasingly functioning on north-south axes. What effect this latter trend will have on Canada's future is one of the great question marks for the next generation.

3 The People

The Canadian people can make no great claim upon the world's notice because of their numbers. Indeed, in an era when the term "population explosion" carries such ominous overtones, these numbers may appear to be almost insignificant. By the Centennial year of 1967 there were some twenty million residents of the country, roughly one tenth of the people living in the United States or the equivalent of about six years of population growth in that country. Three other countries in the western hemisphere (Brazil, Mexico, and Argentina) have more people, as do nearly two dozen countries on other continents, some of them with ten, twenty, or even thirty times Canada's numbers. Nevertheless, although shortage of population has often been a problem, Canadians have no reason to regret the ratio of people to resources and territory which their country enjoys.

Nor can Canadians expect attention as a result of sharply defined national characteristics or of epoch-making contributions to world civilization. The Canadian abroad, at least the English-speaking variety, is sometimes mistaken for an American. It is not clear that the term "Canadian" denotes a characteristic way of looking at the world or at life, a distinctive set of values or way of life. The Canadian says that he is not an American, yet he is clearly something other than a transplanted Englishman or Frenchman. Sometimes he simply takes refuge in the view that the whole concept of a "way of life" is an American invention, with which he will have nothing to do. In the cultural realm Canadians have produced at least their share of talented, educated, and highly competent people, but it would be hard to point to many figures with world reputations in creative phases of art, literature, music, and science. Although the record is far from blank, Canadians appropriately insist that they are a young and not very numerous people, and clearly genius in these directions has rarely reached the highest pinnacles in Canada. Still, the emergence of people with such powers is a mysterious matter, rare and unpredictable. It may also be said that Canadians, with their innate caution and a certain tendency toward self-disparagement, are seldom prone to give excessive, or even sufficient, recognition to those among them who seek to enhance the world's share of truth and beauty.

Yet, if Canadians cannot demand world notice on the grounds of teeming population or the distinctive quality of their civilization, there are still many reasons for knowing more about them. Despite their small numbers, they have imposed order and organization upon half a continent, they have achieved a high standard of living and become one of the world's leading trading nations, their political evolution may fairly be called unique, with an importance extending well beyond their borders, and they have been both tenacious and inventive in establishing civilized life in their part of North America. Not a "Great Power" (for which they can be counted fortunate), they have wielded an influence far beyond that of most countries in their population range. In a phrase that combines Canadian self-deprecation and a North American concern for size, Canada can be described as the world's biggest small nation.

Concern over national identity derives in part from the varied origins of the Canadian people. To be sure, these origins are not nearly so heterogeneous as those of many national populations. Almost all Canadians are of European descent or birth. Considering, for comparative purposes, only the countries of the western hemisphere, Canada exhibits a contrast with both the United States and most of the Latin American nations. In the United States about ten percent of the inhabitants are of African Negro derivation, but this is true of only a small fraction of one percent of the Canadian people. Thus Canadian history lacks, almost entirely, that searing theme, so dominant in American history, of how whites and Negroes are to live together in one society. In Latin American countries, with a few exceptions, the aborigines have survived in large numbers to share national life with the European conquerors, but in Canada, Indians and Eskimos constitute less than two percent of the population (a little more if half-breeds are included). The question of the role of native culture and personality in the national life, so burning in the history of Mexico and other countries to the south, has never been central in Canada. With about ninety-seven percent of its people of European origin, the human scene here is, quite literally, paler than it is elsewhere in the hemisphere; frequently expressed Canadian views on race questions are unfettered by much direct experience of the subject.

Yet Canadian demography is not without variety, distinctiveness, and conflict. The Canadian peoples have never been molded into a uniform, homogenized mass, and they show no tendency to become so. Indeed, Canadians, sometimes with a touch of exaggeration, like to contrast the diversity of their life with the so-called "melting-pot" tendencies thought to be at work in the United States. Distinctive features of the American character, the argument runs, were formed, at a relatively early period, by a predominantly Anglo-American and Protestant population. Political, legal, and educational institutions were developed, and moral and intellectual attitudes were formed, to which for the most part the tens of millions of later immigrants have adapted themselves. Canadians see this process as one that has endowed the American nation with enormous momentum and strength. Sometimes they have been moved to thoughts of envy and emulation, yet the facts of Canadian life have always forbidden any full-fledged imitation of the American example.

Some of these facts derive from geography, as we have already seen: relatively small numbers of people stretched along a four-thousand-mile ribbon, broken for several hundreds of miles in several places, are not likely to rub corners off one another to any marked extent. But diversity is also rooted in the forces and motives that lay behind Canadian settlement, especially the existence of two European "founding peoples" (in contemporary Canadian terminology), and not one, as in the United States. This fact dominates Canadian life and history and is the key to an understanding of the country. Each group, respectively of British and French origin, has entrenched political, legal, and social rights, which are written into the constitutional fabric and are sanctioned by usage and law. In addition there is still another group, amounting to nearly a quarter of the population, of continental European immigrant derivation, and, as in the United States, it is a factor of much significance in the national life.

The most numerous of these three groups is that of British origin, yet this group is so varied that it can be regarded as coherent only in the broadest demographic sense. Some are descended from settlers who arrived two and a half centuries ago, others came only yesterday. Some of the settlers left directly from the British Isles; others reached Canada only after they or their forefathers had spent several generations elsewhere in North America. They were, and often have remained, English, Scottish, and Irish: the distinctive characteristics still so noticeable among the inhabitants of the several parts of the British Isles are somewhat more evident in the Canadian population than among the Americans of British origin. The British in Canada have never needed to adopt new ways to become good Canadians; indeed, there was often strong encouragement to hold as strongly as possible to the old ways and to try to plant them in Canada.

These various elements of British origin, as far as the 1961 census could make out, numbered at that time just under eight million people or 43.8 percent, proportionately smaller than the component of British origin in the American population. (In both countries the census has its problems, for there has been so much mating across group lines that estimates of ethnic origin are only approximate.) Lumped together in the census statistics are the descendants of such groups as the following: the westcountrymen and the Irish who started to fish off Newfoundland's coasts several centuries ago, the English and the New Englanders who had reached Nova Scotia by the middle of the eighteenth century, the American loyalists (of miscellaneous and often non-British origin) who settled New Brunswick and the St. Lawrence–Great Lakes plain after the Revolution, the non-loyalist Americans who came into Upper Canada in the post-Revolutionary years, the Scottish crofters, the Irish peasants, the English half-pay officers and all the other elements of that torrent of humanity that swept across the Atlantic in the generation after the Napoleonic Wars, the many thousands of Americans bound for the Canadian West in the fifteen years before 1914, and the even larger English movement to the cities and farms of the same years, and, finally, the several hundred thousand who have come out since the Second World War. The list is far from exhaustive, but it serves to suggest the diversity of the population of British origin.

Nevertheless, despite the remarkable persistence of national traits, particularly among Scots in certain rural areas, the people of British origin are decreasingly identifiable as coming from the "old country." The great majority of them are Canadian born, many with roots in the country or the continent that go back for many generations. French Canadians often refer to them as *les anglais*, but in fact most of the people of British origin think of themselves as Canadians, are thoroughly North American in customs and attitudes, and have no memories of the homeland of their forebears. The history of the country is strewn with tensions between the older North American population, loyalist and non-loyalist in origin, and newly arrived immigrants from the British Isles. The recent arrivals were sometimes accused of expecting some kind of special treatment, and they in turn complained of discrimination. "No English Need Apply" signs are said to have been posted at places of employment, early in this century. But strains of this kind, while frequently noticeable, have never been deep-seated or persistent, because the English (and even more the Scots and the Irish) have never taken long to establish themselves in North American society.

There is a remarkable contrast between the "British origin" group and the group of French origin. The first group, as we have seen, reached Canada from widely separated points, of both place and time, and have little sense of solidarity, one with another, except as English-speaking citizens of Canada. They do not easily differentiate between the loyalties and values which they hold dear and those which should be binding upon all Canadians, of whatever ethnic origin. In this respect they are reminiscent of Northerners in the United States before the Civil War, who did not distinguish between their own sectional interests and the American national interest as a whole, a view which outraged Southerners. In short, Canadians of British origin, like their cousins in the Northern states before 1860, have frequently believed that their norms are those to which other groups must eventually adjust.

But the group of French origin has had a different history and has a different outlook. They are readily recognized as belonging to an identifiable group, although there are some difficulties because a goodly number of people with British names have been absorbed into the French-language community while the reverse has also happened, with or without change of name. By the census of 1961 there were just over five and a half million people of French ethnic origin in the country, constituting thirty percent of the population, nearly all of whom listed French as their mother tongue. Most of these people, about four and a half million, lived in the province of Quebec; close to six hundred thousand lived in Ontario, to the west, and another two and a quarter hundred thousand lived in New Brunswick, to the east. Between fifty and sixty thousand were scattered in the other Atlantic Provinces and about two hundred thousand in the four western provinces. In Quebec about seventy percent of them listed French as their only language, but in the other provinces large majorities declared they they could speak both French and English.

The most striking fact about this group of French language and origin is that nearly all of them (and to their numbers could be added well over a million people living in the United States) are descended from a relatively small number of settlers who were already established along the shores of the St. Lawrence by the early eighteenth century. Most of the six million North Americans of French origin derive from the approximately fifty thousand residents of New France at the middle of the eighteenth century. In the more than two centuries that have ensued Canada has received relatively few French-language immigrants to reinforce the original band. In seniority order among North Americans they share first place with the descendants of the original settlers of Virginia and Massachusetts; but for the most part the latter have long since melted into the American population as a whole, whereas the French Canadians have never ceased to be visible as a distinctive entity. No other distinctive group has such deep roots in the continent's life.

Their survival (*survivance*) in the midst of an English-speaking community of such size may seem remarkable, yet it should be remembered that in their homeland of Quebec they have always been overwhelmingly the majority. For a century and a half before the British conquest of 1760 they were in sole possession of the St. Lawrence valley, a long time in which to knit closely the bonds of their society. After the conquest, despite initial British hopes, English-speaking settlement was relatively small, and most of it was confined to Montreal and to the Eastern Townships (between the St. Lawrence River and the American border). There was recurrent talk over the years that the French Canadians would or should be assimilated, but in fact large numbers of them rarely saw or heard an English-speaking person from one year's end to the next. Even if they had wanted to be assimilated, they were, as one of their historians has put it, "condemned to survive."

But of course they did want to survive, and they have consciously striven to achieve this goal. They have clung to old institutions — and have fashioned new ones — for this purpose. They have followed, often unswervingly, the trusted leaders who arose to champion their cause. Foremost among these have been the Roman Catholic clergy, who did not desert them in 1760; it has always been very difficult to distinguish between loyalty to the faith and loyalty to the French-Canadian collectivity. The Church has provided a wide range of opportunities for the expression of the French-Canadian personality. It has also sponsored or encouraged the development of numerous intermediate institutions (that is, between the individual and the state) that are fundamental to the organization of this community: schools and universities, patriotic, fraternal, and service organizations, financial institutions, labor unions, cultural associations, and so on. Not all of these originated directly from the Church, but all have affiliations with it. If, in the future, the organization of French-Canadian life becomes less intimately connected with the Church, it will remain true that for over three centuries this connection was the focus of "survivance."

Nor should the role of the state be forgotten. For more than eighty years after the conquest French Canadians had at best a very partial control over the political apparatus, but it was one that became stronger in the 1850's and 1860's. With Confederation in 1867 and the re-emergence of Quebec as a separate province, now with local self-goverment, French Canadians had control of a weak but distinct government, which could be used to protect the life of the community. For a long time this government was used more to repel than to develop, for negative rather than for positive purposes, but in recent years there has been a growing insistence that its scope be widened. The role of this government has been a strong reason why French Canadians in Quebec have to a large extent avoided the fate of their compatriots in other provinces, minorities now partially assimilated.

Finally, among the main groups of the Canadian population, we should look at those of European but non-British and non-French origin, slightly less than a quarter of the population in the 1961 census. Like such elements in the American population, these people are of very diverse and mixed origins, and many of them are thoroughly assimilated to the North American environment. Some, particularly among those of German derivation (the largest group), have lived in Canada, and before that in the United States, for as long as any of the so-called British group (with whom they are often considerably mixed.) The first large movement from continental Europe to Canada did not come, however, until the quarter century before the First World War. Prominent in that migration were Ukrainians, Russians, and Scandinavians, who did much to people the western plains, and central Europeans from many countries, who came to the cities. After the war the movement continued on a considerably lesser scale, drying up in the 1930's. It resumed after the Second World War, with renewed German and eastern European immigration and with a notable influx of Italians. In several years after 1958 Italians were the largest single ethnic group entering the country, and in the 1961 census, except for those born in the British Isles and the United States, Italians led in the category of those born outside Canada.

The large immigration since the Second World War has made the Canadian scene, particularly the urban scene, more varied than it used to be. Not only have new skills been introduced, but a leavening influence has been discernible in respect to restaurants, recreation, and many other aspects of culture. On the other hand, a trifle paradoxically, this immigration has served to strengthen the English-speaking element in Canada, for in time nearly all the European immigrants, or their children, learn English. A generation ago it was possible to make projections, based on birth-rate statistics, that looked to a time when French-speaking Canadians would outnumber English-speaking Canadians. But immigration combined with an evening out of birth rates has postponed that day until the Greek Kalends. It is not surprising that French Canadians have often shown little sympathy for the immigration policy of the federal government.

Of non-European groups, native Indians and Eskimos number about two and a quarter hundred thousand, or a little more than one percent of the population, and there are about half that many people of Asiatic origin. The native peoples are not a vanishing race; their numbers have nearly doubled in the last generation, and there are now probably as many of them as there were when the white man arrived. About three quarters of the Indians live on more than two thousand reserves, occupying about six million acres, and are under the protection of the federal government, which provides money and facilities to further their education and their employment opportunities. Of the approximately twelve thousand Eskimos many still follow their traditional nomadic life, but increasingly they too are turning to schools and to regular employment. Both groups have often been bruised by contact with the white man's world, but the discernible trend toward integration is certain to continue.

Canadians of Asiatic origin stem mainly from Chinese and Japanese immigrants of the last third of the last century. As in California, these people were, in British Columbia, the object of intense hostility, leading to effective steps to halt the inflow, which has never been more than a trickle since. During the Second World War the Japanese were harshly uprooted and dispersed across the country, another unfortunate parallel with American events. Today Canada has no official policy of excluding non-European immigrants, but in fact few seem to be able to meet the requirements set.

Turning to other phases of the Canadian population scene, we should note that there is a significant movement back and forth across the Canadian-American border. While Canada has been receiving immigrants from Europe it has also been losing as many as twenty percent of them, by re-emigration to the United States. Particularly disquieting has been the departure of considerable numbers of native-born citizens. Together, these two groups amounted to an annual exodus of at least thirty thousand persons, which sometimes rose to sixty thousand, or a total in the vicinity of half a million, for the twenty years after 1945.* This phenomenon is by no means new, for it has been going on for a century and a half; the United States census of 1960 disclosed

*This movement was sharply curtailed following the United States immigration law of 1965.

three and a quarter million persons who were Canadian-born or the offspring of Canadian parents. But in recent years there has been concern over the loss of large numbers of highly trained and educated young or fairly young people attracted by higher salaries, wider research opportunities, warmer climate, and what was thought to be a more stimulating or more exciting social environment. Yet the "brain drain" has not gone all the one way. Many of the younger people have returned after a period of training or experience in the United States, while tens of thousands of skilled Americans have moved north, either temporarily or permanently. In the largest sense, the free movement of human beings across the border is in the interests of both countries.

Movement of people has also taken place within Canada, from one province to another and from one occupational setting to another. To a marked extent, population has been moving into four provinces, Ontario, British Columbia, Quebec, and Alberta, and out of the remaining six. The Atlantic Provinces have suffered a steady outward flow, only the latest phase of a century-long movement, and Manitoba and Saskatchewan, since the 1930's, have also had a net migration loss, much of it in the direction of the Pacific coast. In large part this has really been a movement from farm and small town to the large city, one that has been going on simultaneously within each province, notably in Quebec and Ontario. Quebec, once thought to be the land of the *habitant* tilling his small plot, is now about seventy-five percent urban; indeed, there are more people living in the metropolitan area of Montreal than on all the farms of Canada. Present indications point to a population eighty percent urban by 1980 in the country as a whole. Rural poverty continues to be a serious problem on marginal lands in several provinces, as in parts of the United States, and from an economic point of view there are still many farms that should be abandoned. Most of the large cities are near the American border, and thus it can be argued that the movement from the farm brings Canadians closer to the United States. (In that country, however, much of the movement is toward Florida and toward the southwest, away from the Canadian border.)

Lastly, we should comment briefly on some salient features of the religious life of the Canadian people. Like Americans, and unlike the citizens of some European countries, Canadians are almost unanimous in thinking of themselves as a religious people. At any rate, to the 1961 census question "What is your religion?" over ninety-seven percent of the population professed that they had one, although the extent of church membership and the degree of affiliation were not disclosed. By far the largest denomination, claimed by nearly forty-six percent, was the Roman Catholic Church. The largest Protestant denomination (twenty percent of the population) was the United Church of Canada, a church formed in 1925 by Methodists, Presbyterians, and Congregationalists. The Anglican Church of Canada was represented by thirteen percent, and other major Protestant denominations by about the same number. One and a half percent were Jewish. It is interesting to note that American-originated denominations, notably the Mormons and Christian Scientists, are well established and that nearly all denominations have ties, sometimes very close ones, with sister organizations in the United States.

It is official doctrine in the United States that there is a "wall of separation" between church and state, but this view has never prevailed in Canada, particularly in the school system. Generally speaking, there is much more religious instruction in publicly financed schools than is to found in the United States; the picture is varied, however, because education is a provincial matter. In the province of Quebec there are two school systems, Catholic and Protestant (the latter being, in effect, non-Catholic), and although educational institutions in that province are under vigorous review, the confessionally organized school system still continues. In Ontario, Saskatchewan, and Alberta, legal provision is made for Roman Catholic "separate schools," which are supported by taxes; in Manitoba and the three Maritime Provinces such schools also exist in areas with large Roman Catholic populations. Newfoundland has an entirely denominational system: five major denominations operate their own schools under the general supervision of a department of education. Only in British Columbia does the American practice fully prevail: parochial or private schools must operate without support from taxes. Finally, an important current issue is the widespread feeling in the province of Quebec that Roman Catholic minorities, especially the French-language ones, are not treated so well in the other provinces as Protestants and Jews in Quebec.

In summary, then, Canadians share important characteristics, as a people, with their American neighbors and, at the same time, exhibit some differences. Most Canadians believe that they live in a classless, mainly middle-class, society, but, in fact, as in the United States, their social structure is both complex and elaborate. Like Americans, Canadians believe that theirs is a land of opportunity where the highest positions are within the reach of all, but perhaps even more than across the border, success and status depend heavily on ethnic background, social class, and education. Canadians believe that they are an undemonstrative, law-abiding, reasonable sort of people, and it is probable that there is at least as much truth in this favorable self-portrait as in most.

4. The Political System

The institutions and practices of government in Canada resemble those of the United States closely enough so that a casual observer might be excused if he could not detect significant differences. Like its neighbor, Canada is governed through a federal system, which divides power between a central government on the one hand and the several components of the federation on the other; this division is set out in written form in a constitution, with a supreme court as final arbiter of differences. The central government has a powerful executive, at the apex of a large and ramifying bureaucracy; it has a bicameral legislature, with a lower house based on direct popular election and a senate, where the provinces are represented (although by appointment, not by election); and it has an appointed and independent judiciary. The provincial governments, like American state governments, have such large and growing responsibilities, particularly respecting education and social welfare, that they are frequently desperate for revenues. Government at both levels is organized and given momentum by political parties, which are nationwide in scope, represent diverse regional and group interests, and lack distinctive ideological coloring. Elections, based on a secret ballot and universal suffrage, are marked by partisan and sometimes demogogic appeals. The citizen has a low opinion of the "professional politician," yet often shows remarkably little vigilance in performing his civic duties.

Statements of this kind could be multiplied to demonstrate that Canada and the United States share a tradition of constitutional and representative government having its origins in medieval England, and now encased in a federal framework as required by a continental environment. Nevertheless, the Canadian political system is not a replica of the American: it is at once older and newer, it represents a response to Canadian conditions and problems, and at many points it exhibits a deliberate rejection of American models and precedents. Beneath certain similarities of political tone are to be found many striking differences of structure and action.

We come to the most fundamental of these differences at the very outset when we meet the word "constitution." There can be no doubt what is meant by the phrase "Constitution of the United States." It is a document that was drawn up by a convention in 1787, ratified by the states in the following year, and put into operation in 1789. Along with its amendments, and read in the light of subsequent interpretation and practice, the constitution is a distillation of fundamental law for Americans: it limits the power of governments, federal, state, and local, and it cannot be formally changed except through clearly prescribed procedures, which allow the will of the sovereign people to be expressed.

In the American sense of the word, Canada does not have a constitution at all. The nearest equivalent is the British North America Act of 1867, with its amendments in the form of subsequent British North America Acts enacted since that year. But all these acts are statutes of the British Parliament; none of them was ever submitted to the Canadian people, or their representatives, for approval or ratification.* Since 1949 the Parliament of Canada has had the power to amend the British North America Act in matters that do not touch the provinces, but even this power is conferred in the form of a British statute, and the procedure to be followed (simple legislative enactment) violates American ideas of how a constitution should be amended. In matters that affect the provinces the federal and provincial governments of Canada have so far failed to work out amendment procedures for use when the British North America Act, or its successor, shall be a wholly Canadian document.

Nor does the British North America Act of 1867 throw much light on the actual workings of Canadian government. It states simply that the provinces to be "federally united into one Dominion under the Crown of the United Kingdom of Great

---

*With one exception: the Act of 1949 admitting Newfoundland into the Canadian Confederation was preceded by a popular referendum in that province.

Britain and Ireland" are to have "a constitution similar in Principle to that of the United Kingdom." No attempt was made to describe how that constitution actually operated, either in Britain or in Canada in 1867. Instead, the Act declares, again very simply, that the executive authority "of and over Canada" will continue to "be vested in the Queen," who will be represented by a governor general appointed by her. Acting in her name, the governor general appears to have full control of the government: he may appoint and remove his advisers, appoint judges, senators, and provincial lieutenant governors, call and dissolve the legislature, and disallow legislation, both federal and provincial, and no money bills may be passed without his recommendation. Nowhere does the Act refer to the prime minister or to the cabinet, to the relations that must exist between the governor general and the cabinet on the one hand, and the cabinet and the legislature on the other. No mention is made of the real powers of the two houses of the legislature in respect to one another. No mention is made of the role of political parties (also true of the American constitution). Thus, a literal reading of the British North America Act gives not only an incomplete but also a very misleading picture of Canadian government.

The explanation, of course, is that the Act was never intended to provide an explicit picture; it was never intended to be a constitution in the American sense. In the British (and Canadian) sense, a constitution cannot be found in any one document and its amendments. On the contrary, the constitution is a vast body of custom, precedents, statutes, and common law, stretching back for centuries and constantly evolving with or without formal amendments. In this sense the constitution was a well-understood phenomenon in 1867. What was wanted in that year was not a new constitution, but a means by which the existing constitution, already in use in the Canadian provinces, could be adapted to the needs of the federal system about to be formed. Thus, the British North America Act was concerned, not with basic principles of government or with placing limitations upon the power of government, but with sketching out whatever new institutions had to be created, with dividing powers between the central government and the provinces, and with entrenching certain religious and language rights within the new framework. Only in these important but limited respects is the Act (and its successors) comparable to the constitution of the United States.

The second of these subjects—the division of powers—is of fundamental interest in any federation. In the Canadian case it is also a subject apparently clear and simple, but in reality complex and uncertain. The intentions of the framers of the Act—the "Fathers of Confederation"—are unmistakable. Reacting against the breakdown of the American federation during the Civil War, they meant to make the federal government much stronger and the provincial governments much weaker than the equivalent governments were under the American constitution. They tried to achieve this goal in many ways, the most important of which was a broad grant of legislative power to the Parliament of Canada, which was empowered " to make Laws for the Peace, Order, and good Government of Canada" in all matters not "assigned exclusively" to the provinces. That is, the provinces were given authority over sixteen subjects, of provincial or local significance, but all other matters, including the so-called residual power, belonged to the federal government—a striking contrast to the American division, whereby certain powers are vested in the federal government and all others are reserved to the states or to the people. In addition, the Canadian federal government was given the power to appoint and pay provincial lieutenant governors and the judges of provincial superior courts and to disallow provincial legislation. Nor did the provinces receive equal representation in one branch of the legislature as American states do in the Senate. Clearly, provincial governments, although they had exclusive jurisdiction in some important matters, notably education, were intended to be subordinate to the federal government, quite unable to aspire to the sovereign status sometimes claimed by American states.

The letter of the law has not been changed significantly, but a century later the two countries seem almost to have exchanged constitutions, as far as the federal balance is concerned. In the United States the federal government has steadily grown in power, whereas the state governments have become relatively weaker and increasingly on the defensive. In Canada the federal government has seen its legislative authority become restricted, while the provinces have greatly expanded theirs. The various techniques for controlling and supervising the provinces have proved to be largely ineffectual. The courts have narrowly interpreted federal powers and broadly interpreted provincial powers. Social and economic changes have given the provinces responsibilities and opportunities unthought of in the 1860's. In the 1960's the Canadian federal scene is so filled with uncertainties as to need fuller discussion in a later chapter. Therefore, leaving aside the relations between federal and provincial governments, we should look now at how these governments actually function, devoting most of our attention to the federal and noting similarities and contrasts with the American system.

In the executive branch we find, at the outset, a striking difference. Constitutionally, the United States is a republic, led by a president who is both chief of state and head of the government and who is chosen by a nationwide electorate for a specified term. Constitutionally, Canada is a monarchy; the Royal Style and Title, as approved by the Canadian Parliament in 1953, reads: "Elizabeth the Second, by the Grace of God of the United Kingdom, Canada, and Her other Realms and Territories Queen, Head of the Commonwealth, Defender of the Faith." All acts of government, federal and provincial, are done in the Queen's name. As chief of state, she is represented in Canada by the governor general and in each province by a lieutenant governor. Since 1926 it has been officially clear that the governor general is not in any sense a representative or official of the British government. In fact, he is appointed by the Canadian government for a term of about five years, which may be somewhat extended, and since 1952 the appointments have gone to Canadian citizens. Lieutenant governors are also appointed by the federal government, for terms of about four years, and appointments nearly always go to political supporters of the party in power at Ottawa, whatever the party complexion of the provincial government may be.

The Queen's representative, at Ottawa or in a provincial capital, is for the most part a purely ceremonial figurehead, without real political power. He is a valuable focus and patron of many phases of social and cultural life. He devotes much of his time to visiting hospitals, opening exhibitions, and encouraging various worthy movements, as well as officiating at the opening and closing of legislative sessions and receiving diplomats. He is a dignified personage, on the outside of politics, who, by performing many necessary but time-consuming duties, relieves the effective head of government, the prime minister or the provincial premier, of some but not all duties of a formal and ceremonial nature.

Theoretically, the role of the Queen's representative is not entirely ceremonial. Conceivably situations may arise when the prime minister's advice will be rejected or when there is real uncertainty as to which political leader should be called upon to form a government. At such times the Canadian political system cannot function effectively without the presence of the governor general or an equivalent officer. As a leading constitutional authority* has put it, "Cabinet government ... presupposes some central, impartial figure at its head which at certain times and for certain purposes supplements and aids the other more active and partisan agencies of government." Yet, on the single noted—or notorious—occasion in Canadian history when a prime minister's advice was rejected by the governor general, during the so-called constitutional crisis of 1926, there was a violent political storm. Now, the combination of Canadian

*R. M. Dawson, *Government of Canada* (Toronto, 1963), p. 165.

appointees and an increasingly democratic political environment further lessens the possibility of collision. These statements are equally true of the lieutenant governors in the provinces.

We come then to the central figure in Canadian politics, the prime minister. (And what follows applies also to the provincial premier or prime minister.) According to British traditions of cabinet government the prime minister is a prominent political figure, usually the recognized leader of his party, who is asked by the sovereign whether he can form a government that can command the support of a majority of the House of Commons. Having accepted the commission, the prime minister holds office for as long as he retains the confidence of his colleagues in the cabinet and his government is sustained in the House. Such statements, although not inaccurate, do not suggest adequately the strength and power which the prime minister has come to exercise in Canadian government.

In the first place he is more than simply the recognized leader of his party. He is on a plane far above all other figures in the party, even the most prominent. He has reached this pinnacle as a result of selection by a national political convention, to which delegates come from all parts of the country. Thus he owes his party leadership not solely to a parliamentary caucus or to a small group of influential politicians but to the party faithful as a whole. In an election campaign he is, to be sure, a candidate only in his own constituency, but in fact campaigns increasingly center on the personalities and records of the party leaders. In constituencies throughout the country, not only are voters choosing their own members of parliament, but they are also registering choices among the party leaders. The leader of the winning party may thus legitimately feel that he has received a personal mandate from the electorate to add to that previously received from his party followers. It is now a commonplace to hear it said that Canadian elections are taking on some of the characteristics of an American presidential race.

Thus the leader whose party has won the election is in an

extremely powerful position when he is asked by the governor general to form a government. And his position is further strengthened as he proceeds to choose his cabinet. The initiative is in his hands: to choose this man, to reject that one, to fill posts as he sees fit. When the cabinet is completed, it will be clear that the prime minister is not the first among equals, but the acknowledged master. As long as he is prime minister it is almost impossible to dislodge him from the leadership, as was demonstrated in the unsuccessful revolt against John Diefenbaker in 1963. And even when he loses an election, the party chief, unlike a defeated American presidential candidate, usually remains in firm control of his party.

This is not to say, however, that the prime minister has a completely free choice in selecting his cabinet, not even the choice open to a newly elected American president. All members of his cabinet must have seats, or find seats, in parliament, which in practice means the House of Commons. Only on very rare occasions will a cabinet post involving supervision of a department go to a senator. Therefore, the prime minister must confine himself to active politicians of his own party, whereas the president will sometimes appoint such nonpolitical figures as business men and generals. Moreover, the prime minister cannot easily pass over prominent politicians of his own party, even though he may not always give them the posts that they would have preferred. But the most serious limitation on his choice comes from the custom that the cabinet must be federal in character. If possible, each province must be represented, as well as major and minor interests in the larger provinces. Traditionally, the minister of agriculture comes from the Prairie Provinces and the fisheries minister from one of the coastal provinces. Adherence to these and other usages makes cabinet-building an extremely intricate trade. Putting together a balanced yet capable cabinet and then maintaining control of it test all the skills of a prime minister.

In theory, the prime minister and his cabinet are, on the one hand, the advisers of the governor general and, on the other, accountable to the House of Commons for the advice thus given. In reality, the cabinet, headed by the prime minister, is the moving force in Canadian government. Although the Queen, acting through her representative, is the legal executive, the real power to make policy and implement decisions is in the hands of the cabinet. Furthermore, the legislature does its work under the immediate direction and supervision of the cabinet, a fact which makes for a very significant difference between the Canadian and the American political systems. Cabinet ministers sit in the House of Commons; they determine the order of business; they introduce the major legislation, including all money bills; and they secure support for their measures from their disciplined followers, who sit in the rows behind them. Once in power with a clear majority in the House of Commons, the Canadian executive branch can count on the adoption of its measures to an extent that is beyond the fondest hope of the American executive. Party support is loyal and firm, and the opposition's ability to delay and obstruct is severely limited. Yet all this can change and the prime minister's position can become weaker than the president's if his parliamentary majority is not effective.

Turning to the legislature, we will look first at the Senate, which must surely be a great puzzle to American observers, for it is not at all like the body of that name in the United States Congress. More than a puzzle to most Canadians, it is an object of ridicule and derision, and few believe that it can last much longer in its present form. Yet it has had this form for a century, and Senate reform is one of the bad jokes of Canadian politics. In the measured words of the closest student of the institution, it "has been the most disappointing feature of our federal constitution ... the butt of wits as a home for the aged and a paddock for the old wheel horses of the party."

There are a hundred and two members of the Senate: thirty from the Atlantic Provinces, twenty-four from each of Quebec and Ontario, and twenty-four from the four western provinces.

There are no elections, and appointments were for life until 1965, when retirement of senators at the age of 75 was provided for. These appointments are made by the federal government, that is, in the last analysis, by the prime minister. In theory, and with the exception that money bills may not be introduced there, the Senate is equal in power with the House of Commons. In reality, it exercises no real power, and only rarely in the last century has it tried to oppose the will of the lower house. As a rule the Senate automatically passes all bills coming from the Commons, even when the party alignments in the two houses are radically different. Because the senators represent nobody but themselves, they could hardly do otherwise in a democracy.

The dilemma over the Senate can be simply stated. In a federal system, where one house is based on direct popular election, with membership determined by population, it is normal to have the constituent units represented in a second chamber. This is true of the American federation, the West German federation, and others; the Maritime Provinces would probably not have agreed to enter the Canadian federation in 1867 without Senate representation larger than that justified by their population. But cabinet government can work effectively only when the cabinet is responsible to one house; for it to be responsible to two, perhaps conflicting, houses would ensure chaos. Therefore, one house has to be strong and the other weak. The Senate cannot be abolished without offending the federal principle, yet measures of reform might strengthen it, leading to the possibility of collision between the two houses.

In consequence, most proposals for altering the Senate tend to be rather modest. Some observers have argued that the Senate could play a useful role in the initiating of private bills and some of the less controversial public bills, thus saving the time of the Commons for more basic matters; in fact, the Senate is already performing these functions to an increased extent. Others have advocated that up to half the senators should be appointed, on a short-term basis, by the provincial governments, in order that changes in provincial administration would be reflected in the Senate, but this suggestion has the defect of strengthening the Senate unless such action were coupled with a limitation on senatorial legislative powers. Thus, the dilemma is real—and unsolved.

Next, the House of Commons. This is a body of two hundred and sixty-five members, although the number may vary slightly because of a highly complicated system of allocating representatives. Generally speaking, the provinces are represented according to population, with adjustments being made after each decennial census. In contrast to the American system, in which the states have the power to draw the boundaries of electoral districts once the number of their Congressmen has been determined from the census, the Canadian procedure is fully under federal control. Provincial authorities have no voice whatsoever in the process. In the past this control gave the party in power at Ottawa a great opportunity; although the gerrymander was invented in the United States, Canadian politicians became highly adept at the art. In 1964, however, it was agreed to take redistribution out of politics and turn the matter over to independent commissions appointed by the judiciary. The work of these commissions should bring the country closer to the ideal of one man, one vote. By contrast, in the United States, this ideal is being approached by pressure from the judiciary upon state legislatures.

The more centralized character of the Canadian federal system is also exhibited in the conduct of elections and in the determination of the franchise. In the United States, there is no federal electoral machinery; state authorities conduct elections for president and Congress and report the results to Washington. In Canada, however, there is a Chief Electoral Officer, independent of the government, who has full supervision of the voting process; no part is played by provincial authorities. In the United States, there is no federal franchise; within certain restrictions, notably those imposed by the fifteenth, nineteenth, and twenty-fourth amendments (respecting Negroes, women, and poll taxes), the states are free to determine the franchise for federal as well as for state elections. In Canada, there have also been periods when the provinces set the franchise, but since 1920 a federal franchise has given the vote to all adults at the age of twenty-one. Certain categories of persons, including federally appointed judges, lunatics, and criminals, are excluded. Provinces continue to set the franchise for their own elections.

But the most striking differences between the Canadian House of Commons and the American Congress stem from the operations of cabinet government. Canada operates on the British model. Canadian M.P.'s are not elected for a specified term; the one certainty is that, excluding a great crisis like a war, Parliament will not last for more than five years. If the parties are precariously balanced, as they were after the elections of 1957 and 1962, Parliament may last only for a year or even less. Moreover, Parliament does not determine its dates of assembling, proroguing, or dissolving. In actual practice these matters are decided by the prime minister and the cabinet. In addition, as we have already seen, the business of the House is at almost every point directed by the cabinet.

It would be tempting to conclude from such facts that the Canadian House of Commons, when compared with the American Congress, is not an independent legislature. In theory the cabinet is responsible to the Commons, but in practice the Commons might seem to be little more than a body used to ratify the decrees of an overpowerful executive. Nevertheless, although such fears have frequently been expressed, notably in the years immediately before 1957, the House of Commons has resources and weapons to use against the executive which the American Congress might well envy: the cabinet has a commanding position in the House, for reasons already given; but from their very presence in the House, cabinet ministers are under much more immediate and continuing supervision than is the American executive branch. True, Congressional committees of investigation have extraordinary opportunities for interrogating officers of the administration; it is also true that if the president stands behind his men they can normally defy the most persistent criticism, and the president himself is not subject to direct and open questioning before committees. At best, such a function is performed by the press, under ground rules set by the president. The prime minister is not so fortunate. On the floor of the House he and his cabinet must submit to a much more formidable stream of questioning than can ever come from newspapermen. And in the party caucus, government supporters who appear to be docile in the House are often biting critics. In the last analysis, the cabinet know that their great powers can be abruptly terminated if they lose the confidence of the House. Such a possibility is extremely remote, if only because the M.P.'s have no desire to hurry on elections, but the possibility can never be ignored. The most subservient-seeming House can, if aroused, turn savagely against the most powerful-seeming government. In each country the major trends of modern government inexorably strengthen the hand of the executive and produce exasperation and frustration in the legislature. In the United States these trends frequently result in open conflict and collision; the tension is less noticeable in Canada, but it is always there.

Lastly, there is the third branch of government, the judiciary, which plays a less prominent role in the Canadian political process than does its American counterpart. In the United States all governments, federal, state, and local, are limited by the letter and spirit of the constitution, and it has become the duty of the judiciary to pass upon the complaints of those who allege that a branch or level of government has gone beyond the limits of its constitutional powers. The American courts, and above all the Supreme Court, are intimately and continuously involved in the conduct of public affairs. In Canada, however, the tradition of parliamentary sovereignty narrows considerably the scope of judicial review; while the courts may frequently have to pass upon the meaning of a statute, they are much less likely to have to pass upon its constitutionality. For example, the American Bill of Rights places limitations not only on the federal government but on state governments as well, whereas the Canadian Bill of Rights, simply a statute and not enacted until 1960, does not affect provincial governments. There is only one major area in which Canadian courts exercise judicial review somewhat on the American model: federal-provincial relations. In earlier times, especially when appeals could be carried to the Judicial Committee of the Privy Council in Great Britain, court decisions did much to determine the balance of Canadian federalism. Today the Supreme Court of Canada plays an influential role in the federal system, albeit a less dramatic one than that often played by its American counterpart. One reason for the difference lies in the fact that the Canadian Court will hand down advisory opinions in advance of legislation or of the application of legislation when requested to do so by the federal government or by provincial governments. Such opinions, which the American Court has never supplied, are necessarily less charged with impact than those which overturn a law that may have been on the statute books for some time.

The structure of the Canadian court system provides another illustration of the centralized nature of Canadian federalism. Instead of two parallel and separate court systems, federal and state, as in the United States, there is in Canada only one system, part federal and part provincial. The Supreme Court of Canada and the Exchequer Court of Canada are the two purely federal courts, established, appointed, and paid by the federal government. Below the Supreme Court are superior, district, and county courts in the provinces; the provinces set up these courts, but the federal government appoints and pays their judges. Minor courts are the responsibility of the provinces. All these courts interpret and apply a criminal law that is uniform for the entire country, because criminal law is one of the subjects expressly reserved to the federal parliament. On the other hand, there are two systems of civil law, that of Quebec, which derives from Roman law, and that of the other provinces, which is based on the English common law. The law concerning commercial relations tends to be the same throughout the country, however, because in this area the Quebec civil code has been much influenced by common-law concepts.

Such, then, are some of the leading features of the Canadian political system, an adaptation to North American conditions of the British parliamentary tradition. Homage to this great tradition is paid by a careful respect for the age-old customs and usages of the Mother of Parliaments. But behind this scrupulous observance of forms the Canadian system has developed many distinctive lineaments deriving from the federal framework, from the nature of Canadian social and economic life, and from the operation of the system by the national political parties that have flourished in the last century.

5 Economic Life

When seen solely against an American background the Canadian economy may appear to be weak and vulnerable. With a population about one tenth the size of its neighbor's, Canada has a gross national product only about one twelfth to one fifteenth as large. Much of Canadian economic life is centered on the extraction of raw materials for export; its secondary manufacturing industry is relatively small, and much of it is owned and controlled from the outside. The standard of living is somewhere between twenty and twenty-five percent lower than the American average. Because of their intimate economic ties with the United States and their immediate knowledge of life in that country, Canadians are particularly prone to see their economic performance in comparative terms.

Nevertheless, such a perspective, however understandable and perhaps inevitable, can be misleading. From any other point of view, Canada is both a highly fortunate and an extremely successful country. Its people have the world's second highest standard of living, although their claim is sometimes challenged by the Swedes. In economic production they equal what is done by about twice their numbers of British or French or Germans. They are able to carry on a greater trade with the United States than does any other country in the world; indeed, despite their small population, they are one of the great trading nations of the world. Despite many problems arising out of great distances in a northern climate, Canadians have little reason to envy the economic prospects of any other nation.

Americans have a particular interest in understanding the workings of the Canadian economy. Canada is their most important cash market, buying more from the United States than any other two countries put together, more than all Latin America. Large sectors of American industry are heavily and increasingly dependent upon Canadian raw and semiprocessed materials. More American capital is invested in Canada than in any other country. Unquestionably, Canada is of prime importance to the United States from an economic point of view.

Yet the influences in the other direction are even more striking. Because of the vast size of their economy, Americans can remain relatively unaware of even so vast an association as the one they maintain with Canada, especially because it is rarely disturbed in a way to affect American interests. Canadians, on the other hand, can never be unmindful of how closely they are involved in the American economy. Because over half of Canadian exports go to the United States, the slightest tremor in the American market or the smallest change in tariff or customs policy can have significant effects north of the border. On the other hand, Canada buys even more from the United States than it sells to that country, with the result that in this bilateral trade it has a perennial balance-of-payments deficit in commodity exchanges. American investment has brought large sectors of Canadian industry under outside ownership and control. The two economies have become so intertwined that Canadian monetary and fiscal policy must normally adhere to the larger outlines of the American pattern. Thus, although Canadians are fully aware of the advantages which they derive from proximity to the vigorous and advanced American economy, they also see many difficulties and problems in this close association. In short, Canadians often seem to fluctuate between rejoicing over their economic prospects and lamenting the trend toward economic satellitism. The background of these hopes and fears should become clearer as we look at some of the main features of the Canadian economy.

Certainly its most striking feature, now as in the past, is its reliance upon the export of certain primary resource products. Throughout their history Canadians have lived by supplying outside markets with large quantities of such staple items as fish, furs, timber, wheat, and minerals. With the proceeds of these sales they have accumulated the funds needed to buy goods that could not be produced at home. They have also attracted capital from the outside for the development of these and other resources and for the improvement of their vitally important transportation system. Finally, they have sought to achieve a degree of diversification through the processing of some of these resources behind a protective tariff.

Of Canada's primary resource industries, agriculture has always been central, because it provided the basis for a growing population, but the period of its full ascendancy was mainly confined to the century following the 1820's. Before that time the fur trade, fishing, and lumbering outranked farming as wealth producers, while during the last generation and more the mining and forest industries have been overtaking agriculture, particularly in the vitally important export figures. The country's farming base has ceased to expand; in certain areas, it has been contracting. Although lands are still available that could be improved, much discussion of agriculture centers on the problems of existing farmers, many of whom are in a serious economic plight. The farming scene is increasingly marked by glaring contrasts between prosperity and poverty, a condition which it shares with its American counterpart.

The Precambrian Shield sharply divides Canadian agriculture into eastern and western sections: for about a thousand miles north of the states of Michigan, Wisconsin, and Minnesota, there are only limited and widely separated areas where successful farming can be carried on. The eastern and western agricultural sections are further restricted by the Shield pressing down from the North, by the Cordillerans on the west, and by the Appalachian highlands on the east. All told, only about seven and a half percent of Canada's territory is occupied agricultural land, and of this land over sixty percent is unimproved, summer fallow, or pasture. Canada's very large agricultural production comes from a small fraction of its total area and from about ten percent of its population.

Although much of eastern Canada is unsuited to agriculture, this region nevertheless contains some of the country's most prosperous farming communities. In the Maritime Provinces, Prince Edward Island and the St. John Valley of New Brunswick are noted for their potatoes, and the Annapolis Valley of Nova Scotia is equally noted for its apples, both crops having substantial export markets. But eastern Canada's richest and most varied farming lands stretch from the plain around Montreal westward to the Detroit River. Favorable conditions make possible the production of a great range of specialized crops: dairy products, fruit and vegetables, feed grains, livestock, and tobacco, to name some of the most important.

Western agriculture is dominated by Canada's most extensive farming region—the prairies that stretch from the Red River to the Rockies—and the prairies in turn are dominated by the wheat crop, although livestock-raising and mixed farming based on irrigation have increasingly provided a valuable element of diversification. Beyond the mountains, in British Columbia, are relatively small but highly specialized agricultural areas concentrating on truck- and fruit-farming as well as on livestock.

Canada has shared fully in the "agricultural revolution" in North America during the last generation; its farm production has been steadily climbing at the same time that the percentage of its population engaged in farming has been declining. As in the United States, this fact has increasingly involved the government in agriculture, especially in the implementing of various price-support programs. This trend has not gone so far as in the United States, but it has involved the spending of many millions of dollars to keep price floors under such items as butter, eggs, and pork, among many others. The most important crop of all—western wheat—has not been supported, but for many years the federal government has undertaken to buy the annual crop and find overseas markets for it. This task has led to frequent disputes with the United States when the American foreign-aid program took on the appearance, in Canadian eyes, of surplus disposal undermining commercial markets. On the other hand, Canada's readiness to sell wheat to Communist countries, particularly to China, has been greeted with little enthusiasm in the United States. Never a major source of friction, the existence of large agricultural surpluses in both countries was for some time a recurring cause of irritation in Canadian-American relations. But this competitive element is being offset by the growing importance in Canadian agriculture of livestock and livestock products, which have their leading foreign market in the United States. This increasing trade, when seen in relation to Canada's very large imports of fruits and vegetables from the United States, suggests that even in agriculture economic ties are being tightened in North America.

This trend is much more evident, however, when we turn to the other main primary resource industries, those emanating from the forests and the mines, because it was the dramatic rise of these industries, from the 1920's onward, that marked the real watershed of modern Canadian economic history. Before that time Canada's leading exports were wheat, cheese, and other agricultural products, destined mainly for British and other overseas markets. Since that time the leading exports have usually been woodpulp, newsprint, and various metals, which have found their main market south of the border. The east-west orientation of the economy has been supplemented and to a large extent overshadowed by a growing north-south orientation.

No one need be surprised that forests bulk large in the Canadian economy, because over half the total land surface is wooded, much of it with productive and accessible forests. Hardwoods are mainly confined to southern Ontario and a belt north of the prairies, but softwoods stretch all across the country from Newfoundland to British Columbia and well into the north. Although the indiscriminate assault of an earlier day has been replaced by a regulated exploitation that takes account of the interests of conservation, recreation, and tourism, the commercial use of the forests, providing Canada's leading exports, is still only a fraction of the wood annually available.

The forests have assumed their present importance because the various kinds of woods cut from them now sustain a great many secondary industries. Sawmills, especially in British

Columbia, supply a wide variety of wood-using industries and support the world's largest export of lumber. But the most striking development has been in pulp and paper production. This industry, centered in Quebec and Ontario and to an increasing extent in British Columbia, has long been the most important in Canada from the point of view of exports, total wages paid, capital invested, consumption of electrical energy, and purchase of goods and services, including transportation. Canada produces over forty percent of the world's newsprint, most of which is exported to the United States. Most of Canada's large pulp export also goes south of the border. For several years these primary and secondary forest industries have usually had a combined export value about three times that of wheat. This factor alone has been fundamental in giving the American market its enlarged significance to the Canadian export trade. And it is not surprising that this industry has been a prime target for the investment of American capital. Many large newspapers seek to assure supplies of newsprint by buying into the industry, and not surprisingly the Canadian economy is very sensitive to American newspaper strikes.

When we turn to the mining industry, we find that a new factor has been emerging to challenge the primacy of the forest industries, for if all mineral exports are combined they easily exceed in value those based upon the forests. Indeed, this industry has been changing so rapidly that only the most general statements remain true for more than a few months. But the trend is generally upward and toward larger imports by the United States, which in recent years has been taking about two thirds of all Canadian mineral exports.

In the second half of the nineteenth century gold strikes in the western mountains, from the American border to the Yukon, provided a valuable stimulus to the young Canadian economy, but the modern history of the mining industry began with the building of the railroads across the Precambrian Shield country of Ontario and Quebec. This activity first uncovered, and provided access to, the richest metallic deposits that have so far been exploited in Canada: nickel, copper, gold, zinc, lead, and silver in or near such places as Sudbury, Noranda, Porcupine, Timmins, and Kirkland Lake. Later on, similar deposits were found much farther to the west, in the Flin Flon area of northern Manitoba. These strikes revealed that the Shield was one of the richest sources of metals to be found anywhere in the world. The mountains of British Columbia also proved to contain more than gold's flash in the pan when lead, zinc, and other finds were made around Kimberley and Trail. Mines here and elsewhere had given the industry a strong base by the time of the First World War.

But in more recent years equally dramatic events have occurred. In the later 1940's and following came the discovery of large petroleum and natural gas fields in Alberta and elsewhere on the prairies. Uranium was found north of Lake Huron. Far to the east, in the 1950's and 1960's, came the most extraordinary development of all when vast iron-ore deposits were found along the Labrador-Quebec border; from being relatively unimportant, iron-ore production, nearly all of it for the American market, has recently catapulted to first place in value among Canadian metals and made Sept Iles, three hundred miles downriver from the city of Quebec, one of Canada's largest ports.

These are some of the outstanding highlights, but many other developments deserve mention. Canada has a large output of structural materials, most of them consumed in the domestic market, but some figuring prominently in the export trade. This is particularly true of asbestos, mined principally in the Eastern Townships, between Montreal and the American border; Canada has long been the world's leading producer of this material, and most of it goes to the American market. Iron, copper, and gold are found in many places other than those already noted, especially in many mines to the north of Lake Superior. A recent and very promising development is the mining of potash in Saskatchewan.

Yet mining is an industry that has its full quota of problems.

Despite large deposits of coal, mainly in Nova Scotia and Alberta, Canada has never been self-sufficient in this fuel because of the distance of these mines from large markets. More recently, as in the United States, coal has suffered heavily from the competition of other fuels and has been a sick industry, although its outlook at present is considerably more promising because of the increasing production of electricity by thermal power. Transportation costs have also limited many other mining developments, particularly those in the more remote areas of the North; many of these will have to await a world shortage of minerals and a resulting increase in prices. In fact, world prices govern nearly all aspects of an industry that exports about eighty percent of its production. Furthermore, technical changes may reduce demand for a given mineral or the course of world events may undermine an industry, as happened when the nuclear test ban sharply reduced the demand for uranium. The course of American policy is very influential: a decision at Washington to accord protection or preference to domestic producers can deal a body blow to a sector of Canadian mining. Even more important is the fact that predominant American ownership and control has the apparent effect of channeling raw minerals to processing plants in the United States, thus limiting Canadian development of this profitable phase of operations. The mining industry contributes much less to the wealth of individual Canadians than export figures might indicate.

The oldest of Canada's primary industries, fisheries and furs, are now so much overshadowed by more spectacular activities that they can receive only a glance here. Canada ranks about sixth among the countries of the world in the quantities of fish caught, with herring and cod predominating in the Atlantic coast fisheries and salmon on the Pacific, although many other varieties are taken off the coasts as well as in the fresh-water fisheries. About seventy percent of the annual production is exported, more than two thirds of it to the United States. As for furs, trapping is still important in the northern forests, but by far the largest production now comes from mink farmers on the prairies and in the central provinces. Both these industries tend to be somewhat unstable, affected as they are by natural conditions and by changing tastes and fashions.

The primary industries, in summary, provide the foundations of an economy that is heavily dependent upon foreign exports and thus upon external supply and demand. When world supplies of minerals, wheat, lumber, and paper are abundant or over-abundant Canadian economic life is immediately affected by lower prices or a drying-up of markets. Canada is more fortunate than some raw-material-producing countries in being able to process some of its materials before the export stage and in having its biggest market near at hand in the world's largest and most expansive economy. But Canada will continue to have a relatively unstable and even precarious economy until it can broaden its manufacturing base and secure some of the wealth that comes from this most profitable phase of economic activity. Before the problems of reaching this goal can be understood we need to grasp the role of transportation and of energy use.

A country of enormous distances, severe climatic conditions, and scattered resources and population is supremely dependent upon adequate transportation facilities. The task of providing them has been both a central theme and a prime condition of Canadian development, and the costs of maintaining and improving them continue to be a major charge upon the economy. Transportation has been so fundamental and so expensive that government has had to play a leading role at every important stage.

The oldest system, water transportation, is still fundamental. In order to make full use of waterways it has been necessary over the years to spend vast sums, mostly in public funds, on port improvement, harbor installations, ferries, ice breakers, channel dredging, and, above all, canals, with the most striking recent event being the building of the St. Lawrence Seaway, in conjunction with the United States, in the 1950's. Waterways sustain the movement of western wheat to tidewater, of iron and coal to Canadian and American steel mills, of metals and pulp and paper to American lake ports, and of countless other heavy items. Despite the break in navigation caused by winter ice — now made shorter by the use of ice breakers and other devices — the waterways and especially the Seaway play a vital role in moving goods to market and in undergirding secondary industry. After suffering a decline following the introduction of pipelines and improved roads, the waterways have recently been experiencing a remarkable comeback in relation to the other carriers.

The carrier that has suffered most from the new forms of competition is, of course, the railroad. The nineteenth-century economy, based upon the opening up of the West and the movement of goods on an east-west axis, was built around the railroad, and Canadian governments were prepared to provide extensive financial backing to support the building of transcontinental lines reaching from the Atlantic coast to the Pacific. In fact, excessive optimism early in the twentieth century led to overbuilding, followed by bankruptcies and the need to consolidate several lines into the government-owned and operated Canadian National Railways system, set up after the First World War. The Canadian Pacific Railway, which had also received much government aid, remained under private ownership, with close government supervision. These two systems dominate the Canadian railroad scene, although there are several smaller lines. The C.N.R. and C.P.R. are among the largest transportation systems to be found anywhere in the world, and their interests reach far beyond railroads and far beyond the borders of Canada.

Despite perennial financial difficulties, the railroads held their own as the major carrier until well into the 1950's; indeed, like their American counterparts, they enjoyed a remarkable increase of traffic during the Second World War. Since the 1950's, however, they have been steadily losing traffic to the newer types of carriers, and because of the nature of their equipment and their close supervision and control by government, they have not always been able to adapt themselves adequately to a rapidly changing economic scene. But with the help of subsidies for certain kinds of freight and to certain regions they continue to serve vital national purposes. Railroads will probably go on being relatively more important in the Canadian economy than in the American.

Of the newer forms of transportation, road traffic has had a remarkable increase, particularly between the two central provinces of Ontario and Quebec and between them and American points. Government participation has been mainly in the form of provincial highway-building programs and in federal-provincial cooperation in the four thousand five hundred miles of the Trans-Canada Highway, opened in 1962, when for the first time Canadians could drive in reasonable comfort from one end of the country to the other without dipping down into the United States. Improved roads in the north are making air-freight traffic, in which Canada was once the world's leader, less important, although it is still indispensable in many areas. Recently, however, the most startling transportation development has been in pipelines. In the 1950's the world's longest oil and natural-gas pipelines were built from the Alberta and Saskatchewan fields to reach the Ontario market in the east and Vancouver in the west as well as to link up with the American export market. Quebec and the Atlantic provinces still depend upon foreign oil, mainly from Venezuela and the Middle East.

Mention of pipelines leads naturally to the question of energy, a fundamental factor in any country's economy. In the years before the First World War, when industrial growth depended mainly upon coal, Canada's growth was handicapped, as we have already noted, by the distance of its coal deposits from the markets in the central provinces. Despite subsidized transportation, Canada depended mainly upon imports from Pennsylvania and Middle Western states. But the new forms of energy have changed the picture drastically; not only is Canada second only to the United States in per capita consumption of energy, but it is increasingly an exporter in this field. Apart from oil and natural gas, the most striking development has been in hydroelectric power, particularly in the provinces of Quebec, Ontario, and British Columbia, whose economies have been transformed by the abundance of low-cost electric power. It has made possible the growth of the mining, pulp and paper, and chemical industries as well as many forms of manufacturing. Perhaps the most dramatic example of the impact of hydroelectric power has been the establishment of a large aluminum industry at Arvida in Quebec and at Kitimat in British Columbia, although the raw material (bauxite) has to be brought from the West Indies and the Guianas.

These newer sources of energy have a much greater impact upon Canadian-American relations than did the old. American investment in oil and natural gas has had political repercussions in Canada, as we shall see in later chapters. Many hydroelectric installations are along the border, or cut across the border, thus requiring joint planning and continuous cooperation for their development. Of particular importance on the Canadian side is the fact that many projects cannot be developed, and Canadian consumers supplied, unless the American market can be tapped. For instance, the cost of building pipelines west and south to Vancouver was prohibitive until arrangements were made to export natural gas to the Pacific Coast states. An even more ambitious scheme looks to the transmission of electric power from Labrador via Quebec to the northeastern states. To an increasing extent the exploitation of natural resources requires a continental approach and cooperation among several levels of federal, state, and provincial governments and of large, often international, corporations.

It is against this background of natural resources, transportation, and energy sources that Canadian manufacturing must be seen. As might be expected, the largest and the most efficient enterprises are those concerned with the processing of primary materials, mainly for the export market: pulp and paper mills, smelting and refining and iron and steel mills, petroleum refining (for the home market), sawmills, and so on. The outstanding exception is motor-vehicle manufacturing, but this industry has so far been heavily dependent on parts from the United States, which constitute Canada's largest single import. Secondary manufacturing—that is, producing goods directly for the consumer—faces such obstacles as a small and, in part, scattered market, heavy expenses resulting from long hauls and a severe climate, and labor costs second only to those of the United States. A further factor is that manufacturing takes place behind a protective tariff, which entails high costs, fragmentation, and an output per man hour much below the American average. Some products like whiskey and farm implements are able to find foreign markets, particularly in the United States, but for the most part Canadian manufacturers are confined to the relatively small domestic market. Yet without the tariff many of them, textile producers, for instance, would not survive the competition of foreign imports coming from specialized, large-scale American plants or from overseas units with lower labor costs. In addition, much of the secondary manufacturing is done in branch plants built behind the tariff by American corporations, which are now often the tariff's most ardent defenders. Such plants, aimed at the Canadian market, have relatively little incentive to seek outside customers, for to do so might possibly mean competition with the parent firm, from whom they are often heavy importers of materials.

In spite of these difficulties it is clear that secondary manufacturing must be expanded if jobs are to be found for a growing population, trained people retained, and the standard of living maintained and raised. The high priority assigned to this objective was indicated by the federal government's decision, in 1963, to establish the Department of Industry, with the objectives of assisting manufacturers to adapt to changing conditions and techniques and to promote industrial research, a field to which too little attention has been given in Canada. Tax incentives and direct financial assistance are being provided in an attempt to improve the technical capacity of Canadian industry. Areas with high levels of chronic unemployment are designated to receive particular attention through programs involving cooperation with provincial and local governments and with private industry. It is too early to say how far such efforts can counteract the already mentioned obstacles to a high level of efficient manufacturing.

Finally, we should note that Canada shares with the United States and other developed countries the growing emphasis upon a wide range of tertiary activities. Despite rapidly increasing production, the proportion of the population engaged in primary and secondary activities has been steadily declining. Mechanization and automation have made it possible to increase output with a static or even a decreased labor force. On the other hand the number of people engaged in a wide variety of services — technical, governmental, educational, health, social, advisory, and so on — has become so large that they now make up well over half of all those employed, and this trend seems to be accelerating rather than diminishing. The effects are to concentrate population in large metropolitan areas, close to the American border, to increase the problems of such apparently peripheral regions as the Atlantic Provinces and parts of the Prairie Provinces and to increase job insecurity among those lacking relevant training. On the other hand those who are able to adapt themselves to the new society and the new economy enjoy a rising standard of living and an easier, although not necessarily a more satisfying, life than their pioneer forefathers could have imagined. At the center of these changes is the electronics revolution. It emanates from the United States, but its impact upon Canadian-American relations is only beginning to be grasped. We may reasonably think, however, that it will accelerate economic integration on a continental plane and that Canadian procedures will increasingly be adapted to American models. In short, the age of the computer and the business machine may increase the tendency to think of Canada as one of the continent's regional economies, comparable, say, to California or the North Central states.

III

THE PAST:

HOW CANADA

SURVIVED IN

NORTH AMERICA

Any adequate understanding of the fact of Canada's existence today as a separate nation in North America is impossible without some knowledge of its history. That history is radically different from the United States' in many important respects; indeed, it may seem extraordinary that two countries which are thought to be so much alike should be so dissimilar in origin and development. Any attempt to write a history of North America would have to stress contrasts as much as comparisons, not only between the countries on either side of the Rio Grande but between those separated by the Canadian-American boundary. Moreover, for the first two hundred years, and more, of Canadian-American history the prevailing condition along the boundary was hostility punctuated by open warfare, followed in turn, after 1815, by two generations in which tenseness and bad feeling were more noticeable than amity and civility. Despite the firmness of Canadian-American friendship in our own day, it is scarcely surprising that memories of this long tradition of animosity still linger in the folk-mind of the weaker country to caution against too close an association with the mighty neighbor to the south.

Enmity, antagonism, and competition long precede the emergence of the United States or of Canada as a national entity. They appear at the very beginning of the first European attempts to exploit the resources of North America and to establish footholds on that continent. But imperial rivalry is not the whole, or even the main, story. From a very early period colonists in the New World were consumed by ambitions which led them to quarrel and fight with their neighbors even when the mother countries back in Europe were not at war. Nothing would be more inaccurate than to think of peaceable pioneers, desiring only to live in Arcadian harmony but embroiled in overseas power struggles. On the contrary the early settlers strove mightily and often ruthlessly to dominate as much of the continent as they could grasp. In the long run, as we know, they proved to be too much for the European powers, which were ejected in the developing contest.

The French and the English were relatively slow in establishing themselves in the New World. After the early explorations made by John Cabot, Jacques Cartier, and their successors and after the first failures in colonization, contact with America was mainly for the purpose of pursuing the fisheries. It was not until the beginning of the seventeenth century, a century after the start of the Spanish and Portuguese empires, that the French and English secured footholds on the western continent that proved to be permanent: at Port Royal (in Nova Scotia), at Jamestown (in Virginia), and at Quebec. A few years later came the *Mayflower's* famous voyage and the founding of New England. In the beginning the two European powers, and their peoples, shared many common goals in their approach to the New World—desire for commercial gain, missionary zeal, geographical curiosity, and patriotic fervor—but it was not long before the two empires in America began to show marked divergences, caused both by the influence of North American geography and by contrasting political and cultural traditions.

In the English empire the dominant characteristics were diversity, growth, and local autonomy. Before the end of the seventeenth century a dozen colonies stretched along the Atlantic seaboard from Massachusetts to the Carolinas, some with royal governors, some under proprietors, two electing their own governors, and all with elected assemblies. Despite a certain tightening up of imperial control at the end of the century, all these colonies enjoyed a remarkable degree of self-government. Population was of varied national origins and numerous religious faiths, and it was rapidly growing. In contrast to other new colonies, these engaged in a wide range of economic activities, which were bringing into prominence an aggressive merchant class, a planter aristocracy, and a large number of substantial yeomen farmers.

But to the north the scene was different in almost every respect. In the Atlantic regions—Newfoundland and Nova Scotia—the fishery was still so dominant that settlement had

barely begun. In Newfoundland official English policy discouraged permanent settlement. In Nova Scotia there were only a
small number of Acadians farming along the Bay of Fundy, the
French hold on the region was very tenuous, and New England
interest and influence in the region were already very strong and
soon to become more so.

The center of French power in North America was far to the
west of the Atlantic coastal regions. It was on the shores of the St.
Lawrence River that the colony of New France had its start when
Samuel Champlain founded Quebec in 1608. Like the English
colonies to the south, especially Virginia, New France was
founded with the backing of merchants who hoped for a return
on their investment. As Virginia came to depend upon the export
of tobacco, so New France came to depend upon another
staple — furs — for which there was a ready market in Europe.
Paradoxically, this dependence was at first nearly the colony's
undoing, for, in an attempt to secure furs from the Hurons,
Champlain took the side of this tribe in its wars with the Iroquois, whose attacks kept New France under a state of siege for
many years. Moreover, the career of the colony appeared to be
abruptly terminated when an English attack in 1629 forced
Champlain to surrender Quebec.

Nevertheless, the precarious early history of New France
resumed when England gave up Quebec in a treaty of 1632 and
Champlain returned with a hundred colonists. He founded a
second nucleus of settlement at Three Rivers a year before his
death in 1635, and a third center was founded at Montreal in
1642. The colony continued to be drawn into the interior by men
who combined exploring and the fur trade and by Jesuits who set
up missions to the Hurons south of Georgian Bay (the great
eastern arm of Lake Huron). By the middle of the 1640's these
two groups — traders and missionaries — had established ties with
the Indians that reached well toward the Lake Michigan country.
As a result the Iroquois, who had formerly relied on furs from
north of the Great Lakes for their trade with the Dutch on the

Hudson River, became increasingly desperate. Their attacks on New France increased in ferocity, and in 1649 they succeeded in wiping out the Jesuit missions south of Georgian Bay. The fur trade by which the colony lived was utterly disrupted, the merchants who had been given a charter in 1628 were close to ruin, and the government at home was too deeply involved in European troubles to provide much help. The colony hung on, almost by a thread, sustained by a determined clergy, who drew support from the church at home, and by the adventurous young men (*coureurs de bois*), who went into the woods to re-establish trading contacts with the Indians north and west of the upper Great Lakes. In 1663, after more than fifty years, the colony was still alive, with a population of about two thousand five hundred, but they were a weak and shaken outpost when compared with the tens of thousands of settlers in New England and in the Chesapeake region. On the seaboard the picture was even darker, for the New Englanders, with Cromwell's approval, had captured the main French settlements in Acadia in 1654. And yet, at the beginning of the 1660's New France was on the threshold of a long generation of growth and consolidation that would ensure the survival of the "French fact" in North America in spite of all later defeats and vicissitudes.

The starting point of this great change lay in the mother country, which, after a generation of war and internal dissension, was entering upon an era when it would be the unrivaled power of Europe. At the beginning of the 1660's, with the death of Mazarin, Louis XIV resolved to make himself the real ruler of his country, and he placed the conduct of economic policy in the capable hands of Jean-Baptiste Colbert. This zealous minister, who was determined to realize more wealth from overseas colonies, as an offset to the maritime power of England and the Netherlands, sent out military reinforcement and some colonists, put out of business the nearly defunct company, which had had responsibility for the colony, and placed New France under direct royal supervision. In contrast to the English colonies to the south, the growth of New France was stimulated, in large part, by infusions of strength, both human and financial, directly resulting from official government policy.

Under the indefatigable Colbert, new policies were adopted and agents sent out to implement them. The institutions of the colony were reorganized: to the governor, as the King's representative, was added the intendant, charged with internal administration, and on a separate but equal plane, there was the bishop, who saw to the spiritual and educational needs of the people. In the minds of Louis and Colbert, these officials were to work together to defend the colony, to mold its economy to the requirements of French mercantilism, and to make it into an authentic French province. In particular, because the French West Indies were concentrating on sugar and other semitropical items and could not feed themselves, New France and Acadia must emphasize the production for export of cheap foodstuffs and lumber, which otherwise would have to come to the Indies from outside the French Empire. Thus New France was to have a planned economy stressing the development of industries needed to ensure a degree of self-sufficiency and the agriculture that would provide a surplus for export. In this conception there was relatively little place for the fur trade; energies were to be concentrated within the settled regions rather than dispersed into the woods.

Nevertheless, these conceptions were never fully realized. To be sure, a considerable force of regular troops defeated the Iroquois so severely that these foes remained at peace with the colony for several years. A determined immigration policy more than tripled the population by the middle of the 1670's. (Most French Canadians of our own day are descended from the settlers who had arrived by this period.) A vigorous and capable young intendant, Jean Talon, sought to encourage diversification of economic activity and the concentration of settlement. But, despite these successes, the colony was often an exasperating disappointment to the tidy minds of the bureaucrats in Paris. The colonists, both the leaders and the lead, could not or would not play the roles required of them. Instead of working constructively together, the governor and the intendant were frequently locked in bitter quarrels, while the ultramontane-minded bishops, first Laval and then St. Vallier, refused to become mere agents of the royal will. During the bitter and prolonged clash of imperious personalities, the detailed instructions of the Paris government were often ignored or slighted.

Nor were the humbler members — the habitants — more malleable. They were not, as were so many in the English colonies, dissidents who had fled to America to build a life denied them in the Old World, nor were they insistent upon a high degree of political activity. They were loyal subjects of the King, faithful sons of the Church, and ready to accept those in authority. But they were passive rather than subservient. When Church tithes seemed to them to be too high, they simply did not pay them, and the tithes eventually had to be reduced. Efforts to group them into villages failed; the habitants insisted upon a lot with a river frontage, and so settlement continued to be strung out along the St. Lawrence and the Richelieu, a pattern, later carried into the west, that made for strip farming rather than diversified developments. The habitant held his land under the seigneurial system and owed certain duties to the seigneur, who himself had obligations which were quite expensive to him. The seigneur, despite a certain position of prestige, was a harassed landlord rather than an overbearing aristocrat, and the habitant was far from being an exploited serf. European feudalism took no deeper roots here than elsewhere in America.

Above all, it proved to be impossible to reduce the significance of the fur trade in the economy of New France, for this trade promised a richer return than any other enterprise. In Colbert's plans the trade was to consist of an exchange that should take place at the edge of the colony between Indians who brought down the furs and government-designated traders, but the pressures toward expansion proved to be irresistible. Even Talon, faithful as he was to Colbert's design, encouraged this trend by supporting explorations aimed at the discovery of new resources; it was the old resource — furs — that was tapped by these explorations. And after Talon's return in 1672 New France gave itself almost wholly to the western trade. Once again the mother country was deeply involved in Europe and thus unable to provide stimulus toward diversification, whereas the new governor, Count Frontenac, had private reasons, arising out of his mountainous debts, for pushing the trade with every effort.

Moreover, the colony was driven in this direction by pressures from both the north and the south. By this time the English were establishing themselves on Hudson Bay, a move that allowed them to tap some of the richest fur country, and to the south they had turned New Netherland into New York and with cheaper and better goods were attracting a growing trade to Albany, a trade on which the Iroquois heavily depended. Squeezed in this way, the French had little choice but to break through into the Great Lakes and beyond for the purpose of establishing and protecting a far-flung commercial empire. A fort was built at Cataraqui (now Kingston) at the northeastern end of Lake Ontario, and posts at Niagara and at Michilimackinac (the junction of Lakes Huron and Michigan). Far to the southwest La Salle tried, unsuccessfully, to make the whole of the Mississippi Valley tributary to his fur-trading ambitions. In the northwest Montreal traders spread their network of trade beyond Lake Michigan and toward the western prairies. Thus the small colony on the St. Lawrence was reaching out halfway across the continent and down to the Gulf of Mexico at a time when the far greater wealth and population of the English colonies were still concentrated on the Atlantic seaboard.

New France's daring, even reckless, expansion was a prelude to conflict which would last, with intervals of uneasy peace, for nearly three quarters of a century. Within the colony religious authorities, particularly the Jesuits, strenuously opposed the fur traders' use of brandy in their bartering with the Indians, a practice which made almost impossible the Christianizing and civilizing mission of the missionaries. It was a campaign that the Jesuits were doomed to lose: increasingly powerful interests in the colony profited from the growth of the fur trade, while the missions themselves depended upon French influence in the west or at least upon the Iroquois' being held back from attack. As for the Iroquois, they felt growing alarm at the sight of their hinterland falling into the French orbit and reacted by attacking the western Indians who were trading with the French. In turn, the leaders of New France worked to strengthen the western posts and made defensive thrusts which culminated in open war after Frontenac resumed the governorship in 1689. With England and France now at war, the Iroquois fiercely attacked the outskirts of Montreal, and Frontenac retaliated with bloody raids along the northern border of New York and New England. After years of sparring, the two empires, their colonies, and their Indian allies were now locked in mortal combat. Neither New France, on the one side, nor New York and New England, on the other, felt safe as long as the other existed.

The first round of the struggle, which lasted through most of the 1690's, proved to be inconclusive. Far to the east, the weakly held French settlements in Acadia suffered heavily when Frontenac's successes in the interior led the New Englanders to seek revenge by a series of coastal raids. But the men from Boston made their greatest effort in a naval expedition which came into the Gulf and River of St. Lawrence in 1690 and put the fort of Quebec under siege. It did not fall, and the baffled New Englanders had to retire to wait for another day. New France rebounded from this near-disaster by inflicting a series of defeats upon the Iroquois, while combined French and Canadian forces struck successfully at the New Englanders in Acadia and Maine and the English in Newfoundland and Hudson Bay. When peace came in 1697 the French empire in Acadia, along the St. Lawrence, and in the west was still fully intact, and it now controlled most of Hudson Bay. The people of New France, nearly all native to the country, were now Canadians rather than French colonists. They felt that they had given a good account of themselves in the struggle with the English to the south who outnumbered them fifteen or twenty to one, and they looked ahead confidently.

Moreover, the imperial policy of Louis XIV now favored the expansionism that Canadian leaders had always wanted. Looking to control of the Spanish throne and to the possibility of a link with Spain's American empire, Louis aimed to hem the English in along the eastern coast and to extend French power in the direction of Mexico. In 1698, Iberville, a Canadian leader who had been prominent in the recent victories, was sent to establish a base at the mouth of the Mississippi and to keep the English from moving out beyond the Alleghanies. Coureurs de bois, who only recently had been ordered out of the west, were now encouraged to range up and down the Mississippi, to strengthen ties with the Indians, and to keep English traders out of the country from the Great Lakes to the Gulf of Mexico. Missionaries were also supported for the purpose of winning Indians over to the French side. The policy of Colbert, who had died some years before, was thus totally reversed as the eighteenth century dawned, and the French set out to control a vast region stretching from Newfoundland and Hudson Bay down to Louisiana and perhaps beyond.

It was a rashly ambitious scheme which threatened to drain the energies of New France. The mother country's full and energetic support combined with continued division in the English colonies would be necessary if there was to be any chance of success. But Louis was almost at once involved in the War of the Spanish Succession (1701-1714) against a formidable coalition and unable to spare much strength to send to America. For a time, while Marlborough's great battles were being fought in Europe, there was truce in America, at least in the interior. Neither side was ready to see the savage raids resume. But after a few years the English, unable to bring France to its knees in Europe, turned to

America, and their northern colonists were more than willing to join the struggle. Indeed, along the Atlantic, where Massachusetts and Acadia had exchanged raids and counterraids, the truce had been intermittent at best. And the New Yorkers were ready now to move north before the Canadian hold on the western trade became too firm. Once again the New Englanders took Port Royal, which henceforth, as Annapolis Royal, would remain in English hands and once again a naval expedition was sent against Quebec, in 1711, only to come to grief in the Gulf of St. Lawrence. In fact, the English attacks came to relatively little, yet it was by the Treaty of Utrecht (1713) that the French empire in America began to contract on its northern and eastern sides. The English regained their position on Hudson Bay and in Newfoundland, and, to the great satisfaction of New England, the French gave up Acadia, although they retained Cape Breton. As for the west, it was stated that the Indians could trade with either the French or the English, a prospect that clouded the future of the Canadian fur trade.

Nevertheless New France itself was still intact, and it was to have a generation of peace in which to strengthen itself before the inevitable resumption of conflict. During that generation its population more than doubled, to pass beyond forty thousand by 1740, and nearly all through natural increase. At a time when the English colonies to the south were attracting a large and varied immigration, including Scotch-Irish and Germans and people of many religious faiths, out of which a "new man," an American, would emerge, the Canadian, while also a man of the New World, was strengthening the bonds of a closely knit society that was wholly French and Catholic. Although many of its people were strongly attached to the soil, its tone was by no means entirely rural or traditional. At least a quarter of them lived in towns, and the farmers, unlike American frontiersmen, were in easy communication with each other along the rivers on which their lots fronted; sociability rather than isolation marked the life of the Canadians and further helped to bind them together.

Moreover, the fur trade and the means needed to protect it lent a commercial and military atmosphere to the community, and the rise of an artisan class made for further diversity. Like the colonists to the south the Canadians of New France believed that their way of life was both different from and better than that to be found in Europe, yet they also had little in common with those other North Americans in New England, New York, and beyond.

Moreover, these people, especially the New Yorkers, were dangerous competitors who threatened the trade on which New France so heavily depended. With cheaper and better goods and with an improved art in dealing with the Indians, the New Yorkers were increasingly successful in buying up many of the furs coming down toward Montreal. As well, the English were back on Hudson Bay to attract furs in the other direction. Even the sister French colony of Louisiana made difficulties by drawing furs down the Mississippi. Thus the St. Lawrence route had rivals at the south, the northwest, and the southwest, and the Canadian leaders determined to react both by protecting and by extending their western commercial empire. Posts and forts were built or strengthened at various points on the Great Lakes to protect consignments to Montreal and to influence the Indians, and in the 1730's and 1740's La Vérendrye and his sons built a line of forts between Lake Superior and the Lake Winnipeg country, reaching toward the lower Saskatchewan River. This extension, in which we see eastern and western Canada first linked together, meant carrying on a trade over a precarious and dangerous route of some two thousand miles, yet New France had no other option.

Far to the east, on the Atlantic shores, the reduced French empire was very much on the defensive. The English now had title to Nova Scotia, but except for a garrison at Annapolis did not occupy the peninsula. The French-speaking Acadians stayed on, attached to their land and determined to be neutral toward the international rivals. In this near-vacuum New Englanders became more and more dominant as they strove to use Nova

Scotia to strengthen their hold on the Atlantic fisheries. For their part, the French sought to hold their place by building Louisbourg, an imposing but far from impregnable fortified town on Cape Breton, by cultivating ties with the Indians, and by retaining some contact with the Acadians. At best it was a French presence which might keep open the eastern approaches to the continent, but it was one which the Puritan New Englanders regarded as a great menace: a threat to their fisheries, a source of privateering, and a place where the mass was said. When war between England and France finally resumed, the first main action was a New England expedition which, with British naval help, readily took Louisbourg in 1745.

This third conflict for the control of North America, which the English colonists called King George's War, proved to be indecisive, and its end was a mere truce foreshadowing the greater struggle to come. French attempts to retake Louisbourg failed as did Canadian attacks on Acadia; similarly, New York and New England plans for expeditions against Quebec and Montreal came to nothing. As before, the Canadians tried to keep their much more numerous opponents off balance by joining with the Indians in terror raids across the border. On their side, New York and New England came out of the war, which ended in 1748, convinced that their people could never live in peace until Canada was destroyed and outraged that Britain had handed back Louisbourg to France at the negotiating table. After a war which had raised such passions, there could be no real peace. Each side turned quickly to prepare for the next phase. The people living in North America were taking a more and more prominent part in the struggle for the continent; increasingly it was their struggle as much as that of the imperial powers in Europe.

This war was barely ended when it became clear that the country between Lake Erie and the Ohio River was now to be a main zone of conflict. It was a region in which some of the English colonies had claims deriving from their vaguely worded charters but in which they had hitherto not been very active. Now their people were beginning to move across the Alleghanies, never a real barrier, to prepare for land speculation and for trade with the Indians (at which the Virginians and Pennsylvanians were becoming increasingly adept). These outward thrusts were immediately seen by the Canadians as a clear danger; they had already been disturbed by New York's erection of Fort Oswego on the south side of Lake Ontario, and they realized that if they continued to be hemmed in, their wide-ranging fur empire was doomed. As the weaker but better organized side, they reacted with outward thrusts of their own to control the southwestern trade and guarantee communications between Canada and Louisiana. They asserted the French King's title to the Ohio Valley, built forts near where Erie and Pittsburgh now stand, and, with the Indians, cleared the Pennsylvania traders out of a post southwest of the present city of Toledo. On two occasions, in 1754 and 1755, a young Virginian, George Washington, tried to warn them off, but each time he was repulsed, the second time with force. Canada and Virginia moved toward war on the Ohio although the two mother countries were formally at peace. But England and France now, in 1755, took a hand by sending large reinforcements of regular troops to fight in uneasy conjunction with the colonial militia of each side. The shortcomings of European soldiers for American guerrilla fighting were illustrated when Braddock's British army was destroyed on the way to Fort Duquesne (Pittsburgh) and when Dieskau's French regulars were mauled near Lake Champlain. Although welcoming the European soldiers, the colonial leaders on each side were maneuvering energetically for Indian allies.

While the stage was being set south of the Great Lakes and the St. Lawrence the lines were also being drawn in Nova Scotia, where the Canadians were trying to stem the English advance. With the French once again at Louisbourg, the Canadians sought to control the overland passage between that fort and Quebec by occupying the mouth of the St. John River and by building Fort

Beauséjour on the narrow isthmus between the present provinces of Nova Scotia and New Brunswick. For their part the British had to respond to New England's anger at the retrocession of Louisbourg and did so by establishing the stronghold of Halifax in 1749, the first imperial base ever to be deliberately established by Britain in America. Fort Beauséjour was answered by Fort Lawrence, a few miles away. The British command then turned to the intractable problem of the French-speaking Acadians, who insisted upon their neutrality but who in English and New England eyes appeared as a source of potential danger. When they once again refused to take the oath of allegiance, Governor Lawrence, urged on by the New Englanders, took in 1755 the then unprecedented step of ordering their deportation. This harsh and probably unnecessary removal was soon followed by a large influx of New Englanders, who had long been coveting these lands, and, in 1758, by the calling of the first representative assembly in what is now Canada. In that same year Louisbourg was again taken by a British fleet and army, and henceforth Nova Scotia would remain firmly in British hands, with the Yankees from New England later to assume the neutral role which the Acadians had played before them.

By this time the British counteroffensive in the interior was also beginning to make its weight felt. For two years, in 1756 and 1757, the Canadians and the French, under the command of the French general Montcalm and the Canadian governor Vaudreuil, had won several successes. They had taken Fort Oswego, long an affront to them, and captured Fort William Henry, at the southern end of Lake Champlain, thus strengthening their control of the water approaches to Montreal. But Canadian and French power was waning while that of the British and of their colonists was inexorably growing. Anglo-American forces took Fort Duquesne and retook Oswego, although Montcalm staved off the advance on the Lake Champlain front. New France was now cut off from the west and could only await attack on its St. Lawrence homeland from a vastly stronger enemy whose control of the seas precluded any possibility of reinforcement from France. In 1759 a British fleet and army under Wolfe came into the gulf and up the river to attack Quebec. Such expeditions, by the English and the New Englanders and New Yorkers, had failed in 1690 and in 1711 and had not even got started in the 1740's, and for nearly two months it appeared that the Quebec defenses would hold until the approach of winter forced the invaders back down the river. But on the night of September 12, Wolfe was able to put his men ashore above the city and in the morning four thousand five hundred of them were in position on the plain before Quebec. Leading his men out to battle, Montcalm was killed, as was Wolfe, and the French army was forced to give up the town. Quebec had fallen, although the victory was not clinched until a British fleet with reinforcements came up the river in the following spring. Elsewhere French posts, at Niagara and on Lake Champlain, were also forced to surrender, and the ring was closed at Montreal, which capitulated in 1760. After more than a century and a half of valorous, skillful, and often ruthless effort, France's American empire lay in ruins. With approaches on the Atlantic and a base on the St. Lawrence a few thousand men had reached out to Louisiana, to the prairies beyond Lake Michigan, to Hudson Bay, and even to the far Saskatchewan. But their reach had exceeded their grasp. One by one the extremities had been cut off and now the central homeland was surrendered. The fleur-de-lys gave way to the Union Jack, which now flew from the Arctic wastes to the Florida keys. The colonists to the south gave prayerful thanks for the fall of their papist foes who had raided their frontier homes and thwarted their ambitions.

Accepting defeat, the French went home, to take up their struggle with the British on other and later battlefields. But the overwhelming majority of the Canadians stayed, some seventy thousand of them. Whatever flag flew, Canada was their home and had been for several generations; problems of cooperating with the French in the recent war had shown how distinct they had become from the people of the mother country. (The colonists to the south had been discovering the same fact in the same way.) Now the Canadians must live on under a conqueror with an alien language, an alien religion, and alien laws and customs, their land, it would appear, open to penetration from those New Englanders and New Yorkers whom they had been trying to drive back for more than a century. But a century and a half of effort in North America had equipped Canadians to resist such pressures. In time, as the struggle for survival sharpened, they would be powerfully reminded that they had come of men and women who had done great things on this continent and who had built civilization in a wild land. They would remember Champlain, La Vérendrye, and the less renowned explorers, missionaries, soldiers, merchants, and plain farmers who in their time strode the land as free men. Some had been "Caesars of the wilderness," some had been devoted workers for the Church, some had been masters of far-flung enterprises, and many had been tenacious pioneers. Whatever else they were, the Canadians were not a people without a history, and as that history was told in later years they would see it as an epic to which they must remain true.

7 Revolution and Separation

For fifteen years after the French armies along the St. Lawrence surrendered in 1760 Canadian and American history
appeared to converge. All the continent east of the Mississippi
and north into Hudson Bay was now under British control, with
the title confirmed by the Treaty of Paris of 1763. The struggle for
dominion over this portion of North America, which had raged
intermittently for a century and more, seemed to be over. As the
British people contemplated their greatly enlarged empire, vic-
torious in India as well as in North America, they were tempted
to refer disparagingly to the Romans of old as mere pigmies. The
American colonists, more than a million in number, and proud to
be part of this great empire, also looked forward to an expanding
future now that the French enemy was defeated. Yet the glorious
victory, instead of bringing unity to the continent and harmony to
the conquerors, was soon followed by rumblings that grew into
an earthquake. Once again there was long and bitter war, a civil
war within the Empire, in which Americans fought Americans as
well as the British, in which the French again took part, this time
on the side of their old enemies, the Americans, and in which the
Canadians were mainly neutral. When the smoke of battle lifted,
the old divisions had reappeared under a new form of political
geography, and Canadians and Americans resumed their separate but closely linked paths, with the British now joined with
the Canadians instead of the Americans.

So vast a cataclysm had many and diverse origins, but it was
precipitated by the very victory over which the British and the
Americans had greatly rejoiced. This enormous empire could no
longer be governed by the rather haphazard methods of earlier
years. To the old problems that cried out for attention, new ones
were now added. The continent had to have a firmer organization
imposed upon it. The British authorities tried to provide it and
failed. Americans then seized control and eventually imposed
their own organization, but they were unable to realize the goal
implied in the title of their first governing body, the Continental
Congress. Some pieces stayed out and some people came out. In

time, the northern remnants would be fashioned and enlarged into a second transcontinental nation that would, at first with British help, impose its own organization from one ocean to the other.

When the British government surveyed the North American scene on the morrow of victory, at the beginning of the 1760's, they could see at once that the close of war left them with many problems. Hitherto, their concern with their American empire had never extended very much beyond the water's edge: by means of the Navigation Acts they had sought to regulate the oceanic trade of the colonies, but these colonies had been substantially self-governing in their internal affairs. Such arrangements no longer sufficed in the greatly enlarged empire of the 1760's. The interior regions between the Appalachians and the Mississippi had to be organized and protected, and a policy had to be found for the new colony of Canada. Imperial reorganization would also affect the old seaboard colonies, whose conduct, in British eyes, had left much to be desired during the late war with France.

Canada was a particular puzzle. How could a homogeneous, deeply rooted people of some sixty to seventy thousand French-speaking Roman Catholics be fitted into an English-speaking Protestant empire? It is not surprising that a policy was slow in evolving. At first, responsibility lay with the military commanders, whose concern was naturally with the maintenance of peace and order until it was decided whether Canada was to be kept and, then, how it was to be governed. Adopting the accepted principle that military conquest in itself did not disturb the domestic arrangements of the conquered, the commanding generals in 1760 made it clear to the French Canadians that their way of life, at least for the time being, was to continue unchanged. The military issued any necessary directives through the accepted leaders of the Canadians, and for some three or four years after 1759-1760, the people of the colony experienced no real disruption in their lives. Quite the contrary. With hostilities ended, they were able to return to peaceful activities; and far from being uprooted during the military regime, the Canadians, fully accustomed to living within an imperial system and under a monarchy, were able to return to normal during these years of peace under sympathetic rulers. As an added boon they were now free of the grasping corruption that had disgraced the last years of the French regime.

But by the latter part of 1763 the British government was ready to declare a policy, in the famous Proclamation of that year, which seemed to promise that Canadian life would indeed be changed. The limits of the province, now renamed Quebec, were greatly reduced from those claimed by New France. All the northwest and southwest were sheared off, with a western and southern boundary roughly following that of today's province of Quebec. Everything to the southwest, below the Ottawa River and between the Appalachians and the Mississippi was for the time being to be kept as a vast Indian reserve, in which white settlement was forbidden until the Indians were pacified and treaties with them could be negotiated. The Proclamation also looked to the gradual transformation of Quebec into a typical English colony, with a government, including an assembly, like those along the seaboard and with English law. The Canadians could have no share in this government, because English law forbade Roman Catholics to hold office. It was expected that emigration from the old colonies would turn north, because the Proclamation of 1763 prohibited settlement beyond the Appalachians and that under the impulse of the ensuing growth and prosperity the Canadians would see the wisdom of becoming English-speaking Protestants. These calculations, which strike us now as both naive and harsh, are better understood when it is remembered that New Englanders at this very time were moving north into Nova Scotia in considerable numbers and that eighteenth century Protestants assumed that a group of Roman Catholics like the Canadians would rejoice at the opportunity to abandon their religion as the province grew and flourished within the Empire.

In any event, the Proclamation was a dead letter from the

beginning. The few hundred English-speaking merchants who had come into the area rejoiced at its terms, but the first governor, General James Murray, who had previously been the military ruler, refused to let the colony fall into their hands; he simply put off calling an assembly. Moreover, this minority remained a tiny minority when the expected immigration did not occur. Equally important, the governor could see, in the months leading up to and during the Stamp Act crisis, that Britain's American empire was beginning to shiver and shake. It was no time to attempt change in Canada; instead, it was a time for stability, in the face of growing unrest and incipient rebellion to the south, and stability would depend upon a feeling of confidence and content among the Canadian population. Yet even a limited implementation of the terms of the Proclamation—for example, the enforcement of English common law among a people who did not understand it—caused confusion. Clearly another approach would have to be found.

In addition, the country to the west and south also demanded attention. With white traders moving in to do business with the Indians some system of government was necessary to preserve law and order. Yet in the growing mood of suspicion between the old colonies and the mother country it was impossible to reach agreement on this question. After several years of consideration the British government could see no answer but to re-annex this country (stretching from the Ottawa south to the Ohio) to the province of Quebec in order to bring it under the same government. Thus, under British auspices, the old fur-trading empire of Montreal was being restored.

This step was taken in 1774 in the Quebec Act, which also dealt with the vexed question of the government of the province. By this time the governor, now Guy Carleton, was convinced that Quebec would, barring a great catastrophe, always have a French and Catholic population and that it should therefore have institutions appropriate to such a population. The British government accepted his advice, which was embodied in an Act of Parliament. The boundaries were extended as mentioned, although with the careful stipulation that the boundaries of other colonies were not to be affected. The province was given a legislature, to consist of an appointed council in which Canadians might sit, because the Act included a special form of oath which Catholics could take. There was to be no elected assembly: one in which the French-speaking Catholic population could not be represented would be a travesty, yet the British Parliament was not ready to see one controlled by this population. The tangled problem of the legal system was dealt with by prescribing English criminal law and by restoring the French civil law subject to amendment by the governor and council. This arrangement allowed the Canadians to keep to their accustomed laws, but made it possible for the English-speaking merchants to conduct commercial transactions as they had always done. Finally, the Roman Catholic clergy were to be free to collect tithes from their own people, although various limitations were placed upon that church in Quebec. The authors of the Act probably expected that anglicization would take place, but if so, it would come slowly and humanely. Moreover, such expectations were frustrated at the outset by the governor.

This man, the aristocratic Guy Carleton, was determined to win the confidence of the French Canadians, but his hopes were not wholly fulfilled. Believing in a neatly ordered, hierarchical society and thinking erroneously that he was living in one in Quebec, he gave so much trust and confidence to the seigneurs and upper clergy that these groups appeared to have more influence that they had ever had under the French regime. The habitants had no intention of giving their willing support to such a turning back of the clock. Carleton also antagonized the English-speaking merchants by failing to make the promised changes regarding commercial law. Thus in these two important classes the Quebec Act produced irritation and suspicion instead of satisfaction and contentment.

Yet this reaction was mild compared with that raised by the Act in the colonies to the south. There, the developing crisis, temporarily damped down for a few years, had flared up to a new intensity with the Boston Tea Party of 1773. Although it had twice before retreated in the face of American resistance, the British Parliament now resolved in 1774 to bring Boston, and indeed all of Massachusetts, to obedience by passing four Acts of Parliament usually known since as the "Coercive" or "Intolerable" Acts. These measures were thus passed in the same year as the Quebec Act, and although the latter had been in preparation for many years Americans inevitably associated it with the Coercive Acts as part of a grand program of tyranny. The extension of Quebec's boundaries into what they regarded as their own back-country, the lack of an assembly, the adoption of French laws, and indulgence toward the Roman Catholic Church—all these took on a most sinister light when they appeared in the company of the Coercive Acts. The disappearance of French power in Canada had contributed to the spirit of resistance in the old colonies by reducing their sense of dependence upon British protection, yet after a century of hostilities, they were still conditioned to see an enemy to the north. Now in that strange and foreign colony it seemed that hostile measures were again being prepared against them. Thus British policy toward Canada was a factor in bringing on the American Revolution.

Canada was also high on the agenda of the Continental Congress after hostilities broke out in the spring of 1775. In the previous autumn and winter the Congress had already made appeals and sent agents to the Canadians and to the Montreal merchants, urging them to join in the resistance, and then, in June 1775, as its first major military move, it authorized invasion, aimed both at Montreal and at Quebec. This "struggle for the fourteenth colony" gave promise of success because the British had only a few scattered troops in Canada and the mass of the French Canadians, seeing little to choose in a contest between the British conquerors and their old enemies to the south, remained neutral, for the most part. Although some joined the militia, at Governor Carleton's call, several hundred went over to the invading Americans. In consequence the army that came down the traditional Lake Champlain–Richelieu route had little difficulty in making its way to Montreal and taking the town. Carleton narrowly escaped down the river to Quebec, where Benedict Arnold's troops appeared in November after a remarkable overland trip through the Maine wilderness. When Arnold was joined by the army that had taken Montreal, it appeared that Quebec was certain to fall, because Carleton's defense force was a small and miscellaneous assortment of regulars, militia, and Indians. But as the weeks wore on, the plight of the besiegers became worse than that of the besieged, and a desperate attack at the end of the year was a blood-stained failure. The Americans hung on until the spring, when the appearance of a British fleet in the river forced them to retire. Even if they had taken Quebec, they would not have been able to keep it in the face of British sea power. Still hoping for conciliation, Carleton did not pursue the retreating Americans, whom he considered to be "deluded subjects," as vigorously as he might have.

Nevertheless, a few weeks later, the Continental Congress crossed its Rubicon on July 4, 1776, with the issuance of the Declaration of Independence, and it was henceforth clear that the contest would have to be decided on the field of battle. British control in the former colonies was now largely confined to New York City, and it became increasingly clear that Canada was a logical base from which to launch a British attempt at reconquest. A considerable army was collected near Montreal, made up of regulars and Hessian mercenaries, and in 1777 under General John Burgoyne it started south with the purpose of cutting off New England to the east and drawing on the strength of New York, which was heavily Loyalist. But once again a European army proved to be ineffective in the North American forest. Burgoyne's troops lost their momentum and in September at Saratoga were forced to surrender to American regulars and militia under Gates and Arnold. It proved to be a decisive battle of the war. Henceforth Canada was no longer a threat to the American cause. Even more important, the result convinced the French government that the time was now ripe to come out openly on the American side and thus led to the Franco-American treaty of 1778. It remained to be seen how the former French colony of Canada would be affected by a war which had taken such a turn.

Meanwhile, there had been the question of how far the Revolution could reach to the northeast. Not to Newfoundland, to be sure, for this island was too far away; its slender population was fully engaged in the Atlantic commercial world and barely aware of the affairs of the continent. But Nova Scotia was another matter. By 1775 three quarters of its population was made up of New Englanders who had moved in within the last fifteen or twenty years; they might be expected to sympathize with the cause of their friends and relatives. And Massachusetts, which had always had an eye on the peninsula, might be expected now to try to reach out to it.

Yet Nova Scotia was not drawn in, despite prevailing sympathy for the revolutionary cause. In 1776 there was one attempt by a group of "rebels" to take a British-held fort, but it was poorly prepared and it failed. Otherwise the New Englanders were too scattered to think of taking any concerted action and too immersed in the struggle to establish themselves in their new homes. With New England now out of the imperial system, the people of Nova Scotia began to see new trade opportunities, which more than once brought them into conflict with New England privateers. In effect, these Nova Scotia New Englanders, like the Acadians before them, turned to neutrality. Being good New Englanders, their consciences were sorely troubled in this time of divided and shifting loyalties, and they sought relief in a great religious revival that swept the province toward the end of the Revolution. There was also balm in the wartime prosperity. Nor could the Revolution reach out to Nova Scotia. George Washington saw this from the beginning. In view of his limited resources he firmly opposed all suggestions to deflect any part of them to the northeast. He realized that as long as the British controlled the seas Nova Scotia was beyond the American orbit.

After the battle of Saratoga, the province of Quebec also ceased to be a decisive factor in the outcome of the War for American Independence. Henceforth most of the major fighting would be in the southern states, with Quebec on the far periphery. From time to time the Americans and their French allies discussed the possibility of another invasion, but usually more immediate and pressing tasks were at hand. Moreover, these two allies viewed each other warily where Quebec was concerned; the new friendship could not entirely obliterate memories of the past struggles for control of the Lakes and the River. American leaders had no intention of supporting a campaign which might lead to the restoration of the French Empire on the St. Lawrence. Equally, the French, for all their support of the American cause, did not want to see it engulf their former colonists nor did they want to see the new nation completely dominant in North America. If Canada remained in British hands, the United States might be more dependent on France. As for the people of Canada, some had shown sympathy for the revolutionary movement, but for the most part, these adherents had left with the retreating Americans in 1776. In the long run certain elements of the Canadian population were undoubtedly influenced by the ideology of the Declaration of Independence, as would be shown in the later political history of the province, but in the short run the effect of the American military occupation of 1775–1776 was to give an anti-American hue to Canadian neutrality. Occupation troops are never popular, and these had been bigoted Protestants who had, moreover, made payments in paper money. After they left, the British firmly re-established themselves, under Carleton and his successor, General Frederick Haldimand, continuing their close ties with the leading elements of Canadian society. Thus, for various reasons, there was no response along the St. Lawrence to the invitation contained in the Articles of Confederation, which stated: "Canada, acceding to the Confederation and joining in the measures of the United States, shall be admitted into, and entitled to all the advantages of the Union."

Although the fighting on the northern front did not prove to be decisive in determining the outcome of the war, it was nevertheless continuous, bitter, and often savage, for in large part it was a civil war. Its starting point was in the Mohawk Valley of Upper New York, where for a generation Sir William Johnson had been the leading figure in organizing settlement, conducting Indian diplomacy, and carrying on the fur trade. He died in 1774, but his family connection, including his son, his nephew, and his brother-in-law (Joseph Brant, the Mohawk chief) continued to provide leadership. With the outbreak of war the Johnson family remained staunchly loyal to their oath of allegiance, as did the whites and Indians of their community, and there then followed a contest with their neighbors who adhered to the Congress. In this struggle the Johnsons and their followers were driven out and had to fall back westward toward Niagara and northward toward Montreal. After reorganizing and refitting themselves for counterattack, they and their enemies carried on a partisan warfare for several years, each side accusing the other of unspeakable atrocities. Such fighting made impossible any kind of reconciliation when peace came, with the result that the loyalists had to find new homes in the province of Quebec. There were only a few thousand of them, but they gave the province its first non-French population of any size. They were a very miscellaneous lot: Scots, Dutch, Germans, Huguenots, and even some English, and representing half a dozen religious persuasions. But most of them were small farmers by background, and although many of them signed their names with a mark, they knew how to start life over again in the North American forest.

Elsewhere, especially in New York and Pennsylvania, there were many other inhabitants of the colonies, now states, who clung to their British allegiance. It is impossible to know how many of them there were, partly because there were infinite gradations of loyalism, from the most active and belligerent to the most circumspect and wavering. As among the Canadians and the Nova Scotians, there was also a good deal of neutrality. But with the end of the war and the recognition of the independence of the United States by the British government, all residents of the new nation had to make a choice. The neutrals and most of the loyalists elected to stay on and made their peace, either quickly or gradually, with the republic. But there were over fifty thousand who left, either because they were forced out of their homes or because they were determined to live under the British Crown. It was a larger proportion of émigrés than that produced by the French Revolution a decade later. It was probably as large as it was because it was possible to start life again without leaving North America.

These loyalists, although most of them were from New York and Pennsylvania, came from all sections of the country, from New England to Georgia and from tidewater to frontier. They came from all classes of society and from all ethnic groups. Yet they were not quite a cross section of society, because for the most part they represented elements that were somewhat out of the mainstream of American life: newcomers, non-English groups, pacifists like the Quakers, Scots merchants tied to the mercantilist economy, opponents of the tidewater merchants and planters who were so prominent in the revolutionary movement, and others who for one reason or another tended to be on the fringes of the American world or who felt closer to British authority than to the groups that had led the resistance. The greatest concentration of them was behind the British lines in New York City, where the British commander, now Sir Guy Carleton, made plans for their evacuation at the end of 1782 and in 1783. Some of them, including the most highly placed, made their way to England, Bermuda, and the West Indies, but the majority, about thirty thousand, boarded ships for Nova Scotia. As a group they may have had a somewhat more substantial background than those who were collecting near Montreal and at

Niagara, yet for the most part they were farmers, artisans, and tradesmen. As we shall see later, their arrival significantly affected the political and social life of Nova Scotia.

By this time, 1783, the peace treaty had been signed and ratified after long and sometimes difficult negotiations, which, on the American side, had been brilliantly conducted. Led by Benjamin Franklin, the American negotiators realized that the British were anxious for a quick peace and one that would lead to Anglo-American reconciliation. Hoping to gain at the peace table what had not been attained on the battlefield, Franklin tried to persuade the British that the cession of Canada would be the surest step to future Anglo-American peace. Although this was asking too much, the British had too little interest in or knowledge of the interior to stand out very strongly against the skilled and determined Americans. Moreover, the British were ready to be generous as a means of detaching the the Americans from the French. After discussing various possibilities, it was finally agreed that the boundary should start along the St. Croix River, on the eastern side of Maine, and go north until it reached the highlands south of the St. Lawrence. The highlands would be followed until they came back down to the forty-fifth parallel east and south of Montreal. At the point where that parallel intersected the St. Lawrence, the boundary would continue along the river and through the Great Lakes. From a point on the north shore of Lake Superior it was to continue westward through the Lake of the Woods until it reached the Mississippi River. The basic outlines of this border for the eastern half of the continent still stand to this day, but time was to show that these clauses of the treaty contained enough ambiguities and inaccuracies, resulting from inadequate geographical knowledge, to provide for numerous boundary disputes over the next half century and more. More immediately, as we shall see in the next chapter, a boundary settlement that was intended to lead to Anglo-American reconciliation very nearly produced another war within the next dozen years.

The peace treaty dealt with many other questions, in addition to the boundary. One of these, which would long be prominent in later Canadian-American relations, was the complex subject of the fisheries, in which one of the American negotiators, John Adams of Massachusetts, was particularly interested. For a century and a half the people of his region had been using the waters and shores of Nova Scotia in carrying on the fishery; after hard bargaining, Adams secured for them permission, within certain limits, to continue their accustomed activities, even though New England was no longer within the Empire. Two other sensitive questions related to the loyalists, who had suffered much loss of private property in the bitter civil strife of the war years, and to the debts, many of them of long standing, which Americans owed to British creditors. The treaty acknowledged that the loyalists and the creditors had the right to redress and recovery, but it was also clear that the United States Congress had no power to enforce this provision. It could do no more than earnestly recommend to the states that justice be done. Failure on the part of some states to honor this obligation adequately laid the basis for much bad feeling as well as diplomatic maneuvering in the following years.

And so, with the independence of the United States, the continent was again partitioned. In a great and astounding reversal, the British Empire was now left with colonies which the French had started, while the old English colonies, or at least thirteen of them, were embarked upon a new national existence as a loose confederation soon to become "a more perfect union." To the north of this new nation was an odd assortment of separated and dissimilar communities and settlements, having nothing much in common except rather primitive and dependent economies and the same experience of having been rejected or spurned. The breach between Quebec and France would soon be widened by the French Revolution. The Nova Scotia New Englanders were cut off from their parent society. The refugee loyalists, an extremely diverse group (among whom the Six

Nations Indians must not be forgotten), were scattered from Nova Scotia to the Detroit River. For the development of their economies all these elements needed British trade, yet except for the seaboard areas there was no certainty that Britain had much interest in what was left of its empire. They also needed British protection, but it was not clear how far Britain could or would commit itself to these distant and little known regions, especially those in the interior. There were some loyalist visionaries who already dreamed of bringing these peripheral remnants together, but the materials were certainly very unpromising.

The end of the War of American Independence was followed by a generation of crises and tensions, of revolution in Europe from which North America could not be insulated, of wars and rumors of wars. The new American nation, although its political fabric was strengthened through the adoption of the constitution of 1787 and its leadership was by turns both prudent and brilliant, faced threats of disunion, suffered from bitter political dissension, and eventually, as a divided country, came into a war against a great power for which it was almost totally unprepared. The British North American provinces to the north, were politically disoriented by the results of the American Revolutionary War, their trading patterns were disrupted, their dependence on the mother country was made precarious by the long French Revolutionary and Napoleonic Wars, and they faced invasion from a wealthier and more populous antagonist. It was not until the settlement following the War of 1812 that the decisions of 1783 were confirmed, as well as extended, and that the various North American communities became relatively free to concentrate on growth and development.

The problems of transition were less dangerous and less fundamental in the Maritime Provinces, but they must be noted briefly. The immediate and pressing task was to cope with an influx of loyalist refugees that within a few months had approximately doubled the population of Nova Scotia. The British authorities were committed to the finding of homes for these people and otherwise assisting them until they were established. In the best of circumstances this would have been a difficult mission for the provincial authorities, but it was further complicated by the fact that the loyalists were far from friendly in their attitude toward the existing population of New England origin, who in their eyes had been disaffected or at best neutral in the late conflict. The loyalists had no wish to settle down among such people. Besides, they wanted to be in a community which they could control. It was against this background that the decision was taken in 1784 to divide Nova Scotia, thus forming a new province, New Brunswick, in the unoccupied country across the Bay of Fundy. This was the loyalist province par excellence and in it the majority of the maritime refugees found homes. Any idea that a loyalist province would be decorous and deferential was, however, soon dispelled, for the refugees brought with them the traditions of vigorous public debate which they had been used to in the Thirteen Colonies. In fact, New Brunswick was long to be noted for its tumultuous political climate, although Nova Scotia too had a full share of constitutional controversy.

From an economic point of view, the first years after the peace were disapppointing. With the independence of the United States and its consequent exclusion from the British imperial system, many people in the Maritime Provinces, including the loyalists, hoped that these provinces would be able to take the place in the empire long occupied by the old colonies, especially New England. In particular, it was hoped that the Maritime Provinces would be able to supply and carry products, including food and lumber, to the West Indies. But Nova Scotia and even more the infant New Brunswick proved to be quite inadequate to this large role, and the persistent New Englanders continued to get an important part of this trade. The situation became even worse after 1793, when Britain and France went to war, because French privateers made the seas hazardous for the ships of British colonies. As we shall see later, it was not until the latter stages of the long European war that the Maritimers were to benefit from it.

When we turn away from the maritime regions to look at the province of Quebec we see at once that the end of the American war made a deep and shattering impact on both the economic and the political structure of the colony. Within less than a decade the rush of events had overtaken the Quebec Act of 1774 to make it obsolete in several important respects; still, there was little agreement on what form reorganization should take.

The economic consequences of the peace of 1783 caused the most immediate reaction. In the previous twenty years, since the

French defeat, the old fur-trading empire had been maintained with relatively little alteration. English-speaking merchants, among whom Scots were increasingly prominent, joined with the French Canadians to continue and to extend the lines of communication and the Indian connections which were organized from Montreal. The restoration of this empire appeared to be confirmed and consolidated by the extension of Quebec's boundaries south to the Ohio in 1774. But then in 1783 the Montreal merchants were horrified to learn that all their vast and profitable commercial empire south and west of the Great Lakes had, by the stroke of a pen and without warning, been snatched from them and handed over to the United States. Without warning, because there had been nothing to indicate that the Americans might secure this region which they had never controlled, either before or during the recent war. They had acquired it only through the British desire to secure American good will. Moreover, the decision had been made without any attempt to consult the Indians who lived there. These people, who regarded themselves as allies, not subjects, of Great Britain, rejected the view that their lands could be thus signed away and were outraged at being abandoned by the British and left at the mercy of the Americans, who were known to covet their territories. Just as French abandonment of the Indians had led to Pontiac's uprising in 1763, there was now the fear that British abandonment would lead to renewed bloodshed and, perhaps, appalling results on both sides of the border.

Such was the background out of which western policy evolved in the years after 1783. Despite the treaty, British authorities resolved to retain contact with Indians living on lands ceded to the United States, in the hope that the frontier would remain at peace. In practice, this meant that British garrisons remained in forts and posts along the Great Lakes that were now on American soil, and a pretext for this violation of the treaty was found in the American failure to honor promises regarding loyalist claims. Nevertheless, the British presence, although it was a stabilizing force in the interior, raised many hopes and fears. The Indians, resolved at all costs to repel the American advance, deluded themselves by hopes of effective British help. The fur traders, when they saw the first American advances defeated, dreamed of some sort of neutral Indian barrier state between the Lakes and the Ohio River where they would again be influential. And Americans believed that the British were deliberately inspiring and supporting the continued Indian resistance in order to revive the fur trade. Thus the peace treaty was followed by a decade of tension and hostility along and below the Great Lakes boundary.

Despite their flickering hopes of restoring the trade in this region, the Anglo-Scottish merchants, who now directed Montreal's commercial empire, had for some years been making their main effort in the far northwest. With improved organization they returned to the old French objective of getting behind the Hudson's Bay Company to tap the rich beaver lands beyond the Saskatchewan River. The most dramatic accomplishments are recalled in the young Scot, Alexander Mackenzie, traveling for the North West Company, who, in 1789, reached the Arctic along the river which bears his name. Disappointed at not having reached the Pacific, he organized another expedition which took him across the Rockies and to the western ocean in 1793, the first overland crossing of the continent. Skillfully and energetically the Montreal merchants worked to exploit the continental commercial empire of the northwest until, after a quarter of a century, they were defeated by impossibly high transportation costs and forced to amalgamate with the more strategically placed Hudson's Bay Company.

While the traditional economy of the St. Lawrence was undergoing its last and greatest expansion, the old province of Quebec had to face a totally new condition, the presence of a considerable population of English-speaking settlers in the form of the loyalists. These people, who were assigned lands along the St. Lawrence, above Montreal, on the north shore of Lake Ontario, and at either end of Lake Erie were soon busy hewing new homes out of the wilderness. But they were not too busy to make known their dissatisfaction with the institutional framework provided by the Quebec Act. Having demonstrated their loyalty to the British Crown, they now demanded their rights as British subjects, which, they felt, could not be protected and guaranteed by the government at distant Quebec. Most immediately, they wanted English laws, particularly English land laws, not the French seigneurial system, about which they knew nothing. On the other hand, the government at Quebec remained convinced that the French Canadians, still by far the largest part of the population, must have institutions to which they were accustomed. For several years there was uncertainty and deadlock while officials on both sides of the Atlantic wrestled with the problem.

By 1791, however, a decision had been made: to divide the province of Quebec in two, and to provide each with a new constitution. Division appeared to be a fair and practical answer, because the loyalists and the French Canadians were, for the most part, separated by the Ottawa River. Beyond this river, except for a small section between its lower reaches and the St. Lawrence, would rise the new colony of Upper Canada (the ancestor of the modern province of Ontario), where English laws and institutions could flourish. From Montreal downriver, where French Canadians had lived for nearly two centuries, there would now be the colony of Lower Canada, where the guarantees of the Quebec Act relating to laws and religion were still to be respected. But in their political framework the new constitutions superseded the Quebec Act, and they were the same for each province. For many reasons it was decided to return to the normal British pattern, which included a representative assembly, and this could not be given to one province and not to the other. Yet the British government had no intention of reviving unchanged the system of colonial government that was thought to have brought on the American Revolution through the almost unchecked powers of the assemblies. To curb the growth of democracy in this second British Empire in North America, it was provided that the governor and the appointed branch of the legislature would be relatively stronger and the assembly relatively weaker than had been true in the pre-1776 colonies. In particular, the executive would not be so financially dependent on the assembly as he had formerly been. Thus was laid the basis for a prolonged constitutional struggle that was not to end until almost the middle of the following century.

The struggle did not start immediately, however. The nature of the system did not fully reveal itself for several years, and, besides, more pressing and more dangerous questions held the center of the stage for some time, in particular the danger of renewed war with the United States. In the early 1790's there were many sources of Anglo-American tension, but the oldest of these was the Indian question. A decade after the peace the British still held posts on American soil, notably at Niagara and at Detroit. American attempts to make good their title to the lands beyond the Ohio were twice turned back by humiliating defeats at the hands of the Indians, who continued to expect and demand British help. They did not get it, except unofficially through some individuals, and an American army under Anthony Wayne finally broke the back of Indian resistance south of Lake Erie at Fallen Timbers in 1794. But this battle was fought within gunshot of a British garrison not far from the present city of Toledo, Ohio, and only restraint on both sides prevented a clash that might have had irreparable consequences.

This contest in the interior was only one phase of a general deterioration in Anglo-American relations. In addition to other problems left over from the treaty of 1783, notably the delineation of the Maine–New Brunswick boundary and American non-payment of debts owing to British creditors, a whole new cluster of issues arose as the French Revolution led into war between Britian and France. Despite existing ties with France and much pro-French feeling in the United States, the administration of President Washington sought to remain aloof from the struggle.

But it was not long before there was bitter dispute over American charges of violation of their neutral rights by the British navy. Seizure of American ships and impressment of seamen were only the most conspicuous in a long list of grievances which led many Americans into a violently anti-British mood. Nevertheless, the administration aimed for a peaceful settlement by sending Chief Justice John Jay to London in 1794. For various reasons the resulting treaty fell considerably short of American hopes and was highly unpopular in the United States; nevertheless, it is an important landmark in the triangular relations of Great Britain, the United States, and the British North American colonies.

Most fundamental, perhaps, Jay's Treaty was a significant stage in the consolidation of the United States as an independent nation. Even though it failed to realize many of its objectives, the government of the new country did secure a wide-ranging treaty from a great power that had previously treated it with almost open contempt. Thus the treaty was an important acceptance and confirmation of its role and place in North America and in the world. It succeeded, also, in liquidating most of the issues left over from 1783, even though it failed to settle the new ones relating to neutral rights on the high seas. By agreeing to withdraw their garrisons from the western posts, the British acknowledged that the United States could make good its title to the interior and that the boundary of 1783 would stand. The treaty was also a pioneering instrument in the peaceful settlement of international disputes, for it provided that the debt question and the Maine–New Brunswick boundary controversy should be submitted to joint commissions for study and recommendation. Although power and force would continue to be fundamental in maintaining and defining the boundary, here was an early indication that arbitration and judicial settlement would also have a place.

Jay's Treaty was followed by nearly a decade of relatively harmonious Anglo-American relations, combined with worsening Franco-American relations, the emerging states rights controversy in the United States, and growing American concern with the southwest. All these factors made for an easing of tension along the Canadian-American border and an opportunity for the northern provinces to establish themselves.

In the new colony of Upper Canada the most remarkable development was the influx of American settlement. Trending in a southwesterly direction from the Ottawa River to the Detroit River, Upper Canada was readily accessible from nearby American states and for a time was a prime target for American pioneers. Its first governor, John Graves Simcoe, welcomed them for he believed that there were many people in the United States who at heart were still loyal to the British crown or who could be won back to loyalty. For this reason, and because the province's greatest need was an increased population, he made good land available at nominal rates to settlers from the United States, and the policy was continued by his successors. Land speculators were also a force encouraging this movement at a time when overseas immigration was largely cut off by the French Revolutionary and Napoleonic Wars and when, in any event, Americans were thought to make the best pioneer farmers.

And Upper Canada was an attractive goal to settlers who were more interested in good land than in the flag which flew over it. It was easily reached by way of the Niagara River. Its lands were said to be cheaper than in some competing regions of New York State, and it was free of the Indian troubles that still menaced the country below Lake Erie. There were communications with markets by way of the Lakes and the St. Lawrence. As a result, the north side of Lake Ontario and Lake Erie was settled somewhat in advance of the south side. Some of the settlers were described as "late loyalists," but their loyalism often contained a large element of land hunger. Others were Mennonites from Pennsylvania who needed to provide for growing families. But for the most part the settlers were simply the northern arm of the westward-moving frontier. For about twenty years Upper Canada lay across its path, and on the eve of the War of 1812 about three quarters of its population consisted of American settlers. Contemporary observers could see little to distinguish the province from many another American frontier region. Some of the established loyalist leaders and the provincial government officials began to feel alarm at this large influx, arguing that it was better to have a slower growth than an undependable population, a feeling that grew as the War of 1812 approached. Although the American settlers were too occupied with immediate and personal tasks to concern themselves much with politics, they did remain an unknown quantity as the crisis mounted.

While the infant province of Upper Canada was taking on this American character, the long-established lower province was seeking to adjust itself to its new constitution, which required the operating of British parliamentary institutions in a community over ninety percent French-speaking in 1792. From the beginning French Canadians were in a strong majority in the elected assembly, where they soon showed an easy familiarity with English legislative procedures. Nevertheless, they were not in control of the government. The governor was, of course, from Britain, and the two appointed councils, executive and legislative, both had slight majorities of English-speaking members. Clearly, the British authorities were not disposed to place full trust in the French-Canadian majority and were even less ready to do so after France and Britain went to war in 1793. After some Canadians expressed sympathy with the ideals of the revolution and support for France in the war, local officials redoubled their determination to keep the appointed branches of the government under English-speaking direction. In turn, with each election, the assembly became more self-consciously French Canadian, particularly when the executive appeared to be using the management of land policy to enrich itself and to encourage English-speaking settlement. The earlier view of some English authorities — that the conferring of English institutions would lead the French Canadians to become English in outlook — was being confounded. Instead, the French Canadians were seizing

upon their control of the assembly as a weapon to protect themselves against threats of assimilation. Cooperation and trust
between English and French, which had often been evident
before 1790, were giving way to suspicion and antagonism and to
the rise of a self-conscious French-Canadian nationalism in the
first years of the nineteenth century.

This nationalism was closely related to social and economic
changes in Lower Canada, as will be seen more fully in the next
chapter. The traditional leaders, the seigneurs and the upper
clergy, remained firm supporters of British authority, although
always ready to defend their own interests when they saw the
need to do so; but coming to the fore was a new class whose
mood was more challenging. For the most part the new men
were of relatively humble rural origin who, having secured an
education in one of the liberal professions, were trying hard to
establish themselves. Lawyers and journalists to a large extent,
they turned naturally to politics, where they became prominent
in the assembly, often as self-appointed spokesmen of the small
farmers from whom they had sprung. Seeing the control of the
executive government firmly in English hands and the doors to
appointive office closed to them, they became increasingly res-
tive and critical. Responsive to the new waves of nationalism
emanating from the French Revolution, they began to see the
Anglo-Saxons as enemies of their people. It was particularly
irritating to the English-speaking authorities when these new
spokesmen took their stand on British constitutional principles
by demanding that the executive should be responsible to the
assembly for the advice they gave to the governor. The first stage
of this controversy took place from 1807 to 1810, with the governor, Sir James Craig, firmly opposing the nationalist leaders. The
quarrel culminated in a sudden dissolution of the assembly, the
seizure of the nationalist newspaper, several arrests, and other
stern measures. Craig went on to recommend to the British
government that representative government, under forms that
allowed the French Canadians to control the assembly, should

be ended in Lower Canada; but instead London recalled him and sent out a more conciliatory governor on the eve of the War of 1812. This was only the first act of the drama, but a revealing one.

Meanwhile, authorities in both colonies had watched with growing alarm the worsening of Anglo-American relations as the long war with Napoleon continued. After the battle of Trafalgar in 1805 the British were supreme on the oceans and more than ever determined to seek victory through seapower. Again as in the 1790's, this objective clashed with American insistence on their neutral rights, but now the clash was sharper and more dangerous. The United States was, in fact, caught in the titanic struggle between Napoleon's continental system and the British blockade; its ships could not use the high seas without offending one side or the other, particularly the all-powerful British fleet. In 1807 American resentment reached a fever pitch when the British man-of-war *Leopard* stopped the American frigate *Chesapeake* and removed four members of its crew. But President Thomas Jefferson resisted the cry for war and instead sought to defend American rights by economic pressure applied through an embargo on trade. The embargo proved to be a failure and had to be withdrawn just before Jefferson left office in 1809, but under his successor, James Madison, less comprehensive trade restrictions continued. The inability of the United States to secure respect for its rights was a bitter frustration to a mounting sentiment of nationalism, and at the same time the Jefferson-Madison policy produced intense resentment in maritime New England. Nor was the controversy confined to the coastal states. The growing west also felt the effects of the British blockade through the loss of markets; resentment in this region was also fed by reports of continued British intrigue among the Indians. The background of causes was so tangled and the play of interests so diverse that historians still disagree over the explanation for the United States declaration of war against Great Britain in June 1812.

In the context of Canadian-American relations, debate has centered on the goals which American leaders sought with respect to the Canadian provinces. Speeches in Congress can be read to indicate that the so-called War Hawks were more strongly motivated by dreams of continental expansion, aimed at the Canadas and perhaps at Florida (held by the Spanish), than by a concern to redress maritime grievances. Henry Clay asserted that he was not for stopping at Quebec but was for taking the whole continent, while the leading congressional opponent of the war, John Randolph, accused the War Hawks of "agrarian cupidity." This expansionist explanation of the war, though American in origin, has always been popular in Canada because it fits the Canadian view that Manifest Destiny has been a perennial threat. Nevertheless, although many Americans undoubtedly would have welcomed an opportunity to acquire Canada, it is probably true to say that the northern provinces figured more as a means than an end in the calculations of American leaders. As considerations of national honor, national interest, and an unbearable frustration were driving the United States to war with Great Britain, the knowledge that there was one place where the overweening British appeared to be vulnerable was comforting and reassuring. Upper Canada in particular was thought to be ripe for the taking: "a mere matter of marching," as Jefferson put it. Once taken, it could be held as a hostage in the later bargaining, with its eventual disposition to depend upon circumstances. The American declaration of war, in short, was motivated less by expansionism than by exasperation, a sense that all other policies against Great Britain had failed. At the head of a divided and unprepared country, President Madison saw no choice but to "thrust the flag forward," hoping that the people would follow and sustain it.

The political and military leaders in the Canadian provinces were fully aware that they faced American attack. For some years they had been striving to make what preparations they could, but they knew that there was no hope of substantial reinforcements from Britain as long as the latter was fully engaged in the struggle against Napoleon. With only a few thousand regular troops and a population that was not only greatly outnumbered but perhaps not very dependable, the governor-in-chief, Sir George Prevost, determined upon a strictly defensive posture aimed at holding Quebec and, if possible, Montreal. Therefore he refused to commit many of his men to the interior, knowing that as long as Quebec was held there was an entry for eventual British reinforcements. He was also reluctant to strike at the Americans for fear of uniting them behind a war which was so unpopular, especially in New England.

In broad perspective Prevost's strategy was perfectly sound, but it provided little comfort to the commander in Upper Canada, General Isaac Brock, who was anxious to put the Americans off balance before they could organize themselves for attack. There were already signs of disaffection among the predominantly American population, which would certainly increase if the enemy gained striking successes. Therefore, when American forces under General William Hull crossed into the province from Detroit in July 1812, Brock resolved to act. By the time he reached the scene the faint-hearted Hull had already returned to Detroit. With a small and miscellaneous army of regulars, militia, and Indians Brock crossed the river and intimidated Hull into surrendering. Brock then hurried back to the Niagara frontier, where he was killed in the successful repulse of an American invasion attempt at Queenston Heights. These early victories did much to rally the people of Upper Canada to the defense of the province. To be sure, many continued to be neutral or pro-American, but such feeling diminished under the growing resentment against later American raids.

As Admiral A. T. Mahan long ago pointed out, the course of the War of 1812 depended heavily upon naval power, not only on the high seas but also on the Great Lakes and along the St. Lawrence. American supremacy on Lake Erie, confirmed by Perry's victory at Put-in Bay, opened the way in the autumn of

1813 for William Henry Harrison's successful invasion of the western end of the province. On the more crucial Lake Ontario the American naval commander, Captain Isaac Chauncey, had an initial advantage at the beginning of the 1813 campaign, but he did not make full use of it, and by 1814 the two fresh-water navies were about equal in strength. Without naval superiority the American land campaigns came to little in these two years, despite much hard fighting, and at the end of the war the province was practically free of American troops. In the meantime American expeditions against Montreal had had even less success, and by the end of the summer of 1814 General Prevost, having now received large British reinforcements, was finally ready to attempt a local offensive with a powerful army of veterans. Again, however, naval power proved to be decisive and, when the American fleet won the Battle of Lake Champlain, Prevost withdrew his army to Montreal. This turned out to be a decisive battle of the war, because it convinced the British government, acting on the advice of the Duke of Wellington, that further attempts at invasion of the United States would be fruitless. The British attitude at the peace negotiations became less intransigent, and the American negotiators were able to get a more favorable treaty than had earlier seemed to be possible.

Meanwhile, for the Maritime Provinces, the decade following the battle of Trafalgar had been almost a golden age. Now free to use the high seas, as a result of British naval predominance, they proceeded to develop a greatly expanded trade, which was further stimulated by Jefferson's embargo. As New England declined, Nova Scotia rose, aided by Royal Navy expenditures at Halifax. New Brunswick was also awakened when the British government determined to answer Napoleon's continental system by encouraging the production of lumber and timber within the Empire through a system of steadily mounting preferences. The outbreak of war with the United States added still more to maritime prosperity as its seamen turned increasingly to privateering and smuggling even as they expanded their legal trade. Not only were these provinces secure from attack because of British naval supremacy, but in the last year of the war New England was blockaded and a considerable stretch of the Maine coast was under British occupation, further enlarging trade opportunities. Many Maritimers must have felt very little sense of rejoicing when they heard the news that the Treaty of Ghent had been signed.

This treaty, signed on Christmas Eve, 1814, brought the war to an end without settling any of the complex maritime questions at issue before 1812 and with neither side gaining or losing territory. It might appear, therefore, that the war had been another of those human follies that cause much misery but accomplish nothing. For the British, certainly, who had been scarcely aware of its existence, it had merely been an added irritation in the desperate struggle with Napoleon. To Americans and Canadians, however, it had been no comic-opera conflict but one of the most momentous events in North American history.

In American eyes it was seen as a "Second War of Independence." Despite internal disunity, as evidenced in New England's threatened secession, and despite humiliating events, particularly the British raid on Washington in 1814, it was widely believed that the country came out of the war stronger than it had gone into it. There had been many mortifying defeats, but there had also been dramatic single-ship victories over British vessels on the high seas, and at the very end, indeed after the peace was signed, came Andrew Jackson's smashing victory at New Orleans. Altogether, the war proved to be a notable stimulus to the emerging national consciousness of the American people; they saw it as both an assertion and a vindication of the independence won a generation earlier. As one American put it in 1815, "The war has been a vast benefit. It has taught Great Britain to remember and respect our strength. It has taught us to respect ourselves, and to feel a confidence in our own powers and resources. It has strengthened and perfected our independence by improving our agricultural and manufacturing interests."

Indeed, the war had forced a significant diversification of the American economy.

In the Canadian provinces the effects of the war had been equally profound. Large military expenditures had helped to quicken economic development. More important, the war had sharpened the sense of separation from the United States. The change was especially noticeable in Upper Canada, where many American sympathizers had left or been expelled. The vast majority of the American settlers remained, but now they often had bitter memories of the recent invasions and raids. After this ordeal not many of them would be very republican in political outlook. Still more significant, the political and social leaders of the province, partly of recent British origin and partly of loyalist background, came out of the war with a renewed confidence and a renewed determination. For three years they had been in the front lines and had successfully resisted attacks by superior forces. To them it was clear that the United States, having been a real enemy, was still a potential one, and as a corollary it was equally clear that the one hope for safety and security lay in clinging closely to the British tie. It was their fate, as one of them put it, to live beside "a powerful and treacherous enemy" who would seize the first opportunity to repeat the attack. Therefore, the province must be made more British and less American by encouraging immigration from the mother country, and every effort must be made to secure British support and protection. In Lower Canada, which had been less exposed, the repercussions were not so striking. Nevertheless, it was widely noted that the French Canadians had shown a strong determination to defend their homes and had taken an important part in some of the fighting. Soon the tradition would develop, in which some myth entered, of joint English-Canadian and French-Canadian resistance to the invader. Because nationalism develops among a people when they have a sense of having done great things together, it is not surprising that the memory of the War of 1812, when the homeland had been defended, should be cherished and preserved.

Thus the War of 1812 strengthened a sense of identity on both sides of the Canadian-American border. More immediately, it left the need and opened up the opportunity for a fuller settlement than that contained in the Treaty of Ghent. Just as the peace of 1783 had been completed by Jay's Treaty, so the peace of 1814 was completed by later diplomacy, notably the Rush-Bagot Agreement of 1817 and the Convention of 1818. Great Britain was concerned to reach an accommodation with the United States, particularly on matters relating to the interior of the continent, in order to free its hands to deal with European questions, while the United States also wanted to clear the way for further national growth.

In the last year of the war the shipbuilding race on Lake Ontario had reached enormous proportions, and it was in the interest of each side to prevent the renewal of a contest that would be ruinously expensive as well as highly dangerous. Accordingly, the Rush-Bagot Agreement placed limitations on Great Lakes naval armaments, the first reciprocal arrangement of its kind in modern history. The Agreement also served to balance British and American power: although England still remained supreme on the high seas, and a potential threat to American coastal cities, the United States, with its superior resources and population, would henceforth prevail in any contest resumed in the interior. Yet, because it did not produce an "undefended border," the significance of the Agreement should not be exaggerated. Both sides would spend many hundreds of thousands of pounds and dollars on defenses in the next half century.

The Convention of 1818 was more far-reaching. In addition to another round of fisheries negotiations, in which Americans lost the privilege of fishing in Nova Scotian coastal waters but were permitted to use the shores of Newfoundland, there was a further definition of the boundary between the United States and the British possessions to the north. There was now much more of it to define than in 1783 or in 1794, because in the meantime both sides had extended their interests far into the west. On the British side there was the great contest between the Canadian fur trade, based on Montreal, and the Hudson's Bay Company, leading to far-ranging explorations as well as a bitter conflict over Lord Selkirk's settlement south of Lake Winnipeg. British claims on the Pacific slope had earlier been staked by the voyages of James Cook and George Vancouver. On the American side there had also been maritime activity, notably Robert Gray's discovery of the mouth of the Columbia River. But by far the most important event was the Louisiana Purchase of 1803, which doubled the area of the United States and made it into a truly continental power. After the War of 1812 it became the pleasurable duty of the Secretary of State, John Quincy Adams, to negotiate the limits of this imperial acquisition, and in this task he was brilliantly successful. His most triumphant feat came in his diplomacy toward Spain, respecting the southern and western boundary, but he could also be well pleased with the settlement made with Great Britain. By the Convention of 1818 it was agreed that the western boundary, from the Lake of the Woods, should run along the forty-ninth parallel as far as the Rockies. There was, however, no agreement on the boundary between the Rockies and the Pacific, because each side claimed the country north of the Columbia River. This settlement was postponed— until 1846 as it turned out.

But the essentials of the western boundary between the United States and British North America had been defined. It remained to be seen whether they would prove to be permanent, although the question was largely lost to view for another generation. On both sides the far west was for this period the preserve of the fur traders, to whom political boundaries meant little, and Canadian-American contacts were relatively few.

9 Growing Pains, 1819-1849

The long generation from the end of the War of 1812 to the middle of the century was one of rapid growth but also of developing crisis in the affairs of North America. The United States was now less involved in European politics than it had been in earlier periods of its history, a fact which received symbolic emphasis in President Monroe's message of 1823, and it was consequently freer to concentrate upon internal development, which was of breathtaking rapidity and scope. Worldwide commerce, growing cotton exports, the beginnings of industrialization, and a westward expansion that made the United States a transcontinental republic by 1848 were the leading features of a remarkable growth. But this growth was accompanied by the emergence of an increasingly bitter controversy over the place of slavery in American life, a controversy which threatened to disrupt the Union. The British North American colonies, although still a group of scattered and separated communities stretched along the northern side of the United States, began to move away from the primitive economy of an earlier time into an era of internal improvements, expanding commerce, and increased immigration. Yet these developments went hand in hand with bitter political controversy, culminating in armed rebellion, and with fundamental changes in the mother country's imperial policy. Both in the United States and in the provinces to the north the mood was uncertain and the outlook potentially dangerous at the end of this period.

Because our attention will have to center on the provinces of Upper and Lower Canada, the scene of most rapid change and most extensive disturbance, we should begin by a brief glance at the rest of British North America, to the east and to the west.

In later years, the people of the Maritime Provinces would look back on these years leading up to the middle of the nineteenth century almost as a Golden Age. Immigration in the post-Napoleonic era brought a much-needed increase of population, especially to New Brunswick. Shipbuilding and Atlantic commerce flourished as never before, and the relaxing of the

British mercantilist system gave the Nova Scotians a new free-dom to realize their opportunities, although there was worry over the threatened and then the actual loss of preference within the British market. Internally, political debate was vigorous and sometimes acrimonious, but in the end the Maritimers achieved constitutional reform without resorting to the violence that marked these years in the Canadas. T. C. Haliburton's "Sam Slick" might find the provincials rather slow when compared to "go ahead" Yankees, but, on the whole, the Maritimers were content with their place in the Empire and in the North Atlantic world.

Far to the west, at the eastern edge of the prairies, violent events at the very beginning of the period fixed the course of development for the next generation. There, on the banks of the Red River, south of Lake Winnipeg, a colony had been founded by a Scottish philanthropist, Lord Selkirk, which stood squarely athwart the lengthy communication lines of Montreal's North West Company. The Nor' Westers tried to break up the colony but, although almost destroyed, it revived and endured. In the struggle the Montrealers exhausted their energies and resources, with the result that by 1821 they had no choice but to come to terms with their more strategically situated rival, the Hudson's Bay Company, into which the North West Company was absorbed. Henceforth, the trade would be carried on from the Bay, and Canada's link with the West was, for the time being, broken. It remained to be seen whether this link could be rewelded sometime in the future.

Coming back, then, to the St. Lawrence and Great Lakes region, we must see how the two Canadian provinces set out to reorganize themselves after the War of 1812. To the men who directed Montreal's commercial empire it was a time for serious thought and energetic planning. The outcome of the war confirmed once and for all the loss of the old fur-trading empire southwest of the Great Lakes, and the northwest was about to fall from their grasp as the Hudson's Bay Company prevailed in

1821. Clearly, a new economic strategy was needed to replace the old reliance upon the fur trade, and, fortunately, there were attractive possibilities on the horizon. The assault upon the Canadian forest, especially in the region of the Ottawa River Valley, was already well under way, and the expansion of agriculture was also beginning to provide an export surplus of wheat and flour. The Montreal merchants were soon financing and organizing the movement of these products down the St. Lawrence and out to overseas markets. But they also had their eyes on a still larger trade: with the movement of American settlement toward the Middle West, they hoped to attract the exports of this new region down the St. Lawrence. Almost at once, however, they realized that the St. Lawrence route was going to suffer stiff competition from their old rivals to the south, the New York merchants, who, by means of the Erie Canal, were also reaching out to capture the western trade. This canal, started in 1817 and completed in 1825, provided a shorter route into the interior, but the Montreal merchants remained convinced that the St. Lawrence route, if adequately improved, would be able to draw a large share of the western trade.

Adequately improved — that was the great stumbling block. Potentially, the Great Lakes–St. Lawrence route was a magnificent waterway, but it was of little value as long as the rapids at Montreal and above Montreal remained obstacles, and as long as there was no way around Niagara Falls. Obviously, the "canal mania" that was seizing Americans must be matched in the Canadian provinces if the northern economy was to flourish. But the Canadian business leaders soon realized that they were in a very weak position for the accomplishment of their objectives. There was little hope of support from the mother country, which was more concerned to cut down rather than to increase expenditures in the colonies and whose only contribution to canal-building (the Rideau Canal, between the Ottawa River and the eastern end of Lake Ontario) had a military, not a commercial, objective. Far more serious was the fact that the merchants were a small English-speaking minority in a province that was predominantly French-speaking and that the leaders of the majority had little interest in the commercial objectives of the minority. The merchants were well represented in the executive council and in the appointed legislative council but had almost no voice in the elective assembly, where a program of economic development would have to originate.

Such was the background of Lower Canada's constitutional struggle, which lasted for some twenty years and which in 1837 culminated in rebellion. The conflict was by no means purely racial. There were some French Canadians who supported the program of the merchants, and there were a good many English-speaking residents, particularly among the Irish immigrants, who made common cause with the French-Canadian majority. In the beginning at least, the politicians of the assembly, with Louis Joseph Papineau at their head, were convinced that they were fighting a constitutional struggle in the best English tradition. Like Parliament of old, and like the assemblies in the old colonies before the American Revolution, they were seeking full financial control for the elective branch of the legislature and striving to make the executive responsive to the wishes of the people. As time went on, however, Papineau and his colleagues came to believe that there was a sinister campaign under way to destroy the French-Canadian people. In 1822 for instance, the merchants inspired an abortive attempt by the British Government to unite Upper and Lower Canada in such a way that the French Canadians would be outvoted in a united legislature and their language cease to be used in official records and, later, in assembly debates. Protests led to the withdrawal of this bill from the British Parliament, but other ominous events followed. The governor for most of the 1820's, Lord Dalhousie, seemed to be completely in the hands of the English party. The Colonial Office, although apparently somewhat sympathetic to the constitutional aspirations of the assembly, would not support changes that might leave the French Canadians in full control of all branches of government. Measures aimed at weakening the seigneurial system, coinciding with increased British immigration into the province, appeared as evidences of an anglicizing program.

By the early 1830's both sides were almost frantic with frustration. Driven on by an increasingly self-conscious sense of French-Canadian nationalism, Papineau and his supporters were in no mood to be appeased by the rather half-hearted gestures of conciliation emanating from the Colonial Office. Convinced that the latter would never do anything effective to dislodge the merchant oligarchy from its position of control in the two appointed councils, Papineau embarked on a more extremist course that lost him many of his more moderate supporters, both French-speaking and English-speaking. Even so, his support in the countryside remained remarkably steady, because it was a time of serious crisis for the habitants. A combination of bad harvests, uncertain markets, and rural overpopulation in many areas made the farmers discontented and hypersensitive, especially when they saw immigrants pouring in (bringing cholera with them!) and vacant lands falling into the hands of English land speculators. In such a mood they were ready to respond to the nationalist appeals of Papineau and other *"patriotes,"* as the followers of Papineau were now being called. On the other hand, the "English party" were more certain than ever that the French Canadians were so backward, illiterate, and unenterprising as to be unfitted to have political power. They still dreamed of a union with Upper Canada, or of detaching Montreal from Lower Canada, or of other measures to overcome the effects of French-Canadian numbers. In particular, they viewed with suspicion liberal trends in Great Britain during the era of the Reform Bill that might lead to a softer policy toward the demands of the French-Canadian nationalists. They feared, and their fears were soundly based, that the Colonial Office was prepared to go a long way in acceding to these demands; in fact it was only the distracted condition of Lower Canadian politics that prevented the Colonial Office from encouraging a more rapid transition toward colonial self-government in the years before 1837.

Meanwhile, events in Upper Canada had also been moving

toward crisis, although without the overtones of racial conflict found in the lower province. Constitutionally, the problem was much the same: a little oligarchy, soon to be called the "Family Compact," was entrenched in the two appointed councils, and its point of view was usually adopted by the governor sent from Britain. The elected assembly was powerless to prevail against this oligarchy, even when it had a strong mandate from the voters for a change of policy. But this constitutional conflict, which could be found in many colonies of the time, was envenomed by many factors unique to Upper Canada. In particular, the leaders of the so-called "Family Compact," partly of loyalist and partly of recent British origin, were convinced that determined measures must be taken to strengthen the British characteristics of the province; although it had been successfully defended during the War of 1812, Upper Canada seemed to these men to be still predominantly American in tone and manners. Most of the population was of American origin. The largest religious denominations — Methodists, Presbyterians, Baptists — had close ties with their sister churches in the United States. The province was thought to be infested with American schoolteachers, innkeepers, and other agents of Americanism. Hence every effort must be made to strengthen the Church of England, to guide educational development along British lines, and to encourage British immigration. Not only was further American immigration discouraged, but the provincial government held that the American-born settlers were to be regarded as aliens, and thus without the right to vote or hold office, until they had been naturalized and taken the oath of allegiance.

It was this last policy, which not only called in question the political rights of a large element of the population but perhaps also their land titles, that marked the beginning of widespread political controversy. Quarrels over land policy, over the charter for a provincial university, and over the status of the Church of England also added fuel to the fire. By the end of the 1820's the conservative leaders were opposed by a powerful protest movement well represented in the assembly and sometimes in control of that body.

Nevertheless, the political contest was much more evenly balanced than it was in Lower Canada because the opponents of the government were never able to win consistent support from a majority of the voters. Indeed, each election resulted in an assembly with a political complexion different from its predecessor. From an early stage it was apparent that the critics of government were divided among themselves; some were moderate reformers who merely wished a broader political structure that would make for a government more responsive to the wishes of the people, whereas others were of a more radical bent. The more radical were increasingly inclined to cite examples drawn from American practice and to argue for the wide extension of the elective principle. In turn, this tendency made it possible for the supporters of the government to accuse all the reformers of being pro-American in outlook. This raising of the loyalty cry was often effective in a community where memories of the War of 1812 were still vivid. As well, the voters were often disposed to support candidates who would work with the government to secure the building of roads, canals, and other measures of economic improvement. An assembly that simply carried on a bitter and protracted quarrel was obviously ineffective. Yet on the other hand there was a genuine and widespread wish for an end to the narrow and oligarchic system of government, provided change did not weaken the British tie. If Upper Canada could have been moved a few hundred miles away from the American border, its political life would have been more constructive and less confused.

By the middle of the 1830's the sense of frustration among many of Upper Canada's radical reformers was almost as great as that among Papineau and his supporters in the lower province. In fact, the two groups were in close touch and trying to concert their measures. By this time Papineau, under the influence of the traditions of the French and the American Revolutions, had become republican in outlook and increasingly anticlerical. Moderates began to draw away from him, but his continued control of the assembly enabled him to maintain the deadlock between that body and the appointed branches. The final crisis was precipitated by the British government, which despite its genuine wish to satisfy the demand for political reform saw no choice but to use imperial authority to break the financial impasse caused by the assembly's refusal to vote supply. In 1837 resolutions passed by the British Parliament raised the threat that the provincial executive might be empowered to take money from the treasury without the consent of the assembly, and against this threat the patriotes determined to act. Papineau was now being pushed along by men, both English-speaking and French-speaking, who were more radical and extremist than he, men who could count on the support of the distressed farmers of the Montreal and Richelieu River region. Tempers were further inflamed by the provocative words and actions of the English elements who hoped for a showdown. The seething discontent finally erupted in November 1837 in unco-ordinated uprisings north and east of Montreal which were put down after several days of fighting. Most of the leaders escaped to the nearby American states, leaving their followers to face a mopping-up that was often vengeful and brutal, particularly where the English-speaking militia had a hand. The rebellion had never had the active support of more than a fraction of the French Canadians, but its harsh aftermath widened the chasm between the two language groups.

In Upper Canada acute political disintegration also marked the 1830's. In one of the periodic electoral swings the reform group gained a majority in the assembly in 1834 and proceeded to press its case against the Family Compact. Its highly vocal, but less numerous, radical wing was led by William Lyon Mackenzie, a Scottish newspaper editor, who for a decade had been carrying on a personal vendetta against the Family Compact, and they with him. Now the assembly assigned him the chair-

manship of a committee on grievances, of which he made full use
to compile a lengthy record of misgovernment. At the same time
the more moderate reformers were calling for a change in constitutional practice by which the governor would appoint to his
executive council men who had the confidence of the majority in
the assembly. A new governor, Sir Francis Bond Head, made a
move in this direction in 1836 but showed no inclination to act
upon the advice of the reorganized council. Thereupon the
council resigned and the province was plunged into a
hard-fought election campaign, in which the governor openly
sided with the conservative and tory forces and accused the
reformers, moderates and radicals alike, of being agents of
American republicanism. With the conservatives well organized
and the reformers in disarray, the pendulum swung once again,
against the reformers. Mackenzie, who lost his seat, now concluded that the oligarchy would never be dislodged by peaceful
means and began to organize resistance among the farmers north
of Toronto. Taking his cue from the Lower Canadian uprisings,
he led a forlorn march against the provincial capital in December
1837. It was a heedless venture, easily put down without the aid
of regular troops, and Mackenzie was fortunate to escape across
the Niagara River. His call for the establishment of a republican
State of Upper Canada obviously had only the most meager
support in Upper Canada.

These two little rebellions of 1837 are often assigned a greater
importance than they deserve. In general, Canadians have been
so law-abiding that writers have had a natural tendency to pick
out and emphasize the few occasions like these when some sort
of violent protest was lodged against authority. And with the
earlier example of the American Revolution in mind there has
also been a disposition to see these uprisings as revolts against an
imperial authority that was holding these North American communities in colonial subjection. Moreover, because the rebellions were followed within a decade by the achievement of
self-government, it has been tempting to conclude that the rebel-

lions were a necessary prelude to this result. In fact, however, the contest was not between the British government and the colonies (indeed, Britain was anxious to see a larger measure of colonial self-government), but between groups within each colony. In Lower Canada an English-speaking minority, striving for commercial development in the race with their American rivals, desperately opposed change that would increase the political power of the French Canadians. In Upper Canada a British-oriented group, which often had the support of a majority of the voters and which also favored internal improvement, believed that the reform program would break down the already weak barriers holding back American democracy and American republicanism. In each province the recourse to extremism and rebellion probably delayed the process of change by tarring the patriote and reform causes with disloyalty and subversion, and this unhealthy political climate was prolonged by the border troubles that were the aftermath of the uprisings.

These border troubles require brief mention before we sketch the reorganization of Canadian politics in the dozen years after 1837. In each province, and notably in Upper Canada, peace and order quickly returned after the short-lived and abortive resort to arms. A year later, to be sure, Lower Canada was again briefly disturbed by a feebler outbreak, but there was nothing to indicate any danger of significant armed revolt. Nevertheless, for several years both provinces suffered from periodic border raids, which, in the case of Upper Canada at least, produced more casualties and more destruction than the original rebellion had caused and which produced a sharp chill in Canadian-American relations. These raids had their origins in the activities of Mackenzie, Papineau, and other leaders who fled to New York and New England with tales of the cruel oppression under which the colonists were suffering and with pleas for assistance in mounting a war of liberation. These tales and pleas received a sympathetic hearing in many American border communities where it was believed that British redcoats were holding down freedom-loving peoples. Arms and financial aid were contributed to the Canadian rebels, and soon American recruits were joining their causes. For a time Mackenzie set up headquarters on a Canadian island in the Niagara River, where he was supplied from the Buffalo area. These provocative proceedings, in a time of peace, inspired a Canadian militia party to cross the river at the end of 1837, cut out an American ship, the *Caroline,* and send it in flames down toward the Falls, an action which served to outrage many border residents.

Before long, Canadian exiles, who had never been numerous, disappeared almost completely from the groups which were forming to "liberate" the Canadian provinces. But Americans who knew little or nothing about the real situation in Canada continued to flock to them, and soon dozens of so-called patriot societies, notably the Hunters' Lodges, were strung out along the border from Michigan to New England. On several occasions they organized raids, across the Detroit, the Niagara, or the St. Lawrence rivers, which to the people of the provinces appeared as foreign invasions. Further exasperation arose from the feeling that American authorities were doing little to prevent the organization and launching of these raiding parties or that they were even tacitly condoning them. In fact, lack of troops and division of authority between federal and state governments accounted for the ineffective patrolling of the American side of the border in the months immediately following the rebellions. Later on, under General Winfield Scott's direction, quiet was restored, although annoying incidents still occurred occasionally.

The crisis along the Great Lakes–St. Lawrence border, a revival of the dispute over the Maine–New Brunswick border, and the existence of a number of other unsettled questions made it clear by 1840 that Anglo-American relations were in a sad state of disrepair. Each side was making plans for strengthening border defenses, and many voices were being raised in angry and threatening tones. Fortunately for the preservation of peace the year 1841 saw the coming to power in both Great Britain and the

United States of governments that were more disposed and better equipped than their predecessors to seek for a reasonable settlement. This coincidence led to the wide-ranging negotiations carried on by the American secretary of state, Daniel Webster, and the British envoy, Lord Ashburton, which resulted in the treaty of 1842, one of the most important of Anglo-American settlements. Agreement was reached on all controverted boundary questions from Maine and New Brunswick on the east to the Rocky Mountains, and arrangements were also worked out for dealing with the tangled question of extradition. This settlement was followed up in 1846 by the Oregon Treaty, which extended the boundary line along the forty-ninth parallel to the west coast and then around the southern end of Vancouver Island.

These two treaties were highly significant as further confirmations of the political division of North America. During these years many Canadians were greatly disturbed by the rather extravagant expansionist oratory of some Americans who were prophesying that it was the manifest destiny of the republic to extend the sway of the Stars and Stripes from one end of the continent to the other. The course of events which had taken Texas away from Mexico and annexed it to the United States seemed to many in the provinces an ominous pattern that might be repeated to the north. The obvious desire of Great Britain for good relations with the United States, combined with the growing British impatience at the cost of colonies, raised fears that the mother country might be less than firm in resisting American pressures. But these fears were allayed by the two treaties. Although Canadians could cavil at some clauses, where it was felt that the Americans had won more than they deserved, they were reassured by evidence of British support. Modern scholarship has shown that American "manifest destiny" was not so powerful a force as it seemed to many at the time and in any event was not pushing hard against British North American territory, but this is hindsight. The treaties and the firm British stand of the 1840's were needed to convince the provincials that American expansion would not turn northward.

While Canadian-American relations were negotiating the stormy passage of the 1840's, the political institutions of the northern provinces were undergoing a significant change. In a few short years these provinces made the transition from a condition of colonial tutelage to one of effective self-government in their internal affairs. In no period, perhaps, is the divergence of Canadian from American development clearer than in this one, for in contrast to the American tradition that self-government is gained only when the colonial phase is cut abruptly by the gaining of national independence, the northern provinces embarked on a campaign of gradual evolution toward autonomy which envisaged continued close political association with the mother country. As this evolution proceeded, the outlines of the later British Commonwealth began to appear. And because the Canadian determination to hold fast to the British connection owed much to the need for protection against the United States, the U.S. can claim to be a sort of unintentional godfather of the Commonwealth.

Such a transition in so short a time was astonishing because, at the outset, immediately after the 1837 rebellions, the outlook for political progress had been very unpromising. In Lower Canada the constitution of 1791 was suspended, thus eliminating the assembly, the troops were in control, and the English elements were loudly asserting that their worst suspicions of the French-Canadian majority had now been proven correct. In Upper Canada the rash actions of Mackenzie and his handful of followers allowed tories and conservatives to tar the whole reform movement with disloyalty; all suggestions for constitutional change were denounced as American-inspired and subversive. In each province the little oligarchies appeared to be more solidly entrenched in power than ever.

Nevertheless, this appearance was deceiving; there was no possibility that the political life of the provinces could be frozen in a state of immobile reaction. The moderate reformers soon began to regroup their ranks, and as they did so they were greatly heartened to learn that the British government had appointed a new governor in the person of Lord Durham, a man who was noted for his liberal and reformist outlook. Soon after Durham reached Quebec in May 1838, reformers began to bombard him with memoranda to aid him in his inquest into the affairs of British North America and to hold "Durham meetings" advocating political change. For his part, Durham and his staff began an intensive study of Canadian affairs which was abruptly cut short when a quarrel with the British government led him to resign and to return to England in November. But he had been in Canada long enough to gather material for his famous *Report on the Affairs of British North America*, which was issued early in 1839 and which at once became a landmark in Canadian and in British imperial history.

Both in diagnosing the ills of the northern provinces and in prescribing remedies for them, Durham was constantly aware of the close proximity of the provinces to the rapidly growing American republic. As an ardent believer in the doctrine of material progress, he painted a dismal picture of the contrast between the stagnation on one side of the border and the activity on the other. But, he argued, as long as the British North Americans lived in small provincial communities, under narrow oligarchic governments, they had little stimulus or opportunity for moving into the mainstream of nineteenth-century enterprise. They would never rival the deeds of the Americans until their horizons were widened and until they felt assured that government was responsive to public opinion. Therefore, Durham continued, the provincials must have full self-government in their internal affairs (reserving to the British authority only a few matters of imperial concern), and steps must be taken to build a broader nationality by joining the colonies together. To those who feared that these measures could lead to separation from the Empire, Durham replied that the reverse would be true: the

British North Americans would cling more closely to the Empire once their rights were secured and their horizons broadened.

Accordingly, Durham gave vigorous support to the campaign for "responsible government" which Robert Baldwin and the moderate reformers of Upper Canada had been maintaining for several years. As Durham noted, the acceptance of this proposal required no formal change in the constitution; it meant simply that henceforth the governor would rely upon advisers who could command the confidence of a majority of the elected branch of the legislature. When advisers no longer had this confidence they should resign and the governor would have to find new ones. There was nothing strange in such a system: it was cabinet government as practiced in Great Britain, and its adoption in North America would bring the colonies closer to the institutions of the mother country. Secondly, on the matter of intercolonial federation, Durham's first preference was for bringing together all the colonies, but when this scheme promised to be slow and doubtful he adopted, as a second best, the proposal of joining the two largest colonies, Upper and Lower Canada, with the hope that the Maritimes might come in later on.

Durham felt the need for haste in this matter because of his view of the future of the French Canadians in North America. Just as he took over the idea of responsible government from the Upper Canadian reformers, so he adopted from the English party in Lower Canada his attitude toward the French Canadians. These people, although possessing many fine personal qualities, were nevertheless, Durham considered, narrow, rural, and reactionary, opposed to all forward-looking proposals. Moreover, because of the rebellion, they would never again act as loyal subjects of the Crown. Therefore, despite the fact that Durham was committed to the grant of self-government to British North America, he was equally convinced that the French Canadians could not be entrusted with political power. Because they were the majority in the most populous province, this view might appear to pose an insoluble dilemma, but Durham found an answer in his plan for the union of the two provinces. When the English population of Lower Canada was added to that of Upper Canada, the total would outnumber the French Canadians, who would thus be politically impotent and, in time, led to give up their vain ambition of maintaining a separate nationality in North America. As French culture had all but disappeared in Louisiana, so, Durham argued, it should be encouraged to disappear along the shores of the St. Lawrence. There was no place for it in a North America where civilization was to be Anglo-American in tone.

There were few, either in British North America or in Great Britain, who would fully endorse all sections of Durham's eloquent and sharply worded report, but the British government did decide to accept the proposal for the reunion of Upper and Lower Canada, which went into effect in 1841. In the view of the Colonial Office, however, Durham's other main recommendation — responsible government — was unacceptable, for the simple reason that a governor could not serve two masters: he could not at the same time obey his instructions from London and act on the advice of a council responsible to a colonial legislature. What if instructions and advice should conflict? Nevertheless, the Colonial Office, as before 1837, was quite ready to see a more flexible political system develop in British North America.

This readiness was all that the colonial politicians needed for the achievement of the goal of self-government. Although at first the governors tried to delay the process, it soon became clear that Canada — and the Maritimes, too — were moving inexorably toward cabinet government. Before the end of the 1840's, it was in full operation and was accepted by the Colonial Office, despite earlier misgivings. The fact that Britain adopted free trade in 1846 was an important factor in this process, because if the colonies were no longer to have a preference in British markets, thus losing an important economic benefit of the imperial connection, they could scarcely be kept in close political leading-strings. Indeed, there was much anti-imperial sentiment in

Britain, looking to the day when the colonies would be cast off entirely.

Nevertheless, responsible government did not come in the way that Durham had hoped and expected; instead of being swamped by the union of the Canadas, the French Canadians emerged to play an active and sometimes determining role in political life. The simple explanation of this emergence was that political groupings did not divide along purely racial lines, particularly when politicians were thrown together by the union. Soon reformers from Upper Canada were seeking allies among the French Canadians, and, together, the two groups formed a biracial political party which took the lead in securing the adoption of responsible government. The close cooperation in this party of Robert Baldwin and Louis Hippolyte Lafontaine was the first convincing demonstration in Canadian political history that English-speaking Canadians and French-speaking Canadians could work amicably and constructively together.

The demonstration was so convincing, in fact, that by the end of the 1840's the English-speaking mercantile element in Montreal was seized with frantic exasperation. Their hopes for building and controlling a commercial empire seemed to be gone. Despite their record of loyalty, they appeared to be deserted by the mother country, which now seemed to favor French Canadians, so recently rebels. Reacting against the supposed threat of "French rule," many leading figures in the Montreal community gave full vent to their anger. After inciting a Protestant mob to attack the governor general and burn the Parliament buildings, the tory business men of Montreal further expressed their discontent by signing the Annexation Manifesto in 1849. Assuming that the imperial connection was now meaningless, they took the view that Canada's only hope for material improvement lay in political association with the United States. Such a move would also end the threat of French rule: annexation supporters would remain English by ceasing to be British.

Although these spectacular events served to bring one phase of

Canadian history to an end, they represented in reality the temporary frustration of one group rather than widespread conviction. The call for annexation received little response and soon died away. Nevertheless, basic questions remained, which insistently demanded answers. How were the northern colonies to reorganize their economies now that the British preference was gone? What relations were they to have with one another and with their powerful neighbor to the south? Unless constructive answers were found, annexation might in fact turn out to be the only way out, for separate colonies could hardly hope to remain independent of the United States.

10 Disintegration and Integration, 1849-1873

The third quarter of the nineteenth century was a decisive one in the political development of North America. It began with many evidences of disarray and disruption. In the United States the controversy over slavery, following the Mexican War, brought the country to a serious crisis which was patched over by the Compromise of 1850, but only after prolonged congressional debate. In a few short years the dispute reached a new level of bitterness that led directly to the secession of eleven states and to one of the bloodiest of all civil wars. In the northern colonies issues were not so heavily charged with emotion, yet the outlook was filled with uncertainties and hazards. The impact of Great Britain's free-trade policy and its growing determination to lessen its commitments in North America made British North Americans acutely aware that they were vulnerable and exposed. Moreover, the largest colony—the Province of Canada—was soon caught up in acrimonious strife arising out of cultural and religious differences and in a steadily deepening political instability. Nevertheless, on each side of the political boundary the forces of disintegration were stayed and then reversed. In the United States a mammoth mobilization of men and material broke the movement for Southern independence leading to a reconstituted union that was preparing to become the most powerful national state of modern times. To the north a remarkable combination of pressures, both internal and external, brought the colonies together in a federal union which in a few short years became transcontinental. And out of this period of storm and stress came a new ordering of Canadian-American relations on which all subsequent developments have been built.

On each side, the acute tensions of 1849-1850 gave way to several years of optimism and vibrant enterprise, encouraged and maintained by surging new forces of economic growth. While Americans spoke hopefully of the "finality" of the Compromise of 1850, Canadians decided that their prospects were not so dark as the authors of the Annexation Manifesto had painted them. Not only did public opposition to the idea of annexation deepen after the Congress passed the Fugitive Slave Act as part of the 1850 compromise, but it soon began to appear that the mother country had not deserted the provincials so completely as the events of the latter 1840's had suggested. The comforting umbrella of the mercantilist system was gone, but it was replaced almost at once by the invigorating impulses of expanding capitalism. Although British capital had long been flowing into the United States, now, for the first time, it began to move into British North America in considerable quantities to stimulate the emerging boom in railway building that was gripping both the provinces and the states. The services of skilled engineers and contractors as well as a renewed burst of immigration were further British stimulants to a prosperity that was unparalleled in the colonies.

Nevertheless, economic expansion, particularly in the form of lumbering and farming and in the improvement of communications, raised all the more insistently the question of markets for the increased production. Some Canadians were already looking to an answer through intercolonial union, but everyone realized that there were nearer, larger, and more attractive selling opportunities in the nearby states. Nor was the old dream dead of attracting American goods to tidewater via the St. Lawrence; it might be brought closer to reality by a reduction of tariffs along the border. Furthermore, from a political point of view, the governor general, Lord Elgin, believed that the surest way to prevent any revival of annexation sentiment was to increase trade with the neighboring states. Thus began the Canadian pursuit of trade reciprocity with the United States, a pursuit which would have a history both persistent and checkered in the next half century and more.

The British government, ardently devoted to the principle of free trade, stood ready to encourage this project, particularly because increased prosperity might enable the colonies to shoulder a larger share of their defense budget, which was a cause of insistent complaint in the British Parliament. With troubles looming in Europe British authorities were also anxious to allay all sources of dispute in North America. For a time, the American government was indifferent to the reciprocity idea, but then it too began to feel pressures. The Great Lakes states were attracted by the idea of an alternate trade route, but more important, the New Englanders were clamoring for admission to the inshore fisheries of the Maritime Provinces, from which they had been excluded by the Convention of 1818. Some highly effective lobbying in the best North American tradition helped to bring around the doubtful, with the result that the Reciprocity Treaty was easily passed through the Congress in 1854. Additional support came from the employment of contrasting arguments: Northern congressmen were led to believe that reciprocity might be the first stage in the admission of several more free states, whereas Southern congressmen, agreeing with Lord Elgin's view, voted for the bill as a means of preventing such a strengthening of their sectional opponents.

The treaty itself provided for free trade in natural products, for the admission of each side into the coastal fisheries of the other, and for the reciprocal use of several important internal waterways, particularly in the Great Lakes system. The Nova Scotians lamented the fisheries clause, but were appeased by hopes of penetrating the large American market. Scheduled to last for ten years, with each side having the right thereafter to give one year's notice of abrogation, the treaty coincided, for three years, with continued North American prosperity, and many felt that it was a main factor in that prosperity. Although the traditional east-west orientation of their economy was breaking down under the north-south pull set up by the treaty, Canadians rejoiced at the accompanying trade expansion. It is both interesting and significant that the British North American provinces formally adopted decimal coinage at this time.

Meanwhile, however, other events and trends were working against a complete integration of the Canadian and American economies. Of particular importance was the growing involvement between railroads and governments. As in the United States, Canadian railroads which began as private ventures soon turned to government for financial assistance. A classic example of this trend is found in the history of the Grand Trunk Railway, for a time North America's longest railroad, which was built to English standards and in consequence was outrageously expensive in terms of North American distances and traffic. Soon the provincial government had to come to its assistance, and soon that government was searching for revenues to meet its enlarged commitments. Toward the end of the 1850's it was turning for an answer to an increased tariff on manufactured items, not a violation of the letter of the Reciprocity Treaty but, some Americans asserted, a violation of its spirit. This argument would be remembered when protectionism revived in the United States and would play a part in ending the treaty. The Canadian tariff met an even angrier response from free-trade Britain, leading the Canadian finance minister, A. T. Galt, to warn the imperial government in 1859 that it must no longer interfere with Canadian tariff policy. Economic growth was driving the Province of Canada toward a fuller exercise of its powers and a certain definition of its relation to both of its associates in the North Atlantic Triangle.

Along with the problems of economic development there were also warning signs for Canadian leaders to read. The province, from Quebec to the Detroit River, had about reached the limits of growth according to the techniques of the time. Most of the good land had been taken up. The movement of French Canadians to the industries of New England was already under way, and a steady stream of people was leaving Upper Canada for the American Middle West. It was abundantly clear in the 1850's that Canada had no frontier in the American sense, or rather its frontier was in the United States. Yet it was also well known that far off to the northwest there were large quantities of good land under British sovereignty, if only it could be reached, and reached in time. The Toronto *Globe* might exult that "Providence has entrusted us with the building up of a great northern people, fit to cope with our neighbors of the United States, and to advance step by step with them in the march of civilization," but nevertheless the outlook was ominous. This vast western land was still the preserve of the fur trade, and the Hudson's Bay Company was not likely to encourage a large influx of settlers, even if they could reach these distant regions. Yet many Canadians were convinced that, without westward expansion, they would cease to have a viable economy and society and so be absorbed into the United States. They worried, however, that Americans might reach this promised land before Canadians did, and seize it as they had Texas, Oregon, and California. The little settlement at Fort Garry on the Red River (the precursor of Winnipeg) had its main communications with St. Paul in Minnesota, which became a state in 1858, and the discovery of gold on the Fraser in British Columbia led to a large influx of American miners. The isolation of the northwest was ending.

It was against this background that the first moves toward intercolonial union were made in the latter 1850's. The advocates of union sought to join Canada with the Maritime Provinces, and they also contemplated expansion toward the northwest. Railroads were uppermost in their minds: an Intercolonial Railway to Nova Scotia and a stronger political and economic base for supporting the Grand Trunk, now deeper in financial difficulties after the Panic of 1857. But the move proved to be premature. The Maritimes, although interested in a railroad, were not ready for a close political link with Canada, and the Colonial Office refused to encourage a measure that was coupled with requests for British financial support of Canadian railroads. It was clear that the pressures were not yet strong enough to bring about the political and economic integration of the northern half of the continent. Meanwhile, the Province of Canada was fated to continue to try to work a system of government that was increasingly strained and cumbersome; the experiment of linking English-speaking and French-speaking Canadians in a single framework produced sharper conflicts with each passing year. The union of 1841 had been intended to give political supremacy to the English-speaking element, but, as political parties had taken form under the skilled leadership of John A. Macdonald, something very like the reverse seemed to be happening. So at least many politicians of Upper Canada, led by George Brown, believed as they noted that this section now had a majority of the population yet had equal representation with Lower Canada. Brown demanded "Representation by Population," yet he also saw that the French Canadians would never give up the principle of equal representation without effective guarantees. Thus the internal problems of the province of Canada were also driving men to think of some new political structure.

While the northern provinces were wrestling with these problems the greatest storm in the continent's history was brewing on the other side of the border. Convinced that the victory of the Republican candidate in the presidential election of 1860 posed a clear threat to their way of life, seven states of the lower south, led by South Carolina, seceded from the Union in the winter of 1860-1861, and when the new president, Abraham Lincoln, called for troops after the firing on Fort Sumter, four states of the upper south joined the secessionist movement in the spring of 1861. These eleven states organized themselves as the Confederate States of America, with Jefferson Davis as president, put an army in the field, and determined to fight for the recognition of their independence. With equal determination, Lincoln resolved to resist secession and to restore the union of the states. The lines were drawn for a long and cruel war.

The British North American provinces had for years been watching the gathering storm and were bound to follow the course of the conflict with the closest attention, even when caught up with their own difficulties. Provincial attitudes toward slavery were very similar to those in the northern states. Although not accepting the Negro as a social or political equal, British North Americans had long since freed the few slaves in their midst. It was natural, then, that at the beginning of the war, they should have had little sympathy for the side which in the words of Alexander Stephens, Confederate Vice-President, intended to make slavery the cornerstone of its government and society. On the other hand, an antipathy to the institution of slavery did not necessarily lead to any fellow-feeling for the Union cause, because in 1861 this cause was not directed against that institution. Besides, insofar as the British North Americans felt on the defensive against the United States and felt that their interests might be endangered by American expansionism, their feelings were directed more against the nearer northern states. And insofar as the political and social leaders of the provinces frowned upon tendencies toward a boisterous democracy, theirs, too, was a sentiment directed mainly against the North. All told, then, the provincials had little trouble in achieving an attitude of neutrality mixed perhaps with some satisfaction that their power-ful neighbors would for a time at least be fully involved in their own internal problems.

This somewhat aloof stance was rudely shattered before the end of 1861 under the impact of the *Trent* affair, the most serious diplomatic crisis of the war in the relations of the English-speaking world. For a United States naval vessel to stop a British mail steamer and remove two Confederate envoys was a sharp affront to the dignity of imperial Britain which the govern-ment of Lord Palmerston had no intention of enduring. Yet it was a matter for rejoicing by the Northern public, which had seen little but repulses in the first months of the war. Northerners were also intensely irritated by the earlier British recognition of Confederate belligerency and by British coldness or antagonism to a cause which Northerners felt should have the support of free men everywhere. There was a great outburst of anti-British feeling, while across the Atlantic there was determination that the American act must be disavowed and the Confederate envoys allowed to resume their journey. On both sides there was angry talk of the possibility of Anglo-American war.

Such talk, as in the years leading up to 1812, was of immediate and direct concern to the exposed British North Americans, who for many years had been giving little attention to questions of defense. As it turned out, the affair was smoothed over by careful diplomacy, but the tension had revealed how dangerous might be the impact of the Civil War on North Atlantic relations. The crisis also turned British North American feeling from aloofness into a distinctly anti-Northern direction. The passionately anti-British diatribes in much of the Northern press and the talk of attending to the colonies after the Confederacy was subdued led to mounting anger and resentment in the provinces. As a result there was widespread satisfaction and reassurance in the decision of the British government at the end of 1861 to send eleven thousand regulars to Canada, the largest number of troops sent since 1814. During the next three years both sides of the border would be fortified in various places; it was certainly not an undefended border in these years. And the urgency of the defense question led the British government to view the project of intercolonial union in a new light, because that government was as anxious as before to limit its commitments in North America. Thus, while pressing the Canadians to vote more money for defense, the British government also began to see that a broader union might produce more effective action to this end. The American Civil War was building up an insistent pressure for British North American union.

In 1862 and 1863, however, the defense issue was latent rather than immediate, for General Lee and the other Confederate commanders were fully engaging the resources of the North. During these years the politicians of the Province of Canada continued to wrestle with their own problem of government, which became more exasperating with each passing month. Within the framework of the Act of Union of 1841 certain conventions had arisen for the handling of the affairs of English-speaking and French-speaking Canadians, and the most notable of these was that a ministry must be able to command a

majority from each community. With many political indepen-
dents and waverers in the legislature, this system became more
and more difficult to operate, leading to endemic instability in
politics and government. Politicians from each community had
the opportunity—indeed, the necessity—to talk about and vote
on the local affairs of the other in such sensitive matters as
schools and religion where values and methods were widely
different. By 1864 Canadian politics were bitter, frustrated, and
deadlocked just as the prospect of a Northern military victory was
at last clearly in sight. Unable to solve their own political and
economic problems, unable to make a move toward the northwest, worried about the possible moves of a Union army on the
morrow of victory, Canadian politicians and Canadian politics
appeared to be at a dead end.

It was at this nearly desperate stage that the idea of intercolonial union received a new and, as it turned out, a decisive
impulse. Events began with an agreement in the summer of 1864
to call a truce to the debilitating party warfare by forming a
coalition government charged with seeking union. Delegates
from this government in Canada then journeyed to Charlotte-
town in Prince Edward Island, where a conference happened to
be assembling to consider the project of a Maritime union. Using
their most persuasive arguments, the Canadian delegates convinced the Maritimers that their conference should be adjourned
to Quebec for the full and detailed consideration of a scheme for
British North American federal union. There in an October
conference lasting only some two weeks, the "Fathers of Confederation," comprising delegates from Canada and the Atlantic
provinces, including Newfoundland, agreed upon a scheme of
federal union eventually embodied in seventy-two resolutions.
This was a remarkable achievement on the part of men whose
horizons had hitherto been in the main limited by provincial or
even parochial considerations, and it was proof both of the
urgency of the problem and of the extent to which the delegates
shared a common political tradition. Yet after this encouraging

start the movement for Canadian Confederation suffered long and disappointing delays before its completion in 1867.

A review of this movement within the context of Canadian-American relations inevitably raises the question of parallels and contrasts with the movement that produced the Constitution of the United States eighty years earlier. Neither was a widespread popular movement; instead, in each case, the important discussions were kept rigidly secret and the results were approved only after formidable opposition had been overcome. If anything, the Canadian movement was even less democratic than the American, for the Fathers of Confederation had no intention of submitting their scheme to popular ratification. Believing strongly in the doctrine of parliamentary government, they argued that approval by the legislature concerned was all that was necessary. The British North American leaders also had before them, of course, the model of the American federation, and many of them were close students of it. It is perhaps not surprising that in the 1860's it was a model which they sought to avoid rather than to imitate. For many of the Canadian Fathers the American federal system had come to grief because it suffered from the cardinal defect of leaving too much power to the states. Indeed, several of the most influential provincial leaders, including John A. Macdonald, favored a legislative union that would have left the components with only municipal powers. Such drastic centralization was unobtainable, because no French-Canadian leader could accept it nor would the Maritimers make the surrender; nevertheless, there was widespread agreement that the federal government must be made as strong as possible and the authority of the provinces kept to a minimum. Certainly there was no idea of sovereignty being shared between the federal government and the provinces or of powers being "delegated" by the provinces to the central government. There was a conscious determination to avoid what were thought to be the centrifugal tendencies of the American federal system.

In view of this emphasis in the movement for Canadian federation and in the light of later developments, it is clearly important to understand the outlook of French Canadians at the time. Why did they agree to enter a federal system in which they would be in a minority and which would give extensive powers to a federal government that would inevitably be controlled by the majority? To find the answer we must look at the arguments advanced by the most influential French-Canadian politician of the period, George Etienne Cartier.* In the first place, Cartier had a profoundly conservative temperament which was repelled by the disorder and instability of Canadian politics under the existing framework. Moreover, he had an apparently intense fear of annexation by the United States, partly because he disliked republican and democratic institutions and partly because, in common with the Roman Catholic hierarchy, he believed that the religious interests of his people would thereby suffer. Cartier was deeply involved in plans for railroad construction, which he expected to see advanced by Confederation. Like most of his colleagues he also looked forward to a political role on a larger stage. Most fundamental, perhaps, Cartier believed that the proposed scheme provided adequate protection for the interests of French Canada: although the federal government was to have large powers, these were in fields relating to finance and economics rather than to the cultural realm; it would have no authority respecting religion and education. Moreover, the scheme provided that the French civil law was to continue in the province of Quebec and that both French and English would be legal languages in that province, as well as in the federal parliament and courts. Because the French Canadians would be an overwhelming majority in the province of Quebec and would thus control its government, Cartier saw no danger to the customs and institutions essential to the maintenance of the French-Canadian identity. Indeed, it was the English-speaking minority in that province that was most deeply concerned about

*The English spelling of Cartier's first name derives from the fact that he was named after King George III.

guarantees, which were explicitly accorded to it, in the matter of schools. And so Cartier was able to win support for Confederation, although it should be noted that almost half the French-Canadian members in the legislature of the Province of Canada voted against the project.

This vote took place at Quebec in March 1865, after several weeks of exhaustive and often outstanding debate in the legislature of the Province of Canada. Thus the largest and wealthiest of the colonies had given its support to Confederation, but by this time prospects for the project had become much darker than they had been a few months earlier. The legislatures of Newfoundland and Prince Edward Island had decided to stay out, while the premier of Nova Scotia was so uncertain of support that he was delaying consideration of the measure. But the most crucial province was New Brunswick, the vital land link between Canada and the Atlantic communities, and there the government had had to call an election, which had gone heavily in favor of the anti-Confederation forces. Among several factors influencing this outcome was the attractiveness of the idea of improving rail connections with nearby Maine rather than with distant Canada. Thus, as the American Civil War came to an end in the spring of 1865, British North American Confederation was stalled, and the several provinces had to face a possible day of reckoning with an American Union which had successfully come through its ordeal by fire.

There was much to indicate that the authorities in Washington harbored feelings of irritation and even of hostility toward the northern provinces. In addition to resentment at the anti-Northern tone of much of the provincial press, there was indignation over the Confederate activities that had been carried on in the provinces during the war. By far the most notable incident had been the raid of October 1864 on St. Albans, Vermont, by Confederate soldiers, which had been initiated from Canada and which had been followed by the release of the raiders by a Montreal magistrate, for want of jurisdiction. American outrage found vent in more than mere words. The administration gave notice of intention of withdrawing from the Rush-Bagot Agreement of 1817 concerning Great Lakes naval armaments, and followed up this notice by regulations imposing the use of passports along the border. The Congress instructed the president to give the necessary one year's notice to abrogate the Reciprocity Treaty, and there was also talk of rescinding the arrangement by which Canadian goods could be carried in bond to American ocean ports. Looming over everything else was the fact that the United States came out of the war with the most powerful army in the western world.

To be sure, the sharpest phases of the tension were soon eased. All the American measures except abrogation of the Reciprocity Treaty were withdrawn, and abrogation stemmed more from the need for revenue and from mounting protectionist feeling than from a political decision to wound the provinces. The mighty army was largely demobilized within a few months. The American government and public were too deeply caught up in the impending problems of postwar reconstruction to go on nursing very active grievances against their northern neighbors. Nevertheless, the easing of the danger did not mean its disappearance. The ending of reciprocity underlined the need for intercolonial cooperation, and the British government was more strongly resolved than ever to promote Confederation as a means leading to improved defense arrangements and a consequent lessening of its own commitments.

The defense issue also came home to the provincials more vividly than even during the war with the rise of the Fenian movement in the United States in 1865 and 1866. This movement was dedicated to the freeing of Ireland from English rule, but, with a perverse but not altogether insane logic, some of its leaders determined to strike for this freedom by making raids against the British provinces to the north. At the least, they could plague the Empire that they regarded as an oppressor; at the most, they might be able to stir up a crisis leading possibly to an

Anglo-American war. Many of the Fenians were veterans of the Union army who were able to give a good military account of themselves, and American authorities, in the beginning anyway, appeared little disposed to halt their activities. In fact, the Fenian raids were poorly planned and badly led, and in time American authorities became more inclined to break up the movement. But for many months of 1866 (as for several years afterward) they were a constant threat to the peace of the border and a sharp stimulant in reviving the Confederation movement and in encouraging the growth of a sense of nationalism. In particular, they contributed to the calling of another election in New Brunswick, which put a pro-Confederation government back in power. Nova Scotia now also approved the Quebec Resolutions, and the movement was ready for its last stage, approval by the British Parliament, which came early in 1867.

On July 1, 1867, then, the Dominion of Canada came into being. As staunch monarchists, the Fathers of Confederation, particularly John A. Macdonald, now to be knighted as Sir John, wanted to call the new entity the Kingdom of Canada, but some members of the British government felt that this form might give offense to the republican sensitivities of the Americans. The new Dominion consisted of only four provinces, Nova Scotia, New Brunswick, Ontario, and Quebec, the last two made by splitting the old Province of Canada into its pre-1841 parts. Prince Edward Island stayed out until 1873, and Newfoundland remained aloof much longer, until 1949. Of vital significance for the future was the fact that in 1869 the new federal government acquired title to the vast northern and western lands of the Hudson's Bay Company, thus opening the way to the building of a transcontinental federation. Within three years the first province to be carved out of this territory came into Confederation as Manitoba, to be followed in 1871 by British Columbia after the promise of a Pacific railroad.

Thus Canada took mighty strides toward nationhood within half a dozen years of the passing of the British North America Act in 1867. Yet it is important to note that, from a legal or constitutional point of view, Canada acquired no new powers through the passing of this Act nor in fundamentals did it acquire a new system of government. Full self-government in internal affairs had been in operation in the various colonies for some twenty years before 1867; Confederation merely provided for a more effective and concentrated exercise of the system of "cabinet" or "responsible" government. As for foreign or external affairs there was as yet no desire or intention to move into this field, which was still regarded as the prerogative of the imperial government. The extension of Canadian interest and control in this area would develop gradually in the next seventy-five years. Canadians saw Confederation as strengthening, not weakening, the ties with the mother country. In the words of John A. Macdonald, "Instead of looking upon us as a merely dependent colony, England will have us as a friendly nation—a subordinate but still a powerful people—to stand by her in North America in peace or in war."

Talk of war had receded, but relations with the United States were still strained and unsettled. Indeed, in American eyes, Confederation in itself was an added irritation, because it appeared as a fortifying of the monarchical principle on a continent whose destiny should be in the republican direction. Moreover, disputes from the Civil War years were still very much alive, in particular, the question of the *Alabama* claims, arising out of the toll of Union shipping taken by this ship and other British-built Confederate cruisers. The ending of the Reciprocity Treaty added to the tension, not only by restricting trade but, more important, by reviving the old fisheries controversy, because American privileges in the Canadian coastal fisheries ended with that treaty. On the Canadian side there was indignation at the losses caused by the Fenian raids, which were still an intermittent threat. Canadians were also disturbed by a distinct revival of American expansionism after the war. In 1868, for instance, President Andrew Johnson not only defended the recent acquisition of Alaska as a measure for "extending national jurisdiction and republican principles in the American hemisphere," but he also supported "the acquisition and incorporation into our Federal Union of the several adjacent continental and insular communities as speedily as it can be done peacefully, lawfully and without any violation of natural justice, faith or honor. Foreign possession or control of those communities has hitherto hindered the growth and impaired the influence of the United States." With such talk in the air it was clear that sore spots should not be allowed to fester if diplomacy could heal them. As after the War of 1812 and after the rebellions of 1837, it was time for another broad Anglo-American settlement. With the United States anxious to settle the fisheries dispute and with Great Britain determined to withdraw its troops from Canada and be on guard to watch the tense European situation caused by the outbreak of the Franco-Prussian War, the ground was laid for the wide-ranging negotiations that resulted in the Treaty of Washington of 1871.

These negotiations were viewed with much apprehension by Canadians, who were quite convinced that the British were in a mood to make surrenders to the Americans, surrenders at Canadian expense. The treaty did prove to be intensely unpopular in Canada, although it was a crucial event in the history of the three North Atlantic countries. Not only was a wide range of subjects dealt with in the treaty, but further support was given to the practice of arbitration by agreement to submit the *Alabama* claims, a west-coast boundary dispute (over the San Juan Islands, lying between the present state of Washington and Vancouver Island), and the question of compensation for the fisheries to three impartial or mixed tribunals. The treaty was a landmark for Canada: for the first time it was represented on a diplomatic commission, in the person of its prime minister, Sir John Macdonald. In the negotiations he strove doggedly, both with the Americans and with his British colleagues, to gain Canadian objectives, but in the end he failed to secure a renewal of reciprocity and he was unable to use the fisheries question as an effective bargaining counter. Moreover, the United States had from the beginning refused to make compensation for the Fenian raids. Nevertheless, Macdonald signed the treaty and secured its acceptance by the Canadian Parliament. Even an unsatisfactory settlement was better than none at a time when, as Macdonald put it, the Canadian federation had not yet "hardened from gristle into bone."

It may be that, on the American side, it was widely believed that in the natural course of events Canada would one day join the Union; certainly many contemporaries can be quoted to this effect. Nevertheless, by accepting the treaty, the United States acknowledged that it did not intend to disturb the political division of the continent. American acceptance of this division was an indispensable precondition for Canada's peaceful and uninterrupted growth. And this acceptance was easier for the United States to accord because it coincided with the withdrawal of British forces from Canada. Although the British connection would for a long time continue to be a source of assurance and strength to Canada, it no longer operated in a way that posed any threat to the United States. The Union victory in the Civil War had thus been quickly followed by tacit recognition of the dominant role of the United States on the continent, a prerequisite for the improvement in Anglo-American relations that came at the end of the nineteenth century, and for the beginnings of a cooperative Canadian-American approach that would come in the next century. The new Canadian Confederation found itself the northern neighbor of a mighty republic that was rapidly acquiring the contours of a great world power. The fundamental requirement for Canadian-American friendship would be recognition of the inequality of power between the two federations.

After solving their crucial political problems in the 1860's, both North American federations gave themselves over to the unrelenting pursuit of national economic development in the following generation. These were years of striking and often harsh contrasts. Wealth was accumulated into aggregations of unprecedented size at the same time that a prolonged and recurring business depression held the continent in its grip. In the United States conditions of material and cultural life improved impressively, yet many of its citizens spoke scathingly of a "Gilded Age" in which progress was accompanied by shocking poverty. In Canada giant steps were taken to make a nation out of a collection of provinces, but bitter internal dissension and dismal pessimism concerning the future also marked the period. It was not until almost the opening of the new century that some of the clouds hanging over Canadian and American life began to lift.

The early years of the Canadian federation were conditioned by the circumstances of its origin. In contrast to the American union of the 1780's, which brought together several large states as well as some small ones, and which contained sections of roughly equal power and influence (New England, the Middle States, the South), the Dominion of Canada, as its name suggested, represented an attempt to extend the influence of the large central section toward the east and the west. There could be no balancing of sections on the American pattern, because the central section contained most of the wealth and population. But there could be, and there were, recurrent manifestations of discontent on the part of the outlying regions concerning the terms of their integration into the federal framework. It was not entirely unknown for this discontent to be joined with hints or even threats of the possibility of making a better bargain with the nearby states. A second, and related, theme of these years turned on whether both cultural groups of the central region, that is, the English-speaking and the French-speaking, were to be able to extend their influence to the growing west. These problems of the association between the center and the ends dominated the first generation of the Dominion's history and also did much to determine its relations with the United States during the same years.

The initial challenge to the new structure came from Nova Scotia, which voted strongly for withdrawal from Confederation in the 1867 elections for the first Parliament. The oldest of the English-speaking provinces, Nova Scotia had a proud sense of its own identity which it did not want to submerge in a union with the remote and turbulent Canadians. Living by oceanic trade, the Nova Scotians also feared the effects on their economy of being brought under the higher Canadian tariff. Many of them felt that they could make better trade agreements with the United States outside Confederation while some at least felt that given a choice between Confederation with the Canadians and annexation to the Americans they would prefer the latter. Already resentful at the pro-Confederation pressure exerted on this loyal province by British officials, Nova Scotia sent a delegation to London to demand that the decision on Confederation be reversed. It was only after this demand was met by a flat refusal that some of the "secessionists" began to make their peace with the new federal government at Ottawa. More generous financial arrangements ("better terms") helped to reconcile Nova Scotia to Confederation, while work on the Intercolonial Railway in the 1870's was welcomed by Nova Scotia and, even more, by New Brunswick. Nevertheless, Maritime, and particularly Nova Scotian, dissatisfaction with Confederation was to find frequent voice in later years.

Far more dangerous was the situation in the west. This vast region, although separated from the settled parts of Canada by more than a thousand miles of the almost impenetrable Precambrian Shield, was crucial to national growth. The federal government moved rapidly to possess this country, fearing that it might fall to the United States, with which it had close ties. Nevertheless, the first attempt to extend Canadian control to the west illustrated both the hazards and the magnitude of the task.

After lengthy and intricate negotiations the Canadian government in 1869 acquired title to Rupert's Land from the Hudson's Bay Company, and it was decided that transfer of authority would take place on December 1 of that year. Long before that date, however, feelings had been growing tense along the Red River where the *métis*, a predominantly French-speaking people of European and Indian origins, feared that their accustomed way of life and perhaps their very property would be endangered by the establishment of government under Canadian authority. The attitude of Canadians who had already come out to the Red River suggested that Ontario's English-speaking and Protestant civilization was to be extended to the west, but not Quebec's French-speaking and Catholic way of life. In an atmosphere of rumor and suspicion, the métis, under their leader Louis Riel, turned back the Canadian governor at the Minnesota border and set up a provisional government to express their point of view to the Canadian government.

The Canadian government was in no position to react strongly to this flouting of its authority. It could not exercise power in this distant country, at least not during the winter of 1869-1870, and, besides, attempts at precipitate action might throw the métis into the hands of a particularly active group of annexationists working in Minnesota. Moreover, it gradually became clear in Ottawa that métis disquietude was understandable and deserved to be allayed. By early 1870 discussions had led to a decision to grant self-government to the region by forming it into the province of Manitoba. It was only a fraction of its later size, and public lands remained under federal control. Nevertheless, guarantees for the French language and for denominational schools were written into the act, which thus held out the promise that both of Canada's cultures would grow with the country's growth. Unfortunately, the settlement did not end the bitterness, especially after it was learned in Ontario that Riel had shot a Protestant from that province. The Canadian government refused to accord an amnesty for this and other acts committed under Riel's leadership, and it also decided to make a show of strength by sending some regulars and militia to the Red River in 1870. This action was intended, in part at least, to discourage annexationist hopes in the United States, but it also appeared to be a means of overawing the métis. Only the first act of the drama on the prairies had been played; a second and bloodier act would come fifteen years later.

Manitoba's entry into Confederation was followed within a year by that of British Columbia. This Pacific Coast region had been a preserve of the fur trade until its peaceful life had been rudely shattered by the gold rush of the late 1850's and 1860's. With jealousy between Vancouver Island and the mainland and with a mixed population that included British, Canadians, and a good many Americans, the colony had no fixed character as yet. It had no tie with distant Canada: many of its residents preferred to remain a British colony; others were ready to explore the possibilities of annexation to the United States. Like the Californians of the decade before, their main desire was for the rapid building of overland communications with the east, and they were dubious that Canada could or would parallel the American achievement. In 1869 the Union Pacific–Central Pacific railroad link was completed, and the building of the Northern Pacific was underway. Nevertheless, the British Columbians decided to sound out the Canadian government by sending a delegation to Ottawa in 1870. To their surprise and delight the delegates found that the Ottawa government, after its shaky experience with Manitoba, was ready to extend extremely generous terms in order to hold the far west. In particular, the government promised to start a railroad within two years and to complete it within ten years, and on this basis British Columbia entered Confederation in 1871. It remained to be seen whether the limited resources of the Canadian government and people would be equal to the formidable task of building a railroad through three thousand miles of nearly empty country, over half of it in the Precambrian Shield and in the Rocky Mountains where passes were still to be found.

Although the easiest section of the railroad, from an engineer-. ing standpoint, would be the approximately eight hundred miles of prairie between the Red River and the Rockies, this country was a cause of worry for other reasons. According to an agreement dating back to 1818, Canada had inherited a political boundary along the forty-ninth parallel, but this boundary did not coincide with any geographic or economic division. It was not even marked until 1874, and then only by stone markers. Such a boundary was no barrier to traders from the American side, who did a profitable business in selling bad whiskey to Indians north of the line. Their activities, which reflected the geographical unity of the region, were not ended until some years after 1873, at which time the Canadian government set up the North-West Mounted Police, a small force that rapidly gained the confidence and respect of the plains Indians and succeeded in maintaining a high degree of peace and order in the Canadian west, an essential prerequisite for the building of the railroad. The railroad, in turn, destroyed the north-south economic axis of the previous generation.

The government began to make plans for the railroad soon after British Columbia entered Confederation. Adopting the pattern which had been commonly used in the United States in the previous quarter century, Macdonald and his colleagues decided to entrust the enterprise to private capitalists, who would, however, receive extensive government backing in the form of loans, guarantees, and land grants. Again as in the United States and as previously in the old Province of Canada, railroads and politics were intimately entwined as the government tried to balance Montreal and Toronto interests and to exclude American investors. Indeed, the attempt to keep out the Americans helped to produce revelations that brought down Macdonald's government in the "Pacific Scandal" of 1873, not long after it had been re-elected. For the next several years, little progress was made, mainly because the country—and the continent—was in the grip of a severe depression. Moreover, the Liberal government in office from 1873 to 1878 was determined to avoid what it considered to be the extravagance of Macdonald's plans by keeping construction rigidly within the country's means.

In 1878, however, Macdonald returned to power. Not only was he still fully committed to the building of a railroad to the Pacific, but he also saw this project as part of a broader program of national development. It was a program that would be familiar to Americans, because it had been anticipated by Henry Clay (or even by Alexander Hamilton). It involved using the power of the federal government to encourage economic expansion and to protect the economy from harmful foreign competition. Because reciprocity with the United States was still widely desired, Canadians were reluctant to give positive endorsement to the idea of tariff protectionism. But until reciprocity could be achieved, and recent experience was not encouraging, there was widespread support for Macdonald's formula of a "reciprocity of tariffs" that would encourage the growth of secondary industries. As part of his program, Macdonald also looked to the opening of the west through the stimulation of immigration from overseas.

Nonetheless, the railroad clearly had priority among Macdonald's national policies, and soon after he returned to power he succeeded in negotiating an agreement with a syndicate of capitalists, which had Canadian and British backing. The prominent American railroad builder, James J. Hill (who was a former Canadian) left the company because he opposed the idea of building the line around the north side of Lake Superior. It was the old question of whether national or economic consideration should prevail. The government also determined to build the prairie section of the line fairly close to the American border, and to prohibit the construction of any railroads between that line and the border for twenty years; Canada's railroad to the Pacific was intended to impose an east-west axis upon the emerging economic life of the Canadian west. Somewhat ironically, the main task of constructing the Canadian Pacific Railway fell to an American, William Van Horne, who became Sir William Van

Horne in his adopted country, and who pushed the line forward with all the drive and vigor for which American railroad building was already famous. In 1883 the C.P.R. was well across the prairies and preparing to attack the mountains. But by this time business depression had returned, the resources of the company were strained to the limit, and, like earlier American and Canadian lines, it had to turn to the government for more aid. The government had no choice but to respond, although for a time it appeared that both government and company might go under. Macdonald's political opponents objected with increasing vehemence to the large loans made to the C.P.R., and, at the same time, Canadian farmers in the west were beginning to denounce the railroad in terms similar to those heard in the Farmers' Alliance movements across the border.

More serious than discontent among white farmers was the mounting restlessness of the Indians along the Saskatchewan River. Their nomadic life had already been dealt a death blow by the destruction of the buffalo herds, and now they watched the advance of the settlement frontier with growing apprehension. Their fears were also shared by the métis who had retreated from the Red River to the Saskatchewan after 1870 and who felt themselves to be threatened once again. Searching for leadership they turned to Louis Riel; he had for several years been living in Montana, but still felt a mission to save his people. As in 1869-1870 a provisional government was formed. It drew up a list of grievances and then, in the spring of 1885, came out in open rebellion against Canadian authority. This time there could be no repetition of the relatively peaceful settlement of 1870, because Riel had alienated too many elements and the fear of Indian uprising was too vivid to allow for long drawn-out discussions. Troops were rushed westward across the railroad, and before the end of the summer of 1885 all resistance had been crushed. Riel himself was captured and, after being tried in Regina, was hanged in the following November, just after the last spike was driven in the C.P.R. Not only had west and east been joined, but the authority of the government had been enforced. Macdonald's nation-building program had achieved notable successes.

Nevertheless, there were contrasting tendencies during these same years, even as the successes themselves had been gained at a heavy cost. Within a few years of the completion of the C.P.R there was widespread questioning of the wisdom of Macdonald's policies.

One tendency — provincial rights — was as old as North American federalism. Macdonald thought that he had made adequate provision against this divisive phenomenon by the terms of the British North America Act of 1867, but centrifugal forces were soon evident. The relatively wealthy province of Ontario, governed at this time by Macdonald's political opponents, was in no mood to see its resources used to secure political and material advantages to politicians in other sections of the country. Moreover, secession was again a popular topic in Nova Scotia, where the legislature formally endorsed it. The trend toward provincial rights also received aid and comfort from the highest court of appeal in the British Empire, the Judicial Committee of the Privy Council, in London, which in the 1880's began to hand down decisions that strengthened the provinces and weakened the federal government. As in American history, judicial review began to reshape the nature of Canadian federalism and in this instance the British judges appeared to base their understanding of federalism on the American example, the very one that Macdonald had wanted to avoid.

Even more serious was the aftermath of the execution of Riel, which produced a veritable *Kulturkampf* between Ontario and Quebec. Though he had ceased to be a good Catholic before his death and had been opposed by the Church, Riel was seen in Quebec as a martyr who had tried to protect the interests of his people and who had been hounded to his death by Ontario Orangemen. Within a year of the execution a nationalist movement under Honoré Mercier won an election in Quebec and formed a government aimed at protecting the French-Canadian race, language, and faith. When this government proceeded to award compensation to the Jesuits for estates that had been confiscated after the order had been disbanded a century earlier, the outcry in Ontario was vociferous and prolonged. Mercier's action was seen as being another victory for militant, ultramontane Catholicism and as opening the way to its interference in Canadian affairs. The determination to have Canada governed as an English-speaking and Protestant country, in which Quebec was a single (and deplorable) exception, was redoubled and was further strengthened in 1890 when the legislature of Manitoba abolished denominational schools, which had been secured in the Manitoba Act of 1870. In turn, this action was seen as a flagrant injustice, not only by Roman Catholics in Manitoba but by French Canadians in Quebec. It was to spark a long and bitter controversy.

Not only were quarrels over religion, education, and language threatening to tear the country apart in the later 1880's, but Confederation also appeared to be an economic failure. Business depression returned with renewed sharpness, and against it Macdonald's National Policy appeared to be no protection. The steady drain of population across the border, which in most years exceeded immigration, threatened to become a mortal hemorrhage. With insistent force, voices were again raised in favor of economic continentalism. And once again Canadians hoped to use the perennial fisheries issue as a lever, this question being up for discussion with the coming lapse of the fisheries clauses of the Treaty of Washington. Another round of negotiations was held in the American capital, but protectionism in the United States was still too strong to allow a lowering of the tariff. Even the fisheries treaty negotiated by President Cleveland's administration was thrown out in 1888 by an election-bent Republican majority in the Senate.

Nevertheless, the idea of lowering trade barriers refused to die. Developments in transportation and industry were tying the two countries more closely together in an intricate network of commercial and financial relationships, with the result that on each side of the border there were men whose interests led them to see the continent as an economic unit. Some eastern business groups in the United States saw reciprocity as a means of enlarging their influence in Canada, while in Canada the idea of unrestricted reciprocity was taken up at the end of the 1880's as a main plank by the opposition party, the Liberals. Some preferred the term "Commercial Union," which would end trade restrictions along the border and lead to a common tariff against the rest of the world. For a few years the idea of economic continentalism became the most burning issue in Canadian politics.

Among its most persistent advocates was Goldwin Smith, a former professor at Oxford University, who had later taught at Cornell University and had subsequently moved to Toronto. In many articles and in *Canada and the Canadian Question* (1891), the most pessimistic book ever written about Canada, Smith argued that Confederation had failed. The country consisted of four widely separated projections of American regions, which could never be effectively brought together. Churches, labor organizations, reform movements, business corporations, and many other associations were all closely tied to their American counterparts; manners, tastes, and customs were much the same on each side of the line. A Canadian sense of nationality had not developed: Maritimers and British Columbians scarcely thought of themselves as Canadians, whereas Quebec was bent upon the construction of a French and Catholic state. In addition to the compelling economic reasons, Smith argued that union with the United States was necessary because Canada alone did not have the strength to assimilate the French element, which he saw as backward and priest-ridden.

At the other end of the political spectrum, the most fervent opponents of continentalism were the advocates of imperial federation. Sentiment for the Empire had been reviving since the 1870's, both in Great Britain and in Canada, but it was given a powerful stimulus by the movement for commercial union with the United States. Rather than sink their identity into that of the American republic, Canadians should, so the federationists argued, join more closely with their fellow subjects across the sea and share with them the tasks of spreading civilization and maintaining the peace around the world—a nobler vision than a narrowly North American one, theirs was one that would admit Canadians "to full political manhood." Just as Canada had federated its provinces, so it should take a lead in reorganizing and strengthening the Empire as a force for good in the world. Perhaps the United States might come back in some day!

For their part, Americans were little interested in commercial union. Although expansionism was beginning to enjoy a new lease on life in the United States, its direction was outward, into the Caribbean and across the Pacific, rather than northward. Those who did have their eyes on Canada believed that its adhesion to the American union was so inevitable that no action need be taken. Others, like the secretary of state, James G. Blaine, argued that a high tariff would force the Canadians to beg for annexation. But to many Americans of the time closer ties with Canada were not to be welcomed. Midwestern farmers did not want the competition of Canadian agricultural products. The harsh severity of the depression in Canada made the Dominion appear a dubious economic asset. And many Americans had no wish to become involved in Canada's language and religious controversies. In the Populist era the attention of Americans was fully concentrated on their own problems.

In Canada the debate reached its sharpest intensity in the important election of 1891, the last that Sir John Macdonald was to fight. The old leader rejected both extremes, imperial federation and continentalism alike. Although deeply committed to a close association with Great Britain, for both political and sentimental reasons, he had nevertheless always insisted upon Canada's freedom to control its own policy. Moreover, he had no sympathy for the ideal of a kind of Anglo-Saxon Protestant nationality for the Empire, which could so easily be directed against the French Canadians. But in 1891 he felt that the greater danger came from the continentalists, and his last efforts were aimed at turning back their assault upon his national policies. Seeking to touch chords that were deeper than those associated with economic programs, he proclaimed: "A British subject I was born, a British subject I will die. With my utmost effort, with my latest breath, will I oppose the 'veiled treason' which attempts with sordid means and mercenary proffers to lure our people from their allegiance." This emotional appeal, joined with the unsleeping efforts of the C.P.R. management and other interests dependent upon the tariff, proved to be sufficient, although barely so. The result was close, and at the time no one could be sure that a final decision had been made. Nevertheless, the Liberal opposition, which had all along been split over the questions of unrestricted reciprocity and commercial union, moved steadily away from the idea in either form. Many of them concluded that it was degrading to act as suppliants to an American nation that had no intention of departing from protectionism. Indeed, the Congress put the tariff up, not down, in the 1890's. Other Canadians, Liberals as well as Conservatives, felt that commercial union, by bringing Canada under the American tariff, would be a retrograde step as far as the freeing of trade was concerned, while it would almost certainly lead to political annexation. It also seemed to be clear that the Liberals would remain in the political wilderness as long as they continued to alienate the economic interests that had grown up behind the tariff. Thus, Macdonald's National Policy came through its severest time of trial, shaken but intact, and when the Liberals finally returned to power in 1896, they made no real move to disturb it.

Canadian Confederation had thus endured its most difficult generation as far as domestic development was concerned. It owed its survival to many factors, including the determination of its political leaders and the drive of business men who depended upon an east-west economy. Not least, Canadian Confederation had cause to be grateful to the stubborn American devotion to protectionism: it prevented an experiment in continental trade that might have fatally weakened Canada's economic underpinnings. And some contemporary observers professed to find deeper forces at work. A poet-historian, Charles G. D. Roberts, writing in 1897, cried out: "As the sentiment of Canadian nationalism deepens year by year, we realize that to sink our life in another's, to have our country torn apart and swallowed up as so many additional states of the American Union, would be a burning ignominy. It would make vain all the sacrifices of our fathers, all the blood they shed in their country's cause."

Shortly after these words were written, Roberts moved to New York City, where he earned his living as a writer and editor for the next decade.

From the perspective of the second half of the twentieth century, Canadians and Americans have often looked back to the years before the outbreak of the First World War as a time of high hope, tinged with an innocence which can never be recaptured now. After a long generation of cruel depression, often marked by bitter internal strife, the clouds lifted to reveal both a new prosperity and a new political and social era. Progress was the universal watchword and optimism was the prevailing mood. Not only was there a high sense of accomplishment at home, but each country showed a readiness to play a larger role upon the world stage, the United States as a great power, Canada as an autonomous associate of Great Britain. And in their relations with each other, although there were sharp controversies, there were also signs of a cooperative approach toward common problems. The people of North America had never been more convinced that life upon their continent was good and would be better.

Underlying the mood of optimism was the dramatic change in the economic scene. After the severe depression of the middle 1890's, there was a sudden upturn which lasted until the eve of the outbreak of the war in 1914, with only a brief check in 1907. The long years of deflation, which had kept farm prices low, ended when the world's supply of gold was increased by discoveries in South Africa and elsewhere. In Canada the boom was stimulated by the Klondike gold rush in the Yukon after 1898 and by other, more enduring, mining strikes in various parts of the Precambrian Shield and in southern British Columbia. As in earlier American development, mining expansion was both a result of railroad building and a stimulus to it. Before long the opinion was widespread that Canada could not be satisfied with one transcontinental line. Various entrepreneurs were already busy with schemes, and, as always in North America, government was soon intimately involved. Influenced by many considerations, including the search for political advantage, the federal government approved and in large part carried out a program of construction that gave the country two additional transcontinentals before 1914 and twice as great a railroad mileage per capita as in the United States. Later years would show that this was carrying optimism too far.

In turn, the railroad companies, eager for traffic and for land sales, were intimately connected with the sharp increase of immigration that came in these years. After a generation during which Canada not only had not been able to compete with the United States for immigrants but had steadily lost people to its southern neighbor, the Dominion finally became the goal of hundreds of thousands of settlers from Europe and even from the United States. To be sure, the United States was still the great magnet; the fifteen or sixteen years before 1914 saw an average of about a million immigrants a year come across the Atlantic to the republic. Nevertheless, for the first time in half a century Canada began to attract, and hold, a substantial part of the torrent of humanity leaving Europe, one of the greatest movements of peoples of modern history. The novel aspect of the immigration was the large component from eastern Europe, which introduced a new element into Canada's population, in the western countryside as well as in the growing cities. The influx from the British Isles was, however, still larger. And with the American west now beginning to fill up there was a sharpening of interest in the "last best West" beyond the forty-ninth parallel. Many tens of thousands of experienced American farmers followed the great plains across that parallel to seek land for themselves and their sons. At last the Canadian West came into its own as one of the world's great wheat-producing regions. Its political development also kept pace, with the admission of Saskatchewan and Alberta as provinces in 1905 and the subsequent enlargement of the boundaries of Manitoba.

The filling up of the West has usually been considered the most striking economic event of these years, but its importance was at least matched by industrial growth in the east, which caused urban population to rise even more rapidly than rural. After two discouraging decades, during which many had concluded that the National Policy was a dismal failure, the policy of moderate protectionism finally appeared to be succeeding. Manufacturing and other secondary plants began to spring up or to become larger, and resources development, particularly in the mining and forest industries, became more complex and advanced. In retrospect, the most important aspect of these years was the growing interest of American capital and American management in the Canadian economy. American skill and experience, and American financial backing, played a large part in the progress made in realizing the goals of Canada's National Policy. Links between the two economies were also reflected in the affiliation of Canadian labor unions with the larger American organizations. Economic development was bringing a new degree of interdependence and even of interlocking. Despite a preferential tariff accorded to Great Britain in 1898, Canada's imports from the United States increased much more rapidly in the following years than they did from the mother country.

Economic development also brought a common preoccupation with the rise of modern industrialism, but in this respect the two countries appeared to be at somewhat different stages in their reaction to capitalism. American optimism was being increasingly qualified and conditioned by the sharp protests of the "muckraking" journalists, while Canadian comment generally reflected a cheerfully uncritical satisfaction in material progress and a respectful attitude toward the new class of tycoons. At about the same time that President Theodore Roosevelt was beginning to alert his people to the dangerous activities of the "malefactors of great wealth," the Canadian prime minister, in words both vacuous and vaunting, proclaimed: "As the nineteenth century was that of the United States, so I think that the twentieth century shall be filled by Canada."

This optimistic prime minister, Sir Wilfrid Laurier, was much less concerned with the social consequences of developing capitalism than he was with the old problem of relations between English-speaking and French-speaking Canadians. The bitter debates of the decade following the execution of Louis Riel in 1885 had revealed how much antagonism lay just below the surface of Canadian cultural and political life. To Laurier, who came to power in 1896 when the long reign of Macdonald's Conservative party finally ended, a new approach seemed to be vitally necessary, and he had reason to hope that he could help to strengthen national unity. The first French Canadian to head a federal government since Confederation in 1867, he was also thoroughly at home in the English-speaking world of politics and political thought. His appeal was to the moderates of each side, and his hope was that fair-minded compromise would always be possible between the two groups. It was to be his tragic fate to see his career close during a period of intense estrangement, even open hatred, between the two groups.

During his fifteen years as prime minister, the longest consecutive tenure in Canadian history, Laurier tried unceasingly to find common ground on which the moderates of both sides could stand. He was able to make a hopeful beginning when he succeeded in working out a compromise with the government of Manitoba by which French and Catholic schools received a limited recognition. He also succeeded in muting the campaign against "liberalism" which the Roman Catholic hierarchy of Quebec had long been waging. But the impact of outside events was to provide a severer test, and it came first with the Boer War in 1899, when the question arose whether Canada should furnish troops to fight alongside the British in South Africa. Hitherto, military aid had gone all in the one direction, from the mother country to the colony, but now it had to be decided whether the mother country should be offered help.

The resulting debate showed that English-speaking and French-speaking Canadians, for the most part, saw the question from diametrically opposed points of view. It was strongly felt among the English-speaking group that, after having relied for so long upon the British for protection, Canadians should now send troops to fight in South Africa, not because the mother country was in danger, but to demonstrate the solidarity of the Empire. This view did not arise from any sense of colonial subserviency but from an urge for national self-expression and from a belief that the Empire was a force for good in the world. It would be such a force only if it were strong and united. But French Canadians, lacking any deep sentimental attachment to the Empire, particularly in an era when rhetoric about "Anglo-Saxon" fellowship was in the air, could not see that Canada's national interest demanded participation in a distant imperial war. Quite the contrary; participation in this relatively small conflict would furnish a dangerous precedent for the future when larger and more dangerous wars might occur. Canada was a North American country; it should not allow itself to be drawn into the maelstrom of imperial wars by meddling in distant quarrels which it did not understand and on which it could exert no effective political influence. Thus, to the sources of internal friction that had long divided the two groups there was now added a sharp difference over external policy.

In his search for common ground Laurier supported a limited Canadian participation that in effect would allow those who wished to volunteer to do so. But the more ardent English-speaking Canadians saw this policy as letting down the Empire, while Laurier's critics among the French Canadians saw even a token participation as establishing a perilous precedent. The most brilliant of his younger followers, Henri Bourassa, a grandson of Louis Joseph Papineau, broke with the prime minister on the question and sought to rally Quebec, and indeed Canadian, feeling for a more nationalist course; on the other hand, the Liberal government suffered noticeable losses in English-speaking Ontario at the next election. Nevertheless, the majority of Canadians of both groups continued to support Laurier, and the crisis eased with the end of the Boer War. Moderate opinion was also in agreement with Laurier's refusal in the following years to endorse proposals for tightening up the Empire, either politically or militarily. But no one could be certain when a new crisis would appear or what strains on national unity it would produce.

It was at this point that the rather fragile fabric of Canadian national unity was strengthened by an outburst of irritation directed against both of the Dominion's closest associates. The occasion was the Alaska Boundary Award of 1903, which led Canadians to vent strong feelings against the United States and Great Britain. The fact that Canada's case was not of the strongest did nothing to diminish the belief that her interests had been trampled on by these great powers.

The dispute concerned the long strip of Alaska which separates northern British Columbia from the Pacific Ocean. The boundary had originally been set out in a treaty of 1825 between Great Britain and Russia, but later exploration and trading activity in the region revealed many ambiguities in the language defining the line of demarcation. With American acquisition of Alaska from Russia in 1867 and British Columbia's entry into Canadian Confederation four years later, the question became one for Canadian-American relations, although it received relatively little attention until the discovery of gold in the Yukon in 1896. The subsequent rush of miners and the need to maintain law and order in the area convinced the Canadian government that it needed to have an all-Canadian route into the southern Yukon, and unless a long and expensive railroad was built through northern British Columbia that route would have to be by sea, through the Lynn Canal, a long inlet of the heavily indented coastline. It was admitted that the United States had been in undisputed possession of this region for some time, but it was also argued that Canada had a good claim to the head of the inlet according to one line of geographical reasoning . In consequence, Sir Wilfrid Laurier, when he was one of the members on the British side of a Joint High Commission which met in Washington in 1898 to deal with a number of outstanding issues affecting the United States, Great Britain, and Canada, sought without success to settle the question. As on a number of other occasions, Great Britain and Canada wanted to deal with all questions on a give-and-take basis, looking toward a general settlement, whereas the United States insisted on considering each question separately. One can detect at this stage a certain irritation, felt by both the British and the Americans, at the injection of Canadian issues into Anglo-American discussions. Lord Salisbury is said to have compared the Dominion to a coquettish girl with two suitors, playing one off against the other; John Hay called her a married flirt, ready to betray John Bull on any occasion, but holding him responsible for all her follies. Great powers can seldom see why small powers should not be accommodating in international negotiations.

It will be remembered that these years saw "the rise of Anglo-American friendship." Great Britain, in particular, was anxious for improved relations in view of the increasingly dangerous situation in Europe and was ready to go to considerable lengths to remove sources of friction with the United States. One of these was the question of whether the United States should have a free hand to build an Isthmian canal, which would mean ending the stipulation, contained in the Clayton-Bulwer Treaty (1850), that Great Britain was to have an equal interest in such a canal. Because she also wished for Canadian good will at the time of the Boer War, Great Britain sought for some time to trade concessions respecting the canal for a settlement of the Alaska boundary dispute, but again the United States insisted upon separate settlements. With the Hay-Pauncefote Treaty of 1901, by which Great Britain relinquished all claims respecting an Isthmian canal, the Alaska question was finally isolated for distinct settlement, unconnected with any other issue. In the eyes of the new American president, Theodore Roosevelt, who took office in 1901 following the assassination of William McKinley, the American case was unassailable, and the only reason for going through the formalities of negotiation would be to give the Canadians and the British a face-saving avenue of retreat from an untenable position. Accordingly, when it was agreed to put the dispute to a six-member judicial tribunal of "impartial jurists of repute," Roosevelt had no compunction in appointing, as the American members, three political figures who were known in advance to be opposed to the Canadian claim. Doubtless appointments of any other kind would never have been approved by the United States Senate.

It was at this point that Canadian indignation began to rise, because these appointments were seen as signs of a cynical disregard for the terms of the tribunal. Moreover, Canadians could derive little comfort from a scrutiny of the British panel, which consisted of two Canadians, one French-speaking and one English-speaking, of judicial and legal background, and of Lord Alverstone, Lord Chief Justice of England. The tradition had long since been implanted in Canadian minds that, in a serious dispute with the United States, the British placed good Anglo-American relations above Canadian interests. The sorry record of such yielding went all the way back to the Treaty of 1783, according to the interpretation of many Canadians. In the words of a loyalist-descended politician, speaking in 1888, English statesmen had committed "atrocious blunders [in] every treaty, or transaction, or negotiation that they have ever had with the United States where the interests of Canada were concerned, from the days of Benjamin Franklin to this hour." Hence, there was little surprise, but much outrage, when Lord Alverstone joined with the American members to outvote the Canadians, who refused to sign the award of the tribunal and who published a long attack on the majority decision. A fairly typical remark was that of one British Columbia newspaper editor: "perhaps we should be thankful that there is left no territory which grasping Americans can reach for and complaisant British commissioners can give away." Canadian opinion was in no mood to ask whether the Canadian members had been any more judicial in their approach than those on the majority side. Nor were Canadians willing to see that the course of events leading to the establishment of the tribunal had placed Lord Alverstone in an impossible position: not only did the United States have a very strong case, but any other decision on his part would have led to deadlock and to a probable implementation of President Roosevelt's threat to use troops to enforce the American claim. Canada's interest in the inlets of the north Pacific Coast was not important enough to justify the risk of a first-class crisis.

In their first reaction to the award, which was a sore affront to their pride, Canadians unloosed most of their indignation against Lord Alverstone. The incident led many of them, including Laurier himself, to assert that Canadian interests would never be adequately defended until the Dominion had a fuller, if not an exclusive, part in the conduct of its external affairs. But this response soon gave way to the view that the outcome would have been even less favorable without British assistance, and hence there was as yet little support for the idea of full diplomatic independence. The debate reflected an emerging national sentiment, but in the shadow of T.R.'s "Big Stick" this feeling was directed more against the United States than against Great Britain. A growing Canadian nationalism was quite consistent with a continued sense of attachment to the Empire, although this was undoubtedly truer of English Canada than of French. In short, Canada would continue to resist all proposals for imperial consolidation, but she was still prepared to leave large questions of foreign policy to the British Foreign Office.

Nevertheless, in the years after 1903 it became increasingly clear that Canada needed some machinery for collecting and coordinating information on external affairs; there was literally no officer of its government solely charged with this task, and there was no central repository of official records. Indeed, since the late 1890's the under secretary of state,* Joseph Pope, had been bringing this need to the attention of interested persons, and by the middle of the following decade he had some backing, in the cabinet as well as from the governor general. He also had

---

*The secretary of state, unlike the American official of this title, was not, and is not today, a minister of foreign affairs.

the support of the British ambassador in Washington, at this time James Bryce, who regularly had to deal with Canadian-American affairs but who often had great difficulty in securing effective advice on the Canadian point of view. Laurier was at first not much interested in the idea of setting up an office for this purpose but eventually he accepted the proposal, and in 1909 the Canadian Department of External Affairs came into existence. Power of decision was in the prime minister's hands, and in fact in 1912 the constituting act was amended to provide that the prime minister should hold the portfolio. For many years the department was an extremely modest affair and did not aspire to a place in making policy, but a start had been made in giving Canada regular machinery for dealing with matters beyond its borders.

While discussions leading to the establishment of this department were taking place, there was a growing realization that one aspect of Canadian-American affairs, namely, boundary waters, needed special attention. During the previous century most of the controversies had had to do with deciding which waterways actually constituted boundaries and to a lesser extent with rights of navigation. The record of the peaceful settlement of such disputes was reasonably good, although it was also true that settlements had usually been made only after long delays and had often been accompanied by the application of political pressure. By the beginning of the twentieth century the waterways problem was no longer one of locating boundaries (the Alaska dispute was the last of any consequence), but one of regulating the use, above all for hydroelectric development, of rivers and lakes that crossed or straddled the international border. The study and adjustment of this range of questions was the province of technically trained experts rather than of politicians. And these questions could not normally wait upon the leisurely processes of *ad hoc* diplomacy.

In this matter the United States took the initiative. In the Rivers and Harbors Act of 1902 the president was requested to approach the British government with a proposal for the setting up of a joint board, leading to the formation in 1905 of the International Waterways Commission, which was charged with purely investigative functions. In turn, this body recommended that a permanent board with larger powers should be created, and this result was accomplished in the Boundary Waters Treaty of 1909, which established the International Joint Commission, consisting of three American and three Canadian members. This commission, which was provided with a suitable technical staff, was empowered not only to investigate and report upon matters referred to it by either government, but it was also given the power to issue binding decisions upon questions relating to diversion, obstruction, or new uses affecting the natural level or flow of boundary waters. In addition the commission was to have the broader function of acting as an arbitral tribunal for the decision of any problem, not necessarily concerning boundary waters, that might be referred to it with the consent of both parties. The I.J.C. has proved to be a strong and flexible instrument for the adjustment of Canadian-American affairs; since 1909 it has effectively disposed of scores of highly complex questions. It might be noted, however, that the I.J.C. has not been able to deal with one perennial controversy—the extent to which the city of Chicago may divert water from Lake Michigan to its drainage canal—because this question had arisen prior to 1909 and thus was not a "new use" by the terms of the treaty.

In retrospect, these two departures of the year 1909—the establishment of the Department of External Affairs and of the International Joint Commission—were events of outstanding importance for Canada's emerging role in the world and in North America. At the time, however, they were far overshadowed in the public mind by the continuing debate over two questions of high emotional content: Canada's role in the Empire and trade policy toward the United States.

The imperial issue had never entirely died down after the Boer War. Both in Great Britain and in Canada insistent voices were raised in favor of strengthening the political and military ties of Empire, but Laurier's response continued to be negative. He took the view that Canada would come to the assistance of the United Kingdom if the latter were threatened, but he refused to commit himself in advance regarding the nature and extent of such assistance. As for measures to build up Canada's home forces, Laurier felt that there was no longer any point in preparing for defense against an American invasion, and the Monroe Doctrine protected Canada from attack from any other quarter. Nevertheless, the pressure for closer cooperation with the United Kingdom continued to mount, particularly after fears were raised by Germany's program of naval expansion. By 1910 Laurier had to bow to pressure from English-speaking Canadians for a naval contribution to the defense of the Empire, but he was resolved that such a contribution must remain under Canadian control. Accordingly the government brought in a bill looking to the building of a small Canadian navy of about a dozen ships, to be under Canadian command but with the proviso that the force might be placed under the British Admiralty in time of emergency. The measure was of course a compromise, and it invited sharp attack from both the Conservative opposition and the French-Canadian nationalists. The former argued that the "tin pot navy" would be useless against the German menace and in any event would take too long to build; Canada's most effective contribution would be a cash contribution for strengthening the Royal Navy. On the other hand, Bourassa and his associates denounced the measure as one that would inevitably draw Canada into what Laurier had himself once called "the vortex of European militarism." The next step, it was ominously asserted, would be the conscription of French-Canadian youth to fight in far-off imperialist wars. Thus the naval question unloosed a passionate and divisive war of words across the country.

Suddenly, and quite unexpectedly, a new issue — reciprocal trade with the United States — was injected into the national debate, and at first Laurier was convinced that he had a trump card of decisive strength. Although Canadian politicians had given up the active search for free trade with the United States because the idea had apparently been rebuffed by the voters in 1891, and although the question had somewhat fallen out of sight during the years of prosperity and growth, political observers assumed that the majority of Canadians would welcome the lowering of trade barriers. Laurier had reason to know that at least some Canadians felt very strongly on the question, because on a western trip in 1910 he found that farmers' organizations were waging a clamorous campaign against the protective tariff. Thus, later in that year and with understandable satisfaction the Laurier government learned of the Taft administration's desire to conclude a reciprocal-trade agreement that had been under discussion for some months. Such a measure should both satisfy the farmers and take minds off the explosive naval question. Moreover, it had come at American initiative, without any further humiliating "pilgrimages to Washington." In fact, the proposal had originated in Taft's own domestic political difficulties following the outcry against the Payne-Aldrich Tariff of 1909. With both governments expecting political gain from reciprocity, they did not take long to reach an agreement, early in 1911, for free trade in natural and some manufactured products. Because there was no possibility of getting the necessary two thirds vote in the United States Senate, required for a treaty, the agreement was to be implemented by concurrent legislation. By cooperating with Democrats (and at the cost of alienating insurgents in his own party) Taft secured approval of the agreement by Congress in the summer of 1911.

The fate of the measure thus depended upon the action of the Canadian Parliament, and Laurier was supremely confident that it would be widely popular. Even the Conservative opposition, led by Robert Borden, was initially hesitant to criticize it. There was predictable opposition from spokesmen representing interests dependent upon the protective tariff, but such interests could be expected to support the Conservatives in any event and

Laurier had beaten them in four consecutive elections. To Laurier's surprise and dismay, however, the opposition continued to rise and to spread rather than to abate. Prominent members of his own party came out against the agreement, whereas Borden and his party decided to oppose it. Laurier was still convinced, however, that the voters would support him, and he appealed to them in an election called for September 21, 1911.

The ensuing campaign was one of the two or three most memorable in Canadian history. Despite its large majority and despite its early confidence that reciprocity would prove to be an effective issue, Laurier's Liberal government was on the defensive from the beginning. Its attempt to emphasize the economic advantages that would come with freer trade was increasingly drowned out by the opposition's charge that reciprocity would be a first, and a giant, step toward annexation. Soon the atmosphere of the campaign became highly emotional, with the Conservatives and the Liberal defectors appealing more to loyalty and sentiment than to economic considerations. The feeling grew that Canada was at the "parting of the ways" (a phrase used by President Taft himself). The newspapers of the United States were combed for comments that were annexationist in tone, or that could be construed as such, and these were prominently reprinted in Canadian newspapers. Remarks such as those of Champ Clark, Democratic leader of the House of Representatives, to the effect that he was for the agreement "because I hope to see the day when the American flag will float over every square foot of the British North American possessions, clear to the North Pole" were endlessly repeated. All the latent suspicion of the United States, engendered by events as recent as the Alaska boundary dispute or as distant as the War of 1812 or the American Revolution, came to the surface in the slogan "No truck nor trade with the Yankees." By the eve of the election day a great many voters appeared genuinely to believe the words of Rudyard Kipling's intervention in the campaign: "It is her own soul that Canada risks today. Once that soul is pawned for any consideration Canada must inevitably conform to the commercial, legal, financial, social and ethical standards which will be imposed upon her by the sheer admitted weight of the United States." The election proved to be a sharp defeat for Laurier and the Liberals. Reciprocity had been killed in a vote which luridly exhibited the regionalism of Canadian politics.

But reciprocity was not the only issue in the election: in Quebec it received relatively little attention compared with the emphasis given to the navy question. Confronted by the combined opposition of the Bourassa nationalists and of the Conservatives Laurier had to face the charge that his naval policy would lead to the conscripting of French-Canadian youth to serve in imperialist wars, just as, in English-speaking Canada, he was accused of planning to throw Canada into the arms of the United States. The combination, in Quebec, of nationalists and Conservatives, termed an "unholy alliance" by the Liberals, made considerable gains and contributed, although not decisively, to Laurier's defeat. Fifteen years of Liberal government came to an end as the new prime minister, Robert Borden, declared, "Canada has emphasized her adherence to the policy and traditions of the past. She has wisely determined that for her there shall be no parting of the ways but that she will continue in the old path of Canadianism — true Canadian nationhood and British connection. She has emphasized the strength of the ties that bind her to the Empire. The verdict has been given in no spirit of unfriendliness or hostility to the United States and no such spirit exists, but Canada desires and elects to be mistress of her destinies and to work out those destinies as an autonomous nation within the British Empire." Yet an objective analysis must note that a good many factors served to defeat Laurier, including reaction against a government long in power, anti-Catholic feeling in Ontario, and a vigorous well-financed campaign by the protectionist interests.

The new prime minister was faced at once with the defense

issue that had bedeviled Laurier. As he would amply demonstrate during the next decade, Borden was as firm a Canadian nationalist as his French-Canadian predecessor, but he was much more exposed to political pressure in favor of emergency assistance to Great Britain. Accordingly, he introduced a measure to provide for a cash contribution sufficient to pay for three battleships. The Liberals opposed the bill ferociously, and they were joined by some of the Quebec elements that had supported Borden in 1911; it was only after the application of closure* that the bill was passed. It was then defeated in the Liberal Senate, in the most important contest between the two houses in Canadian history. The upshot was that neither Laurier's nor Borden's naval program had been implemented by the time of the outbreak of war in 1914, and Canada was almost wholly without effective naval strength. Moreover, the bitterness of the naval debate was accompanied by despondency over the return of bad times with the business downturn of 1913. There was a certain pause in the exuberance of the previous decade and a half before Canada plunged into the European holocaust.

---

*This term is used in Canada, rather than "cloture," preferred in the United States.

13   War and a New Status, 1914-1931

With the outbreak of the First World War in August 1914 Canada and the United States felt the impact of events in the outside world more directly and more profoundly than they had since the Napoleonic Wars a century earlier. Each country was drawn into the fighting, each put forward a mighty effort that not only affected the course of the conflict in Europe but had vast economic and social consequences at home, and each came out of the terrible but exhilarating trial with an intense feeling of revulsion. In the ensuing decade each country was resolutely, though perhaps naively, determined to cultivate its own garden and to resist any further involvement in Europe's quarrels. This determination became even stronger when the relative prosperity of the 1920's gave way to the almost bottomless depression of the 1930's. Finally, each country found that economic change was tying its business system more closely to that of the other.

Nevertheless, despite these general similarities in the experiences of the two countries, as seen in the perspective of a latter generation, contemporaries would have been more inclined to stress contrasts, particularly at the beginning of the period. Seeking to remain faithful to their long tradition of nonentanglement in European wars and caught up in the climax of the Progressive movement, as embodied in Woodrow Wilson's New Freedom, Americans fervently endorsed the president's proclamation of neutrality and his call for impartiality in thought and action. Over two and a half years would pass before Wilson would reluctantly conclude that he had no choice but to ask the Congress for a declaration of war against Germany. Mobilization and the transport and training of troops would take up most of another year, with the result that the United States was fully engaged on the western front only during approximately the last six months of the war. Yet that engagement was on such a scale and American industrial might so vast that the republic exerted a decisive influence on the duration and outcome of the struggle. On the other hand, Canadians had agreed, before 1914, that when Great Britain was at war, Canada would be at war, although

Canada would determine the nature and extent of its own contribution. Accordingly, Canada was legally in the conflict from August 4, 1914. Furthermore, it soon became clear that the government and people intended to put forth an unparalleled effort. From the early months of 1915 Canadian troops were in the thick of the fighting, where they remained for nearly four years. Casualties were so sickeningly high that they approximately equalled those of the United States, despite a population only one tenth as large as that of the latter. Unquestionably the military effort was the mightiest in Canadian history, outranking relatively that of the Second World War and bringing the Dominion of age as a nation more rapidly than any other conceivable event could have done. Yet, while most Canadians never doubted the rightness of their decision to throw everything into the balance, and while they were justly proud of the role played by their men, it was a harrowing and sometimes a frustrating trial. Not only was the country brought to the edge of national disunity; but as a small power allied with giants, the people were often doubtful whether their contribution was understood or appreciated. At the end, it was a hard lesson in world politics to see their relatively unscathed neighbors acclaimed, and sometimes acclaiming themselves, as the bringers of triumph. The depth and persistence of Canadian exasperation over the phrase "We Won the War," supposedly uttered boastfully by Americans, help to measure how searing and perplexing an ordeal it had been.

At first, it may seem to be surprising that two North American countries, living side by side and sharing many attitudes, should differ so sharply in their initial reaction to the war, the one thankful for three thousand miles of ocean between her and the conflict, the other eager to use the ocean as a highway to reach the fighting. It must be remembered, however, that in 1914, most Canadians did not think of their country as a separate and independent nation, but as a self-governing colony within the British Empire. They rejoiced in the name of Canadians and adamantly opposed any tendencies toward "Downing Street rule"; but, solely as Canadians, they were a small and insignificant people. As British subjects, however, they were full and equal members in what they firmly believed to be the grandest political community the world had ever known — one that was a force for good around the globe. Membership in this community, for all the occasional irritations, had made it possible for Canadians to build the Dominion of which they were so proud; a deep sense of loyalty, felt equally by the far-off Australians and New Zealanders, made response almost instinctive when the center of this civilization was in danger. Response would never again be quite so spontaneous, but neither would Canadians ever again be quite so sure of their place in the world's scheme as they were in 1914. The current search for a "Canadian identity" would have made little sense to men of 1914.

Then, the response was general, felt in some sense in most of the country, but not everywhere of equal depth. If recruiting figures are an indication, it was felt most strongly by the British-born who, because of the large immigration of the previous two decades, included a very considerable number of men of military age. Such men made up a majority of the first contingent that sailed before the end of 1914. The response was also strong among those not more than one or two generations away from the mother country, among those of loyalist stock, and among the city-dwellers more than among the farmers. Immigrants of non-British stock had less direct sense of involvement. The oldest Canadian .group, the French Canadians, lacking the sense of sentimental attachment and thinking of themselves as Canadians rather than as British subjects, did not identify themselves immediately or personally with events in Europe. Their most prominent leaders, lay and clerical, defended the justice of the allied cause and the need to stand by Britain and France, but there was no outpouring of enthusiasm on the part of the rank and file of French Canadians. There was no one in the Borden government who could speak to them with an influential voice, and the growing army, in which English was the sole language of command, appeared as a strange, even foreign, entity. In these circumstances, nationalists of the Bourassa school struck a sympathetic chord when they argued that Canadians should defend Canada, not the distant Empire, and when they asserted that until French-Canadian rights were assured at home it was hypocrisy to talk of fighting for freedom abroad. This last was a reference to a recent regulation of the Ontario government severely restricting the use of French as a language of instruction in the schools of that province. Thus, from the first weeks of the war, Canadian participation threatened to reopen old wounds and to make new ones.

Still, for many months these were only threats. No one had any inkling of the demands that would be made upon Canadian manpower, even as all were agreed that service would be on a voluntary basis. To a considerable extent, in this early stage, the country saw the conflict in economic rather than in military terms, because it was widely hoped that British and French war orders would revive an economy that had begun to flag just before 1914. At first, there was some complaint when the great belligerents appeared to be favoring American at the expense of Canadian sources of supply, and some time was necessary to gear and orient industry and agriculture toward the needs of the war machine. But after a year or so, business was booming, Canada had become a major supplier of munitions, and wheat prices were at unheard of levels.

Meanwhile, the ever-increasing flow of troops to the front was forcing the Canadian government to concern itself with problems of organization and control that were completely novel. At first, Ottawa had been satisfied to see its men as part of the British Army, partly because there were no Canadian officers experienced in high command and partly out of a sense of imperial solidarity. But Sir Robert Borden became rapidly disillusioned with this arrangement. Friction between Canadian soldiers and British officers, a growing conviction that many of these officers were unbelievably incompetent, and Borden's inability to get adequate information from either the British government or the War Office led to a sharp confrontation between Ottawa and London. Because Borden's view of the generals was shared by Lloyd George, there was a distinct improvement of relations after the latter became prime minister in December 1916. Communications became more direct, bypassing both the governor general and the Colonial Office. A Canadian general, Sir Arthur Currie, was placed in command of the Canadian Corps. An Imperial War Cabinet was set up, in which the prime ministers of the Dominions could participate in discussions at the highest level. Without conscious plan or intention, Canada was being forced by its vast war effort to act not as a loyal colony but as a loyal ally.

By the early months of 1917 the responsibilities of an ally were becoming increasingly burdensome. An overseas trip at this time convinced Borden that the flow of reinforcements must be maintained or increased if Canada was to meet her commitments in the face of frightfully high casualties on the western front. Yet it was a brute fact that the rate of recruiting was steadily declining as an expanded industry and agriculture competed for manpower and as the supply of men most strongly motivated to enlist was exhausted. Reluctantly but inexorably the government was driven to consider the imposition of conscription as a solution of the reinforcement crisis, and it was also influenced by other than purely military factors. The entry of the United States into the war with conscription from the outset was a powerful stimulus and example. The Borden government was also in danger of losing significant support if it did not do everything possible to support "the men at the front," and allied to this pressure was the growing feeling in English-speaking Canada that Quebec was not doing its part. It would perhaps be too strong to say that conscription was seen as much as a means of coercing French Canada as it was a means of finding reinforcements, but the former sentiment certainly existed. It was also clear that the government could count on the support of an influential group of

English-speaking Liberals, who had broken with Laurier. Accordingly, Borden formed a coalition government in October 1917 and called an election for the following December. The campaign was bitterly fought, and it appeared to set the one language group against the other, although in fact many English-speaking Canadians opposed conscription while many French Canadians continued to support the war effort, provided the voluntary system was retained. The government was returned, and conscription was enforced. The number of men drafted was relatively small, but the threat of compulsion caused enlistments to pick up considerably. Canada ended the war with the federal government completely in the hands of the English-speaking element and with Quebec feeling helpless and embittered. For the next generation the majority of its voters would regard Conservatives much as Southerners did Republicans after Reconstruction.

The long and savage ordeal of war left an indelible imprint upon the Dominion and its people. Its economy was enlarged and diversified, and its government was forced to play a more complex and positive role, as when it took over several railroad lines out of which were formed the Canadian National Railways. Rapid social change was reflected, as in the United States, by the grant of the vote to women. Above all, there was a new confidence, a new pride in Canada, born of the deeds of the hundreds of thousands of soldiers who fought on the western front. But this burning trial was not one which the two language groups had undergone together: although large numbers of French Canadians had served, the two groups had not shared the experience in such a way as to build a national feeling common to all Canadians. The two groups had been driven apart rather than drawn together. English-speaking Canadians believed that French Canadians had failed to answer the call of duty when civilization had stood at bay; they did not see, and did not want to see, that a hundred and one factors, some reaching deep into history and some arising from immediate circumstances, had made the

French Canadians see the war in a distinctive light. French Canadians believed that the majority group had shown themselves to have a colonial mentality, giving their first loyalty to England rather than to Canada; they could not grasp why English-speaking Canadians had devoted themselves so fully to the struggle nor understand how strongly it had strengthened their sense of nationalism. Each side, looking back on the war, was to have an almost totally separate set of memories: of soul-stirring achievement, of bruising humiliation.

After the end of the war, Canada and the other Dominions insisted upon, and received, some recognition of their new status in international politics. This status was, and for some years would remain, somewhat anomalous, because they did not claim to be fully independent in the legal sense, although they clearly were not dependent communities. When other countries, for instance, the United States, found it hard to understand why, at the Paris Peace Conference, Canada should be part of the British Empire delegation and at the same time, like the other Dominions, have separate representation, the answer sometimes came that the evolution of the Empire (or Commonwealth as some were beginning to call it) transcended logic. Another recognition of the newly acquired nationhood came when Canada, again like the other Dominions, was accorded membership in the League of Nations. At this point a superficial observer might have concluded that Canada was preparing itself to play an active and positive role in world affairs in contrast to its North American neighbor, which refused to join the League. In fact, however, although Canada was eager to be recognized as a distinct international entity, it shared to the full the American determination not to become entangled in the problems and quarrels of distant countries, and Canadians showed little interest in foreign affairs at this time. It has often been pointed out that Canada was as isolationist inside the League as the United States was outside, probably more so, because as a great power the latter assumed certain responsibilities (for example, concerning German recovery) not required of a small power. For its part Canada began an attack on Article X of the Covenant when the draft was being prepared at the Peace Conference and for many years to come kept up the attempts to water down the collective-security provisions of the League. Canada had no more intention of being committed by the League than it had earlier had of being committed by the British Government. In a highly complacent speech of 1924, the Canadian delegate to the League asserted that Canada lived "in a fireproof house far from inflammable materials," and hence should not be expected to pay a very high insurance premium. In fact, those present at League sessions frequently had to endure "the Canadian speech," which consisted of a self-satisfied celebration of the friendly Canadian-American border and an exhortation to the less virtuous to imitate the North American example. Whether countries that were threatened by aggressive neighbors derived comfort from these lay sermons is doubtful.

Thus, one consequence of Canada's rise in status was a stronger emphasis upon its role as a North American nation and as a neighbor of the United States. There had been evidence of this tendency during the war when the need for coordination in economic programs had led to close liaison between the various boards and control bodies of the two governments. Noting that more than three quarters of the work of the British Embassy in Washington related to Canada, at a time when the latter was not effectively represented on its staff, Sir Robert Borden had apparently favored the establishment of separate Canadian diplomatic representation in the American capital, although the only action taken was the appointment of a Canadian War Mission. In 1920 Canada and Great Britain agreed that a Canadian representative should be appointed to Washington, but for various reasons no action was taken until 1926, when the United States and Canada announced that they would exchange legations. Thus Canada had its first diplomatic representation in a foreign country, followed soon by the establishment of legations in Paris and Tokyo.

Beyond its bilateral relations with the United States, which were becoming highly complex and intricate under the impact of modern business, transportation, and communications, Canada was becoming more conscious of the need for compatibility in the policies of the United States on the one hand and of western Europe, especially Great Britain, on the other. Indeed, Borden warned the British Government that "if the future policy of the British Empire meant working in co-operation with some European nation as against the United States, that policy could not reckon on the approval or the support of Canada." Some Canadians began to see for themselves a role as a link, or even an interpreter, between the republic on the one hand and Great Britain and western Europe on the other. Such a role seemed to be highly appropriate to a country located in North America, belonging to the Empire-Commonwealth, and a member of the League. A notable instance of the adoption of this role occurred in 1921 when the Canadian prime minister, who, briefly, was Arthur Meighen, successfully convinced the British Government that it should not renew the Anglo-Japanese Alliance. Meighen's only strong argument was that the alliance was unpopular in the United States: Anglo-American friendship was now seen as more important than any other consideration. Because abrogation of this alliance was one factor in the isolating of Japan that helped lead to Pearl Harbor, one may now question the wisdom of the Canadian intervention. But it did illustrate that an anxious desire to please the Americans was acquiring high priority in the formulation of Canadian policy.

This desire was much stronger in Meighen's successor, William Lyon Mackenzie King, who had become leader of the Liberal party after Laurier's death in 1919. Like the Republican party in the American elections of 1920, the Liberals in Canada benefited from the fact that the opposing party had borne the responsibility for making the many unpopular decisions needed during the war and the immediate postwar years. With the coalition government ended and the Liberal party reunited, King crushed the Conservatives in the 1921 elections, taking one hundred and seventeen seats to their fifty. But his position was far from secure, because these elections had also revealed a formidable uprising of western and Ontario farmers against both the old parties, which resulted in the victory of sixty-five third-party Progressives. King did not have a clear majority in the House of Commons. Moreover, his own party was not a very effective instrument for governing the country. Over half the Liberals came from Quebec, which had gone solidly against the Conservatives, now tarred with the brush of conscription, and these members had little in common with the more progressively minded western Liberals who had escaped the Progressive onslaught. Finally, there was the prime minister himself. As a grandson of the rebel of 1837 and as a Harvard Ph. D. well versed in labor and social questions, he might be expected to press for a program of reform; in fact, however, he soon revealed a caution so deep-seated and pervasive that a generation of historians and commentators has failed to find adjectives adequate to describe it, despite an enthusiastic search. Clearly, a positive domestic program was not likely to emanate from such a leader in such a house. Far better to emphasize the continued growth of Canadian nationhood, on which French Canadians and most English-speaking Canadians might find common ground, even though many Conservatives might cry out that the Empire was being abandoned.

Apart from political calculations (although it is perhaps false to suggest that political calculations were ever absent from King's mind), the prime minister had a strong suspicion that the authorities in Downing Street were seeking to turn back the clock or at least to hold the hands from moving. He asserted that the British government wanted a single policy for the whole Empire-Commonwealth, to be made in London and to commit all the members. He considered his suspicions verified in 1922, when, in a crisis relating to Turkey, Winston Churchill, without prior warning or consultation, asked the Dominions for assistance in the event of war. King replied that Canada could not be committed without the approval of the Canadian Parliament; in effect, he rejected the British request, although, characteristically, he made no claim that Canada would develop a policy of its own and he had no wish that his government should secure the information on which decisions might be based. The reaction was simply negative. But with the constant danger, as he saw it, of being drawn into imperial schemes, King grasped every opportunity to stress Canada's autonomy at the same time that he encouraged a closer relationship with the United States as a kind of counterbalance against pressure from Westminster. Ever since, in Canada, there has been dispute over this alignment, with one school of thought seeing it as a natural and praiseworthy avenue toward the status of an independent North American nation and another seeing it as a weakening of the British connection, a weakening that in time would turn Canada into an American satellite. Perhaps the first school attached exaggerated importance to a development that was largely one of form, and the second would not see that the old stance of an Anglo-Canadian entente to resist American pressures was no longer relevant in the postwar world.

With respect to changes in form, the years 1926 and 1931 provided the great landmarks. On the first occasion an Imperial Conference approved the Balfour Declaration, which sought to sum up and define the relations between the United Kingdom and the self-governing Dominions in light of war and postwar changes. The Declaration defined Great Britain and the Dominions as "autonomous communities within the British Empire equal in status, in no way subordinate to one another in any aspect of their domestic or external affairs, though united by a common allegiance to the Crown and freely associated as members of the British Commonwealth of Nations." Because many phases of the legal and constitutional *status quo* were clearly at variance with this statement, a committee was established to recommend ways of sweeping away the heritage of a colonial past. In 1931 the essence of the committee's report was embodied in the Statute of Westminster, passed by the British Parliament, which removed obsolete restrictions on the competence of the parliaments of the Dominions. In law, as long since in practice, these parliaments were placed upon a level of constitutional parity with the mother of parliaments. That some loose ends and inconsistencies still remained was in part an evidence of the normal untidiness of human affairs. As far as Canada was concerned, it was also an indication of internal difficulties, because inability to agree on a method of amending the British North America Acts of 1867 and of later years forced Canada to insist on a provision in the Statute denying to herself the right to amend her own constitution. The Acts would continue to be amended by the British Parliament, which would act automatically whenever Canadian authorities could agree to ask for changes.

Thus, although there was still much scope for further definition and for changes of procedure, Canada had by the end of the 1920's secured full recognition in the world community: she was a member of the League of Nations, a self-governing Dominion of the British Commonwealth, and a friendly neighbor of the United States. And the best of it was that this new place in the sun appeared to entail no added duties. The world was at peace under the aegis of the League of Nations. As a member, Canada had a sense of being more world-minded than the United States, which had refused to join, while she continued to keep shy of collective-security engagements. Yet at the same time Canada welcomed an American initiative to promote stability when it was agreed that war was to be outlawed by the Kellogg-Briand Pact of 1928, a particularly desirable instrument because it was on the highest moral plane. Great Britain also continued to be a force for world order, but Canada had made it clear that she was not committed by British actions. Commitments suggested military alliances and military preparedness, sordid and antiquated concepts in the new era.

It was a good time to be a young nation, and Canada took pardonable satisfaction in the celebration of the sixtieth anniversary of Confederation in 1927. The old quarrels between the two language groups had left the headlines. With the increase of nationalist doctrine among English-speaking Canadians, there was a good deal of common ground respecting external policy, and nearly everyone was talking a bit like Bourassa. Political stability again reigned at Ottawa; after a rousing election in 1926, in which a British governor general had been ticked off for presuming to exercise his constitutional responsibilities, Prime Minister King had been triumphantly returned to power with a clear majority; the stable two-party system had been restored. Prosperity continued, and the government was able to lower taxes. Capital, mainly from the United States, was stimulating the growth of secondary industry and was rapidly expanding mining and pulp and paper operations. The stock market was beginning to boom to breathtaking levels.

14 Depression and Isolation, 1929-1939

The second of the two interwar decades contrasted sharply with the first as a period of rising prosperity and general peace gave way to sharp depression and to the mounting international tensions preceding the outbreak of the Second World War. Canada and the United States felt the full impact of the economic cataclysm, and for years they were mainly preoccupied with measures to combat it — so much so, that they devoted little attention to the course of world affairs. After the middle of the decade, however, as they became increasingly aware that the world had moved from a postwar to a prewar era, they had to consider whether, or to what extent, they could stay clear of the coming conflict. Despite a strong feeling in each country against involvement, there were nevertheless noticeable differences of policy, with the result that Canada entered the war almost immediately upon its outbreak whereas the United States did not become a full belligerent until more than two years later.

The decade also saw a new intimacy and a new complexity in the range of Canadian-American affairs. In economic relations Canada began by trying to reinvigorate trade with the Empire, but soon saw a steady increase of north-south trade, an axis which has never since been reversed. In the more intangible cultural realm, a self-conscious Canadian nationalism led to a vivid concern for defense against American penetration, resulting in the first protective measures in this area. In foreign policy there was an approach to the concept, which would take form in 1940, of joint cooperation in the defense of North America. Perhaps it was only Canada's earlier declaration of war in 1939 which allowed her to escape from the tight confines of a wholly North American partnership.

When the Canadian economy began to slow down in 1930 after the New York stock-market crash of the previous autumn, Mackenzie King's government was in its fourth year and had soon to face the electorate. Confident that his record would ensure another victory at the polls, King showed no readiness to take positive actions to combat falling prices and rising unemployment; like leaders in other countries, he assumed that the downturn would be temporary. But his confidence showed overtones of partisan arrogance when in an unusual burst of clear statement he asserted that he would not provide a single "five-cent piece" to provincial governments controlled by the Conservative party for the purpose of defraying relief costs. On the other hand, the Conservative opposition, now led by R. B. Bennett, not only pledged direct grants to the hard-pressed provincial governments, but also promised to use the tariff to protect interests suffering from outside competition as well as to "blast a way" into world markets. The electorate was in a mood to respond to such forceful, if illogical, language, and the Conservatives won a resounding victory in 1930. The Liberal government under King was one of the first of many, in America and Europe, to be beaten by the depression. With his usual luck, King went out at the very beginning of the depression, leaving his opponents to grapple unsuccessfully with the worst years of economic catastrophe; in 1935, he would return to start his party on a twenty-two-year run of power. By contrast, the unhappy Republican administration under Herbert Hoover had to face the voters in 1932, when times were much worse, and that party would be unable to regain power for twenty years. Many other factors accounted for party success and failure in each country, but the timing of elections was undoubtedly of considerable importance.

About the only similarities between Bennett and King were that both men were bachelors and both rather aloof in temperament. But while King was a cautious politician, with an academic and civil-service background, who had learned how to weld able men into a efficient administrative team, Bennett was a millionaire corporation lawyer, with little experience in politics, more given to imperious command than to harmonious contrivance, who never discovered how to delegate authority effectively. It would be his somewhat unjust fate, as it was Herbert Hoover's, to be indelibly stamped as the government leader who failed to sense and to cope with the little man's travail in the depths of the depression. Just as Americans talked about "Hoovervilles," so Canadians talked about "Bennett Buggies" (broken-down autos pulled by horses). But if Bennett has gone down in history as a kind of Canadian Hoover, it was he, not King, who eventually tried to copy some of the program of Hoover's opponent, Franklin Roosevelt. The attempt was unsuccessful, as we shall see, and Canada was never to have its own "New Deal," nor a national leader who could rally the people as did Roosevelt. As on other occasions, Canadian-American contrasts would be as striking as the analogies.

There was another important difference between Bennett and King. King had the Liberal's belief in low tariffs as an economic panacea, and in his political orientation respecting Great Britain he was more inclined to stress independence rather than a close working association. Bennett, however, was both a firm advocate of high tariffs and an ardent believer in the Empire. With a deep and fervent sense of personal loyalty to the Crown, he pledged his allegiance to the King of Great Britain as much as to the King of Canada, and he meant—or so he said—to do everything possible to tighten the connection between Canada and the mother country. One of his actions as prime minister was to revive the practice, which had been discontinued in the 1920's, of granting titles to Canadians (King would again discontinue the practice in 1935, and it has not since been revived), and Bennett would eventually leave Canada and end his days in the House of Lords. His was an older conception of Canadian patriotism, already fallen into popular disfavor in his own day, but still attractive to those who feel that monarchy and the British tie are bulwarks of freedom and independence.

Bennett saw the tariff as a practical means of realizing his hopes for closer Anglo-Canadian relations. During the 1920's Canada's trade with the United States had increased markedly, and its economic bonds with that country seemed to be growing tighter. But then in 1930 the United States Congress passed the Smoot-Hawley Tariff, the highest in American history, and, against the advice of a thousand economists, President Hoover signed it. Canada, which far more than its neighbor depended upon foreign exports for economic health, immediately saw its nearest market placed in jeopardy, and Canada's Parliament responded with the highest tariff in its own history. In part, this expressed Bennett's "blasting" policy: the Canadian tariff was to force the Americans to bring theirs down, a vain tactic with a country as large as the United States. But Bennett placed his main hope on increasing exports to Great Britain, and he went to the Imperial Conference of 1930 determined to secure that goal. Like his old friend of early New Brunswick days, Lord Beaverbrook, Bennett wanted the British government to give up "free trade," a doctrine almost a century old, and to impose tariffs against foreign countries. Within that framework it would then be possible to revive the old system of imperial preferences and allow Canada to sell at an advantage in the British market. Bennett found little imperial sentiment in the London of 1930, but he did secure a grudging agreement to the holding of a later conference on the subject. For various reasons the conference did not meet until 1932, at Ottawa, and by then the economic roof had caved in so completely that there was no chance for such a device to work, if it had ever had any merit. Nevertheless, the Commonwealth countries entered into a hard-headed, and sometimes ill-tempered, round of bargaining, out of which came a system of Imperial Preferences. They proved to have some effect in increasing Anglo-Canadian trade, but they played little part in lifting Canada out of its depression. An economy that was increasingly dependent upon exports from the mines and forests had to have access to the American market. In this respect President Roosevelt's 1934 decision to increase the price of gold, taken for purely domestic American reasons, had a far more tonic effect on Canada than did the Imperial Preferences, and Cordell Hull's Reciprocal Trade Agreements Act of the same year started the two countries, as well as others, on the road back to freer trade. At the end of his term Bennett's government, in conjunction with American authorities, laid the groundwork for a Canadian-American trade agreement, for which King would later take the credit. Like many other leaders, Bennett had found reality intractable.

Meanwhile, the country had been sinking deeper into the depression, with the prairies suffering the worst. Still almost entirely dependent upon one crop, the western farmers saw the price of wheat fall to unbelievably low levels, and then, when the price began to rise a bit, the farmers could derive little benefit because, following the worst drought in North American history, they had little wheat to sell. Loyalty to the old political parties, never very strong in the west, weakened further as new movements made their appearance. In 1933 delegates representing farm organizations, labor unions, and disenchanted intellectuals met at Regina, Saskatchewan, to form the Co-operative Commonwealth Federation (C.C.F.), dedicated to the achievement of democratic socialism, somewhat on the model of the British Labour Party. In Alberta discontent was channeled into the emotionally charged Social Credit crusade, which blamed the depression on the banks and the orthodox money system; coming from nowhere it astounded the country by capturing the government of that province in 1935. Nor were the large central provinces content with the existing order. In Ontario the provincial Liberal party scored a political upset in 1934 under a blatant demagogue named Mitchell Hepburn. In Quebec a new upsurge of nationalism was giving rise to the Union Nationale party which would gain power in 1936. In brief, the political scene was somewhat analogous to that across the border where tub-thumpers like Father Coughlin, Dr. Townsend, and Huey Long appeared to be building up large popular followings.

In the United States these movements were in large part defused by Roosevelt's "turn to the left" in 1935, and in Canada there was an equivalent attempt, although with opposite political results. Until the end of 1934 Bennett, as befitted a Conservative politician, had confined himself to limited and orthodox measures to combat the depression. He had strengthened the banking system by establishing a central bank (the Bank of Canada), but the nearest hint of criticism of the existing system was contained in the campaign being waged against price-fixing by the minister of trade and commerce, H. H. Stevens, a campaign for which the prime minister had no sympathy. Then, with apparent suddenness, at the beginning of 1935, a year in which an election must be held, Bennett proclaimed a broad program of governmental intervention in the economy. It is clear that this program was directly inspired by Roosevelt's New Deal, for the prime minister was stimulated to adopt it by his brother-in-law, W. D. Herridge, the Canadian minister in Washington and a close and sympathetic observer of the exciting developments there. Bennett even tried to copy Roosevelt's methods by announcing his measures in a series of radio broadcasts, the first such use of radio by a Canadian prime minister. He then followed up his announcements by securing the enactment by Parliament of several major statutes on such subjects as wages, hours and conditions of work, unemployment insurance, and marketing. In the ensuing election the voters were called upon to endorse the program and to give the prime minister a mandate for further change.

It was, of course, too late, a "death bed conversion" as many said; not many saw the Conservative party as an instrument of reform or Bennett as an effective popular leader. And unlike Americans, Canadians showed a marked reluctance to entrust the federal government with broader powers; the discontent so evident on the provincial scene turned Bennett out but was not translated into an effective demand for national reform. Even the depression did not upset innate Canadian caution, which brought the inevitable Mackenzie King back into office. King had little to offer beyond a promise to secure freer trade. He was able to conclude in 1935 the trade agreement with the United States, which was already substantially prepared, and to negotiate another and broader one in 1938. As for Bennett's "New Deal," King did what an American president would not have been able to do: he asked the courts for an advisory opinion on their constitutionality, and when appeal went to the Judicial Committee of the Privy Council in London, the committee declared almost all the Bennett legislation to be beyond the powers of the federal government. Thus a British court, which demonstrated little grasp of the apparently clear language of the British North America Act, dealt the federal government a body blow at about the same time that the United States Supreme Court was beginning to reinterpret the constitution in the light of modern conditions. It was an ironic reversal of the hopes and intentions of the Fathers of Confederation. Prime Minister King took refuge in a Royal Commission on Dominion-Provincial Relations, which made an elaborate and valuable study of Canadian federalism but which did not report until 1940, when the country was at war and in a new era. The depression held Canada in its harsh grip until after the outbreak of war in 1939.

Before turning to the growing preoccupation with the approach of war, we should look at another phase of Canada's life in the 1930's, vital for an understanding of her relations with the United States: concern over American cultural penetration. This was by no means a new concern at this time. It would be possible to quote endlessly from both native and outside observers, who from the early nineteenth century had been commenting, usually disapprovingly, on the prevalence of American or "Yankee" manners and customs on the northern side of the international border. The purpose of these earlier comments, however, had been to show that the northern communities, although British by allegiance, were not very British in tone and atmosphere. Insofar as they were not British, they must be American, except for the French Canadians, who were a separate case. No one expected to find a personality that was neither British nor American, but instead was Canadian. Back in the 1870's there had been a little "Canada First" movement, of minor significance, but in the following years not much had been done to emphasize distinctively Canadian symbols or attitudes. For a long time debate centered on whether Canadians should cling as closely as possible to British standards and conceptions or whether they should give fuller vent to prevailing continental norms. By the 1920's, however, the pattern had noticeably changed. The fiery experience of the First World War, followed by the development of a new international status, made Canadians much more aware of themselves and much more determined to foster a national consciousness. There was as yet relatively little in the way of distinctive cultural achievement to point to—in painting, the Group of Seven* stood out—but hopes were high. A long list of new and reviving national organizations can be complied, all of them hard at work in these years to promote a Canadian sentiment and a Canadian outlook.

But this new activity in Canada coincided with a mighty explosion of popular culture in the neighboring republic. Hollywood confirmed its dominance of the motion picture industry, and the screen started talking before the end the 1920's. Popular magazines and brightly written newspapers circulated more widely than ever before. The "golden age" of professional sport entranced countless millions. Automobiles rolled off the assembly lines to give the "common man" a new freedom and a new mobility. And perhaps most striking of all, an entirely new medium of mass communication, radio broadcasting, sprang into being. These were only the highlights of a brave new world of immense vitality which influenced the lives not only of the ten million Canadians strung out along the northern border of the United States but of much of the world beyond.

But Canadians were closest to this vigorous outburst, which poured irresistibly across a truly undefended border. Most of them consumed the new culture as readily, and as expertly, as did Americans, yet inevitably their reactions were somewhat different from those of their neighbors. Even while they were being amused and thrilled—in a restrained Canadian fashion, of

*The Group of Seven—among them Lawren Harris, A. Y. Jackson, F. H. Varley, and Arthur Lismer—found distinctive ways of painting the landscapes of the Canadian North.

course—they indulged themselves in a certain sense of disapproval, like a maiden aunt who was titillated but who felt that she ought to be shocked. Many indications of Canadian opinion revealed a strong belief that they were more honest, more moral, more religious than Americans who allowed easy divorce, let gangsters dominate their lives, and tolerated corruption in all phases of their national life. If any of these and countless other deplorable characteristics appeared in Canada, they were merely taken as evidence of insidious American influence. When an extensive survey of Canadian opinion was made in the mid-1930's for a volume in a Canadian-American-relations series, the editors deliberately omitted or softened much of what Canadians had said, in order to "prevent a book in a series designed to promote the course of international goodwill from itself being a source of irritation."*

Some of this spirit of criticism was merely the old sense that Canada could best resist absorption by the United States if her people clung as closely as possible to British traditions and standards. But increasingly a new note was being struck: Canadians must have an opportunity to preserve and develop their own distinctive identity, which was in immediate danger of being stifled. It was a concern shared by French Canadians, because the new forms of popular culture often leaped the language barrier, which in any event scarcely existed in the cities of Quebec, where an increasing number of French Canadians spoke and understood English. Many spokesmen, of both language groups, argued that, just as Canada had once consciously promoted its separate economic development through tariffs and railroad building, now it must take similar action to ensure cultural growth.

Such action could be negative, as in the tax placed on American magazines in 1931, but there was one field where there appeared to be an outstanding opportunity for positive measures:

*H. F. Angus, ed., *Canada and Her Great Neighbor* (New Haven, Conn., 1938), p. v.

radio broadcasting. American transmitters were much more powerful than the Canadian ones, and, besides, the small Canadian
stations could not afford to prepare material with any kind of
distinctive content. Consequently nearly all the programs heard
in Canada at the end of the 1920's were directly or indirectly of
American origin. As a preliminary step in dealing with this
question the federal government in 1928 appointed a royal
commission on broadcasting, which in the next year recommended the establishment of a government-subsidized
broadcasting company. There was then a lull while the country
was concerned with other matters and while the government
hesitated over possible procedures. But a vigorous pressure
campaign, and a decision of the Judicial Committee of the Privy
Council declaring that control of radio was an exclusively federal
matter laid the basis for action. Studies made it clear that the
establishment of a national network was beyond the resources of
private industry; in a slogan of the time, it was a question of "the
State or the United States." Finally, in 1932, legislation was
passed to establish the Canadian Radio Broadcasting Commission, and four years later several changes were made when it was
replaced by the Canadian Broadcasting Corporation. The outcome was a typically Canadian compromise, leading to a publi-
cally owned national system while allowing the continuance of
private broadcasting, a combination of British and American
approaches. The C.B.C. was to become a potent, although
frequently controversial, force in Canadian life.

As a final topic in this chapter, we must note the Canadian
responses to the deteriorating world situation in the four or five
years before the outbreak of war in 1939. It is a highly interesting
period in the history of Canadian foreign policy, because for the
first time considerable numbers of Canadians openly and sometimes heatedly debated whether the long-standing association
with Great Britain should give way to a policy of isolation similar
to that being followed by the United States. Most French Canadians were even more isolationist in outlook than the majority of

Americans. Some articulate English-speaking Canadians argued for withdrawal. They felt strongly the prevailing abhorrence of another ghastly world war, and most of them could not bring themselves to say openly that they would participate if one came. Yet they were troubled, for they could not convince themselves that what happened to Britain or to Europe was no concern of theirs. In such a dilemma it was hard to face facts squarely and to draw realistic conclusions; the temptation to engage in wishful thinking was great.

The central figure in the formulation and implementation of foreign policy was, of course, the prime minister, who was also secretary of state for external affairs. Back in office in 1935, Mackenzie King was vividly aware that much of his political support came from sections of the country, particularly Quebec, which opposed an enlarged participation of Canada in overseas affairs. At the same time he realized that in a world crisis, probably a great majority of the people would not endure a policy that broke with the old close association with Great Britian. Yet he was also conscious of the desirability of good working relations with the United States, which, Ulysses-like, bound itself by the Neutrality Acts of 1935-1937 to resist entanglement in foreign wars. King felt that he had to walk a tightrope; a false step might very well drop him into political oblivion. Hence, he constantly preached the need for "national unity" and for a policy that would preserve at least a surface harmony. He found his magic formula in the phrases "no commitments" and "Parliament will decide," meaning that Canada would not bind itself in advance to any positive course of action and would not go to war without legislative approval. In practice, this formula meant both more and less than the words might suggest. It meant that Canada as a small power would take no active part in trying to find answers to pressing international problems; whatever weight she had would not be thrown into the balance. Yet King never had any doubt, although he did not say it openly, that Canada would support Britain in the event of a major war. Thus Canada was in fact committed, but without any real voice in the decisions preceding the outbreak of war. Again, Parliament would decide, but its decision would be taken at a time when no real choice was open. King kept policy in his own hands as much as possible. He discouraged debate on foreign affairs in Parliament, and his own rather infrequent speeches on the subject, while of extraordinary length, were so diffuse and so cloudy that few of his hearers knew at the end what he had said. His performance was unheroic, even disingenuous, but it was brilliantly successful from a political point of view. He gave his opponents no firm ground on which to stand.

The tone of these four years was set within a few weeks of King's return to office in the autumn of 1935. For many months beforehand Canada, and the world, had been watching the developing crisis centering on Mussolini's aggressive designs on Ethiopia, which had led to the invasion of that country and to the imposition of sanctions against Italy by the League of Nations. In English-speaking Canada there was a rather indefinite feeling that fascism was an evil, but little pressure for strong Canadian support of the League. In French-speaking Canada there was not only strong opposition to such support but instinctive sympathy to the corporatist philosophy of Mussolini's regime; it saw the measures against Italy as an anti-Catholic campaign against a civilized country. Consequently, the new Liberal government announced that although it would continue to support economic sanctions it would undertake no new commitments. Its hand was then forced by its own delegate at Geneva, W. A. Riddell, who, without instructions from his government, proposed an extension of the embargo to items, particularly oil, that were vital to Italy's war machine. In Ottawa the government quickly disavowed the action and the prime minister stated that, while Canada was not necessarily opposed to such an embargo, it was not Canada's place to take the initiative in such an important matter. The incident had little influence on the course of world affairs, for there was no chance that a positive initiative by Canada would have been supported by the great powers, as the announcement of the Hoare-Laval plan soon showed. Many Canadians were nevertheless left with the uneasy feeling that their country had made its own small contribution to the destruction of the League. Still others, however, came out of the crisis convinced that a North American country should keep as clear as possible of the sordid world of European politics. The prime minister was confirmed in his view; as he stated in an interview: "After all we are but 10 millions on the north end of a continent and we should not strive to over-play our part."

That part was indeed kept to a minimum. In the years after the Ethiopian war Canada continued to keep itself clear of involvement whether with respect to the Spanish Civil War, the Japanese attack on China, or the developing crisis arising out of Hitler's expansionist ambitions. True, in a private conversation with the German leader in 1937, Mackenzie King implied that Canada and the other Commonwealth countries would certainly come to the aid of Britain in the event of a war of aggression, but at the same time he was giving full support to the policy of appeasement that was coming into favor in London. This policy would doubtless have been adopted without Canadian support, but, by refusing to support proposals for military cooperation with Great Britain, King helped to strengthen the hands of those in the British government who argued that appeasement was the only possible policy. King himself was convinced, after his conversation, that Hitler would soon be satisfied and would not risk a large war. For the first time since he had become a national leader King found it possible to give public and enthusiastic praise to British policy, when he greeted Neville Chamberlain's words and actions in the weeks leading up to Munich with "unbounded admiration" as a service to mankind. At the same time Royal Air Force overtures looking to the training of air crews in Canada were discouraged, as were British proposals for the accumulaton of strategic materials and munitions. If Hitler was aware of this negative response, he could hardly have taken seriously King's warning of 1937. And London was just as much misled, because it did not know that the Canadian government fully intended to provide support in the event of war. In the name of Canadian unity, King refused to reveal his hand fully to anyone, including the people of his own country.

A major bulwark of King's policy was his firm belief that Canada still lived in a "fireproof house far from inflammable materials." In the spring of 1938 he observed in the House of Commons that "the talk which one sometimes hears of aggressor nations planning to invade Canada and seize these tempting resources of ours is, to say the least, premature. It ignores our neighbours and our lack of neighbours." The attitude of Canada's neighbor to the south became more evident in August of that year when President Franklin Roosevelt, in Canada to receive an honorary degree, stated emphatically: "The Dominion of Canada is part of the sisterhood of the British Empire. I give to you assurance that the people of the United States will not stand idly by if domination of Canadian soil is threatened by any other Empire." With the war clouds darkening in Europe, most Canadians were not disposed to analyze carefully the possible implications of this statement; it was welcomed as a contribution to Canadian security and was followed up by a promise from the Canadian prime minister that his country would do its part in keeping aggressors out of the western hemisphere. This atmosphere of increasing Canadian-American accord was exemplified by a number of specific cooperative actions taken at this time and might have suggested that the two countries would follow parallel policies in response to the world crisis.

Yet, in fact, they did not. In the United States a dogged isolationism was still the prevailing mood; efforts by Roosevelt and Hull to escape from the restrictions of the Neutrality Acts continued to be unavailing. In Canada, however, at the beginning of 1939, the prime minister dismissed any possibility of legal neutrality when he asserted that if Great Britain went to war, Canada would be at war, too. Thus Parliament's power of decision, so frequently emphasized by King, would operate within a very narrow range. After Hitler's occupation of the rest of Czechoslovakia in March, King said that he had "no doubt what the decision of the Canadian people and parliament would be" in the event of an attack on Britain. Some days later he called it "sheer madness" that "every twenty years this country should automatically . . . take part in a war overseas for democracy [and] feel called upon to save, periodically, a continent that cannot run itself." Still, he was opposed to the idea of neutrality which might cause "passionate controversy" in Canada and possibly lend aid and comfort to a potential aggressor. On the other hand, he argued that the day of large expeditionary forces was past, and he solemnly promised that his government would never impose conscription. He had made his bow to nearly every important strand of Canadian opinion. It was his colleague, Ernest Lapointe, the minister of justice, who cut to the core of the matter when he bluntly informed his Quebec colleagues that any attempt to prevent help going to Britain, if that country was attacked, would lead to "a civil war in Canada." Thus for all the references to "no commitments" and "Parliament will decide," the country was in fact going to participate, although many people hoped it would be mainly an economic (and profitable) participation.

When war did come at the beginning of September, King called Parliament to meet a week later. After a day or so of debate, the address in reply to the speech from the throne was approved almost unanimously on September 9. This vote was taken to register approval of Canada's participation in the war, and the cabinet then approved a declaration of war as from September 10. This was exactly a week later than the declaration made by the United Kingdom government, and it was therefore argued that Canada had made its own decision, taken constitutionally after parliamentary debate. Yet it is not clear what Canada's position had been during the previous week. King had told President Roosevelt that Canada was neutral, and Roosevelt had not applied the Neutrality Acts to Canada during this period.

On the other hand the government in these days had taken a number of actions which clearly assumed that Germany was an enemy. Approval by Parliament was thus largely a formality, with English-speaking Canadians determined to stand by Britain and French Canadians trusting in the government's promise that conscription would not be imposed. Each group could place its own interpretation on what participation meant; in the end, that question would be decided by events.

The government and people of Canada had not been very consistent or very clearheaded in these years, but there never had been any real doubt that the old ties were still too strong to be denied. There was also at least some indication that the feeling was more than simply one for the British connection: to remain aloof was impossible when western Europe was threatened. Unlike Americans, who saw themselves as building a new civilization in a new land, Canadians felt themselves to be directly related to the old civilization across the Atlantic. There was, of course, no complete contrast in attitudes. Many Americans had this same sense of implication in the fate of Europe, which would become more vivid in the following two years, whereas many Canadians argued that they should stay clear of Europe's perennial problems.

On another level, Canada's declaration of war was an assertion that the country was not wholly within the American orbit. It may have been the last such assertion. The increasingly intimate cooperation between Canada and the United States, which became strikingly apparent in 1940, and the rapid enlargement of the American world role in the next few years, have worked against another divergence in foreign policies as sharp as that of 1939.

15 War and Cold War, 1939-1949

The mighty upheavals of the decade following the outbreak of the Second World War in September 1939 forced upon both the United States and Canada a fundamental alteration in attitudes and policies toward the outside world and in their relations with each other. From a position of aloofness, to which many Americans held with particular tenacity, each moved, at differing speeds, to join a worldwide alliance of nations united to defeat Germany and Japan. Despite an unprecedented military and economic contribution to the victory, each emerged from the world struggle relatively unscathed, indeed enormously strengthened; but instead of seeking another withdrawal, each joined the new world organization and played a large part in working for international economic recovery and political stability. More than that, and most striking of all, at the end of this decade, the two countries entered into a binding twenty-year military alliance with several countries in western Europe, thus breaking explicitly with the old pattern of nonentanglement and no commitments. Their own bilateral association, in both the war years and the postwar years, became increasingly intimate, involving military cooperation in the defense of the continent, first against the wartime enemies and then against the cold war antagonist, and economic cooperation in developing and managing the continent's resources. Yet the new closeness of their ties did not lead to full integration or absorption by the stronger of the weaker; a combination of forbearance on the one side and of resistance to conscious or unconscious pressure on the other preserved the separateness that had always marked their histories. At this stage, in 1949, Canadians were relatively content or even cheerful about the new relationship, but some were beginning to wonder about its implications.

By 1949, then, Canada's problem, as it would be thereafter, was how to live beside the world's most powerful country, whose interests were rapidly ramifying into all corners of the globe. But in the first months after the outbreak of the war in 1939 it all appeared quite different. While the United States continued as a neutral, Canada was slowly and somewhat tentatively mobilizing during the period of the so-called "phony war." The First Division reached England from Canada before the end of the year, and an agreement was signed with Great Britain for the training of Commonwealth air crews; but economic mobilization was slow, mainly because the British government gave no effective lead in this sphere. For the Canadian government, domestic considerations were still uppermost as it faced, and defeated, attacks from two opposing groups of critics. The first attack came from Quebec, where the premier, Maurice Duplessis, called an election on the ground that the federal government intended to speed up its centralization program "by involving the pretext of war." The federal government saw this move as a direct challenge, which could not be ignored, and its Quebec cabinet ministers, led by Ernest Lapointe, entered directly into the campaign: they warned that they would resign if Duplessis were returned, thus leaving Quebec without an effective voice at Ottawa, and they also solemnly promised, once again, that there would be no conscription. Their intervention was so effective that Duplessis' large majority was turned into an equally large majority for the provincial Liberal party. Quebec had chosen the path of cooperation.

The second attack, at the beginning of 1940, came from Ontario, where the legislature passed a resolution condemning the federal government for not pursuing a more vigorous war effort, a not very oblique injection of the explosive conscription issue into the national debate as well as an incident in the long feud between Mitchell Hepburn and Mackenzie King. King seized upon the condemnation as justifying an immediate election. There had to be an election sometime in 1940 unless the life of Parliament were indefinitely extended through the formation of a coalition government, an idea which King adamantly opposed. Yet he dreaded the last session of a dying Parliament, when his government would inevitably be on the defensive as it would still be during the campaign. He was also reluctant to see an election later in the year when the war might have entered upon a more violent phase. Accordingly, when Parliament met in January, shortly after the Ontario resolution, which he professed to see as a kind of vote of want of confidence, the prime minister secured its immediate dissolution before any business had been transacted or a word spoken in debate. This unprecedented action, which his opponents took as proof of King's contempt for Parliament, brought rich political rewards, because in the ensuing elections the Liberals won the largest majority up to that time and so were secure in office for another five years. As King wrote in his diary: "We really cleaned up in the province of Quebec and I often thought of what Sir Wilfrid [Laurier] said to me . . . when I told him of my intention to stand by him . . . against conscription [in 1917] — that I would have the province of Quebec for the rest of my life."

King's expectation that the phase of static war would not last far into 1940 was soon borne out: two weeks after the Canadian election Hitler unleashed his attacks upon Denmark and Norway, soon to be followed by the invasion of the Low Countries and of France. These catastrophic events brought an immediate sense of crisis to North America, unlike anything ever known before, and they also led to an unprecedented level of consultation and cooperation between Canada and the United States. As one authority has noted, quoting Lewis Carroll:

> But the valley grew narrower and narrower still,
> And the evening got darker and colder,
> Till (merely from nervousness not from good will)
> They marched along shoulder to shoulder.

But there was good will, as well as nervousness. It is worth noting that in April, when on a postelection holiday, King spent a few days with President Roosevelt at Warm Springs, Georgia, where the two men thoroughly canvassed common problems. An acquaintanceship that went back to Harvard days at the beginning of the century quickly ripened into an easy and firm friendship, of inestimable value for the months and years ahead. Roosevelt was thinking of ways to provide assistance to the British, and King was convinced that the key to the whole crisis lay in the role to be played by the United States, a fact which he believed the British did not yet grasp. King may sometimes have exaggerated the importance of his role as "interpreter," but he played it with some degree of skill. Although Canadian Conservatives were extremely suspicious of King's greater readiness for meetings with American than with British leaders, King felt that it was essential "to bring the countries together as one, without which there can be no salvation for any one of the three."

King's role was never more difficult than it was a month later, toward the end of May 1940, when France was reeling to defeat and the question of whether Great Britain could hold out was suddenly on everyone's mind. At this point the government of the United States was visibly alarmed by the possibility that the British might find it necessary to surrender the fleet in order to avoid complete destruction of their islands, and Roosevelt and Hull called upon King to persuade Churchill that the fleet must not be given up. At first, King "instinctively revolted against such a thought" because "it seemed to me that the United States was seeking to save itself at the expense of Britain." Further explorations brought about a fuller disclosure of the American position, and King then sent a carefully drafted message to Churchill stating that, if it became necessary for the fleet to leave British waters, the United States would see to its repair and refitting in American and Commonwealth ports, would extend its defense of the Atlantic, would participate in a stringent blockade of the continent, and, if the Germans attempted to starve out Great Britain, would send food ships under naval escort. "And interference with such ships would mean instant war."

Four days later Churchill uttered his famous words: "We shall never surrender, and even if, which I do not for a moment believe, this Island or a large part of it were subjugated and starving, then our Empire beyond the seas, armed and guarded by the British Fleet, would carry on the struggle, until, in God's good time, the New World, with all its power and might, steps forth to the rescue and liberation of the old."

For some months following, King continued to act from time to time as an intermediary until the two great leaders were fully at ease with each other. This role could not last, of course, and later on Canadian leaders would sometimes have a sense of being left out or ignored in the discussions of the two leading powers.

Meanwhile, the great European crisis of the summer and autumn of 1940 had led to a highly significant development respecting continental defense. This subject had been discussed very tentatively in 1938 by the two countries' chiefs of staff, and then after a considerable interval there were more conversations in the summer of 1940. Each side agreed, however, that closer and more continuous contact was desirable, and after some preliminary diplomatic preparation President Roosevelt, in August, invited Mackenzie King to meet with him near Ogdensburg, New York, on the St. Lawrence River, to look into the matter further. The president was accompanied by his recently appointed secretary of war, Henry L. Stimson, but the prime minister had neither a cabinet minister nor a service officer with him. After a few hours talk the two heads of government announced to the press that they were establishing a Permanent Joint Board on Defense (P.J.B.D.), consisting of four or five members, civilian and service, from each country, which was to begin its activities immediately. The board's role would be advisory: it was to study problems relating to the defense of the northern half of the continent and make recommendations, with implementation to be in the hands of the two governments. The pattern was thus similar to that of the International Joint Commission, set up thirty-one years earlier, except that the board rested upon no formal agreement of any kind. Its existence rested, and still rests, solely upon the press release of August 18, 1940. Mackenzie King's critics have not failed to point out that, although he had spent twenty years before 1940 in resisting all proposals for Anglo-Canadian military cooperation, he now, in a few hours, without consulting his own colleagues let alone Parliament, agreed to a close, and permanent, military association with the United States. His defenders could point out that the crisis was, or appeared to be, immediate, that the board's role was advisory, and that there were few in Canada at that time willing to reject the idea of military cooperation with the United States.

In the next five years of the war period the board made thirty-three recommendations, all unanimous, to the two governments, and nearly all of these were acted upon. In addition, its discussions had an intangible but very real influence in speeding up and making more efficient the war efforts of each country. For Canada the ever-present problem was whether a close association with a country so much stronger and richer would lead to a subordinate or satellite status. This possibility was made more real by the fact that Canada had committed much of its limited resources to the overseas war, leaving little for continental defense, and this at a time when the United States, still neutral, was rapidly building up an immense war machine. Thus Canada had little to contribute to the vast, even grandiose, proposals which the Americans frequently put forward. To some extent, the board was a technique for securing Canadian consent to projects which Americans would carry out on Canadian territory. It was also agreed, in October 1940, that if Britain were overrun or if the Royal Navy lost control of the Atlantic, the United States would assume strategic direction of Canadian forces, but when in the spring of 1941 the American members argued for such strategic direction after the United States come into the war the Canadians refused. At this time King noted in his diary that defense cooperation raised "a real political danger" and that it would be "better to have two peoples and two governments on this continent understanding each other and reciprocating in their relations as an example to the world, than to have anything like continental union."

Among projects flowing in whole or in part from P.J.B.D. recommendations, two or three may be mentioned, relating to communications toward the northwest and the northeast. In the former area the Canadian government had already made surveys looking to the establishment of efficient air communications from Edmonton to the Arctic (the Northwest Staging Route) when the board, at the end of 1940, recommended that transport facilities between the United States and Alaska should be improved. In the next year the Canadian government completed this system, after a fashion, to the Alaska border. At the beginning of 1942 the board then endorsed the project of building an overland highway, linking the airports, to be paid for by the United States and to be turned over to Canada at the end of the war. By November 1943 the Alaska Highway was open to military traffic. Many subsidiary undertakings were also carried out, notably the Canol project for the piping of oil from northern Canadian wells for the use of the United States Army in Canada and Alaska. At the other side of the continent the Canadian government completed the air base at Goose Bay, Labrador, which formed part of the Northeast Staging Route for the ferrying of medium- and short-range aircraft to Europe. It was also decided to supplement this system by the building of the Crimson Route, starting from the center of the continent and reaching Greenland via Baffin Island, but the need for this route declined and it was never completed. These and other projects involved extensive American activities in the Canadian north and some alarm about an "army of occupation."

After the entry of the United States into the war the importance of the P.J.B.D. declined somewhat, because it was now preferable to have direct liaison between the military staffs of the two countries. There was, however, some delay, due to U.S. military opposition, in achieving this end, and not until the summer of 1942 was a Canadian military mission posted to Washington. Its members often had difficulty in finding out what the Americans and the British were up to.

On the fighting side, the Canadian and American war efforts

remained distinct from each other, because the plans and organization of the 1939-1941 period governed the main lines of Canadian action thereafter. The use of British equipment and British-style uniforms further marked off Canadian from American servicemen. Thus, in the North Atlantic, the Mediterranean, and Northwest Europe, although Canadian and American forces cooperated closely, they were not fused. Yet one should note the formation of a fine fighting unit, the U.S.-Canadian First Special Service Force, which campaigned in Italy and southern France. And if the Pacific war had gone on beyond 1945 the line of separation would probably have disappeared. In 1945 a Canadian Army Pacific Force was in training for use in the war against Japan and was preparing to use American equipment and tactics.

In the realm of economic cooperation, the first year and a half of the war saw Canada striving rapidly to increase its capacity to produce munitions for British needs, an effort that required extensive purchases of capital equipment from the United States and led to an adverse balance of payments with that country. Traditionally such an adverse balance had been met by converting the proceeds from sales to Britain into American dollars, but this was no longer possible because of the weakness of the pound in world markets. By the beginning of 1941 Canada's reserves of gold and U.S. dollars were so low that the purchasing program was in immediate peril. At this very time President Roosevelt invented the lend-lease device and secured its approval by Congress in order to meet this same problem in respect to Great Britain and, later, other countries fighting the Axis. After some consideration, the Canadian government decided not to apply for assistance under the lend-lease program, for it wished to avoid dependence upon its powerful neighbor. Indeed, Canada developed its own program of assistance to Allied nations, called Mutual Aid, which, when the size of the two economies is considered, was comparable in magnitude to the American program.

But the problem of the lack of American dollars remained, and after some preliminary discussions by officials, it was solved at a meeting between Roosevelt and King held at Roosevelt's Hyde Park residence in April 1941. The essence of the plan was that the question of war production should be viewed in continental rather than national terms, thus allowing Canada to concentrate on items which she could produce most efficiently. This in turn would lead to increased American purchases in Canada, and thus to an easing or an ending of the currency problem. After Pearl Harbor American procurement in Canada became so large and economic cooperation so close that this problem did not reappear. It cannot be said, however, that either country kept strictly to the spirit of the Hyde Park Agreement, which would have meant that each should remain dependent on the other for items that were more efficiently produced there. Each broadened its productive base to produce items in all, or nearly all, categories. Nor did the economies, particularly the civilian economies, of the two countries become integrated. Normal tariffs continued. Prices were stabilized more strictly in Canada, and at a lower level, thus necessitating stringent export controls by Ottawa to prevent the flight of essential goods to the highly attractive American market. Nevertheless, each side did more business with the other than ever before, and trading habits were developed that were to persist after 1945. In particular, the United Kingdom was never able to regain the place in the Canadian market which it lost in these years.

In summary, despite occasional irritations, Canada enjoyed excellent relations with her American neighbor and her British associate. The high level of competence of her civilian and military leadership was widely recognized and commented upon. The efficiency of her organization for war was nowhere surpassed, with the result that, despite her small population, she came to have an economic and military weight that was much closer to that of the great powers than it was to that of any country outside that group. At the end of the war Canada was the world's fourth strongest military power, with an industrial and agricultural economy to match this position. Nevertheless, throughout the war years nearly everyone in Canada was conscious of the possibility that this immense effort might be disrupted by a return of the national disunity that had flared up so luridly in 1917. It was the firm determination of most leaders, the prime minister above all, that history must not be allowed to repeat itself, but until the very last months of the war there was no certainty that it would not do so.

We have already seen how King met and defeated his critics in both French-speaking and English-speaking Canada in the first six months after the start of the war. For about a year and a half thereafter the domestic scene was relatively stable under a government with a very large majority. In the middle of 1940 Parliament passed the National Resources Mobilization Act, giving the government large powers over the economy and the power to draft men into the army for home defense. The government was, however, still bound by its firm promise not to send conscripts overseas. This restriction appeared not to be serious in a period when the voluntary enlistment rate was good and when emphasis was heavy on economic mobilization. The Canadian army was not in action until the beginning of the Mediterranean campaign at the end of 1942, and the replacement of losses was not a problem; indeed, the Canadian forces felt themselves able to enforce one of the world's strictest standards of physical fitness, thus rejecting for service thousands of men who would have been inducted in other countries.

By the end of 1941, however, the mood was beginning to change. Casualties had still been very low, compared with the same period of the First World War, but the competition for manpower among the several services and in industry was becoming intense. The long period of preparation, of hard work, and of high taxes, with a second front apparently still far off, was producing a noticeable irritation in the public mind. The relatives of those who had already seen long service were disposed to wonder whether sacrifices were being borne equitably. Insistently, the question of conscription for overseas service was pushed to the fore, stimulated in part by the entry of the United States into the war in December 1941. Back of this insistence, as far as some were concerned, was the view that the war provided an appropriate and highly promising opportunity to require a minority to submit to the will of the majority—more precisely, that French Canadians would be brought into line and, if necessary, coerced. Such people seemed to feel that, if they could not get at the enemy, at least they could have it out with their fellow Canadians of the other language and religion.

As usual, when faced with a demand for action, Prime Minister King sought to temporize and to postpone. It was his deeply held belief that his greatest service to Canada had been in the things that he had prevented from being done rather than in what he had positively accomplished. On this occasion he came forward with a remarkable device, a plebiscite to ask the voters to release the government from its pledge not to send conscripts overseas. Without saying that the government either would or would not impose overseas conscription, King asked the voters on April 27, 1942, to answer Yes or No to the question "Are you in favour of releasing the Government from any obligations arising out of any past commitments restricting the methods of raising men for military service?" In the provinces with English-speaking majorities the vote was eighty percent in the affirmative, but in Quebec there was an negative vote of seventy-two to twenty-eight. For the country as a whole the affirmative vote was sixty-four to thirty-six. The Prime Minister then moved another inch by securing legislative approval for overseas conscription, while stating that this measure was only for the purpose of being prepared for future contingencies. A majority of the Quebec members protested, and the senior French-Canadian minister in the cabinet resigned. The sharp and at times heated debate continued through the summer of 1942, with the government standing uneasily in the middle between the For-God's-Sake-

Do-Something school on the one side and the flat negativism of most of French Canada on the other. By stepping up the rate of call-ups for home defense the government helped to stimulate the enlistment in the army and navy of many men who preferred to escape the obloquy which attached to being drafted for home defense only. Thus the government weathered the first storm over the question of how the country's manpower was to be mobilized and used.

For another two years the question remained in the background, although never far from people's minds. Until D Day (June 6, 1944) the Canadian Army was not heavily engaged, except in the Mediterranean, and the air force and the navy were able to meet their needs by the voluntary system. Strenuous efforts were made by lay and clerical leaders to convince French Canadians that they had a stake in the war that required every possible effort. Many, although not all, of the recruiting mistakes of the First World War were avoided. For these and other reasons there was a fuller response than there had been in the earlier conflict. Still, it was nevertheless perfectly clear that French Canadians did not regard the war effort in the same light as did either their compatriots in Canada or their neighbors in the United States. When they were told, either by their own leaders or by Canadian or Allied spokesmen, that the war should take precedence over every other consideration, they simply did not believe it. Instead, they continued to feel that the preservation of their own way of life was their first duty, and they were already sorely troubled by the rapid social change that the war economy was forcing. They held unwaveringly to the bond given in 1939, that participation in an overseas war was a matter of individual and voluntary decision, and they listened sympathetically to orators who gave voice to the prevailing uneasiness. In August 1944 the province's mood of withdrawal was symbolized by the return to power of Maurice Duplessis and his Union Nationale party, after a close election.

It was at this very point, about two and a half months after D

Day, that the minister for national defence began to receive warnings from overseas of a shortage of trained infantry in the reinforcement pools. Eventually, the minister, J. L. Ralston, made a personal investigation in Europe, and in the middle of October he informed the cabinet that trained infantrymen from the home-defense forces should be sent overseas immediately. Ralston had actually submitted his resignation on the conscription issue in 1942, and now he made it clear that unless his recommendations were approved he would leave the cabinet. But Prime Minister King and a majority of his colleagues were determined to canvass all possibilities before turning to the dreaded expedient of conscription. Because the crisis had apparently come upon them suddenly and because the war appeared to be nearing its end, they argued that it was better to make one more attempt to raise the needed men rather than to see the country once again in the grip of disruptive debate. At the beginning of November, Ralston was dismissed and replaced by General A. G. L. McNaughton, and the attempt was made. Before the end of the month McNaughton had to confess failure and, at last, with his government on the verge of dissolution from internal conflict, King decided to issue the order for the despatch of drafted men overseas. There then followed a parliamentary debate, in which all the old positions were stated and restated, but fortunately this debate was relatively temperate nor was there any need for a wartime election on the issue. The approaching end of hostilities had a moderating effect. French Canadians had been required to bow to the will of the majority, but the desire of some English-speaking elements to use this opportunity to isolate French Canada and thus render it politically impotent had been frustrated. As so often, Mackenzie King was the political beneficiary of these developments, of which to a large extent he had been the architect. In June 1945, just after the end of the European war, he and his party were once again returned to power.

King conducted his electoral campaign during an interval of

absence from the sessions at San Francisco where a new international organization, the United Nations, was being formed. For about a year and a half before this time Canada, like other countries, had had to consider what attitude it would take to the proposal, put forward by the great powers, that a new world organization be formed. As in the United States, public-opinion polls and comments by politicians showed much more support for such an organization than there had been at the beginning of the League of Nations. A formal resolution endorsing the project was adopted by the Canadian House of Commons, a month before the opening of the San Francisco meetings, by a vote of two-hundred and two to five. At these meetings the Canadian delegation joined with those of several other countries in an unsuccessful effort to eliminate or weaken the veto which the great powers had reserved for themselves. The Canadians also tried, with slightly more success, to secure some recognition for the so-called middle powers, that is, those countries that did not have permanent seats on the Security Council but whose military and economic strength might entail considerable responsibilities under the charter. In October 1945 the Canadian Parliament unanimously approved the Charter, but the mood was cautious rather than enthusiastic. Everyone agreed that the days of isolationism were gone and that Canada must not hold back in its support of the new organization. Nevertheless, there was little thought that the millennium was being ushered in, for there was already clear evidence that the Soviet Union and the western powers were in fundamental disagreement over the nature of the postwar settlement. Canadians were soon involved in a wide variety of U.N. programs, but they also knew that in the new world that had dawned with the dropping of the atomic bomb on Hiroshima the fundamental answers to the problems of world peace did not lie with the middle or small powers.

For Canada, like the other countries that had spent long years at war, the period following the close of hostilities saw a concentration upon internal and national issues. Canada's problems were, of course, minor compared with those of nations that had been fought over or otherwise weakened during the long struggle; indeed, Canada entered the postwar era with a much more diversified and productive economy than it had had in 1939. Nevertheless, there was the vast task of demobilizing and converting to peacetime procedures, there was the need to deal with questions, particularly those relating to the workings of the federal system, that had been postponed or ignored, and there was a strong impulse to round out and complete some aspects of the national structure. (With no space here to develop these themes, only some aspects of the last one will be noticed in a later chapter.)

In addition, there was the question of economic readjustment, which requires brief mention, for it revealed a problem that was to prove to be endemic. Canada's exports quickly declined when war orders ended and although many of her products, such as food, were badly needed their shipment could be financed only by various forms of credits and loans. On the other hand, pent-up civilian demand and the need for plant modernization and expansion led to a rapid increase of imports from the United States. By 1947 Canada was buying twice as much from its neighbor as it was able to sell, but was unable for various reasons to realize U.S. dollars from overseas sales, the traditional method in prewar years for meeting the deficit in North American trade. In consequence, a first-class dollar crisis suddenly loomed in 1947 and threatened the Canadian government with insolvency. It was met by resorting to drastic measures for the conservation of U.S. dollars, and it was also greatly eased by the coincident adoption of the European Recovery Program by the United States. Under this program the administration was empowered to procure commodities "from any source," with the result that in the early stages a considerable part of British and European needs for food and other bulk goods was filled from Canadian supplies, financed by Marshall Plan dollars. E. R. P. was no long term solution for the problems of Canadian-American trade, because the program soon changed in emphasis and in any event was limited in time, but it did prevent recourse to further harsh restrictions that would have hurt both countries. The basic problem remained.

The other main question in Canadian-American relations in the years immediately after 1945 related to the new configuration of continental defense. It was not many months after the defeat of Germany and Japan that the two mighty victors, the United States and the Soviet Union, began to regard one another as antagonists and then as possible enemies. In this increasingly tense era of the emerging Cold War it was soon clear that Canada occupied a new, strategic, and, potentially, highly dangerous position between the two great opponents. If either attacked the other, it would have to be across her territory; Canada's vast Arctic wastes had become the first line of defense both for herself and for the United States. The Permanent Joint Board on Defense was soon put to work to study the problem in this new light, with the result that early in 1947 an announcement was made stating the principles that would govern continued defense cooperation. It was cautiously made clear that, despite the disparity in power and resources of the two countries, Canada would retain control of all defense installations on its own territory: there would be no American bases in the Canadian north. In the next year or so activity was mainly confined to the building of weather and navigation-aid stations but before the end of 1948 consideration was already being given to the construction of a radar screen. The problem for the Canadian government, at this time as well as later, was to balance the elaborate projects put forward by American military authorities against its own limited capabilities and its decision to retain control of all installations. Clearly, defense cooperation had broader national implications in this new era.

Concern over the consequences of a purely bilateral defense relationship with the United States was one influence governing Canada's attitude toward the most important foreign policy event of this period, the formation of the North Atlantic Treaty Organization. Far more important, however, were other and broader considerations. First among these was the new direction in Canadian foreign policy, forced by the experience of the recent war; the old mood of aloofness was now gone forever. The fullest and most authoritative statements outlining Canada's approach to world affairs came from Louis St. Laurent, who had come into the King cabinet in 1942 to succeed Ernest Lapointe as the government's leading spokesman from Quebec. At the end of 1946 he left the ministry of justice to become the first secretary of state for external affairs to hold that post free of other duties.* In several speeches he made it clear that Canada was prepared to accept international responsibilities and obligations to a far greater degree than had been true of an earlier day. At the same time it had to face the thorny problem of how a "middle power" functioned in a world dominated by great powers. With the return of several important countries to an active role in the world community and the imminent revival of others, Canada ceased to occupy the somewhat inflated position that her part in the war had given her, although she could never again be thought of as a minor entity. Careful consideration had to be given to the framework in which Canada could best function.

For some Canadians, the answer was a simple one: continued cooperation with her associates in the British Commonwealth. But this role did not seem to be sufficient in itself. The Commonwealth was rapidly changing its center of gravity, and if it were to remain a loose organization, on which Canadians insisted, it provided no clear answer to problems of security in a world of competing great powers. Still other Canadians found the answer in the United Nations. But although everyone expressed high hopes for the new world organization it was soon abundantly clear that as long as the great powers were in fundamental

---

*Hitherto the prime minister had always held this portfolio. In 1948 Lester B. Pearson succeeded to this post, and St. Laurent became prime minister upon the retirement of Mackenzie King.

disagreement the U.N. could not be an effective instrument for guaranteeing collective security. In short, despite all the remarkable changes in the postwar world and in Canada's place in it, the greatest need was still the same as before — good relations with the United States and with its friends in western Europe, especially the United Kingdom, combined with concord between the United States and western Europe.

There was, however, a new factor, which was the most immediate and pressing of all, the question of national security. Canadians were less ready than Americans to see the Soviet Union as an expansionist power driven by unlimited ambitions, nor were they so exercised by the dangers of international communism. Nevertheless, in 1947 there was growing alarm over a number of Soviet actions and a great sense of shock when the communists took over Czechoslovakia in February 1948. Soon after this last event Canadian leaders, particularly St. Laurent and Pearson, began to warn that if the U.N. continued to be hamstrung by the veto some other approach to the problem of security would have to be found. There was, of course, the bilateral association with the United States, but it by itself left Canada to deal alone with its friendly but mammoth neighbor. Besides, this arrangement provided no answer for Canada's friends in western Europe.

As 1948 wore on, St. Laurent and Pearson came out more and more explicitly for a North Atlantic regional system. They were perhaps the first prominent western leaders to adumbrate the idea, but this is not to claim that they invented it. It was in everybody's minds. The way had been prepared by the Marshall Plan, because economic recovery and political security went hand in hand. The coming together of the Marshall Plan countries in the Brussels Treaty was an essential first step, although no further progress would have been made without a positive American response. Canada's role was thus limited, but it was consistently employed toward the goal of bringing the two North American countries into a close and binding association with the

Brussels Treaty countries. It was the view of James Reston of the *New York Times* that Canada's part in the negotiation of NATO strengthened American support for a project which, without Canada, would have worn the aspect of merely another plan for aiding Europe. Instead, it appeared as a framework for the protection and strengthening of North Atlantic civilization.

Canada's support of NATO was so strong that she was the first signatory to complete the ratification procedure after a unanimous approval by Parliament. There were some people in the country who saw it as a military pact, sponsored by the Pentagon, that would lead to an intensification of the Cold War. But the prevailing view was that, although a military pact was justified in the circumstances, NATO was, or would become, much more than that. It would be a means of drawing together the North Atlantic countries, sharing common political and cultural traditions, into a closer and more fruitful association. For instance, Canadian delegates had been instrumental in securing the inclusion of Article II, which pledged the members to economic cooperation, and Canadian leaders regularly emphasized the nonmilitary aspects of NATO. It cannot be said, however, that the Canadian interpretation of NATO gained much support from other members, who felt more immediately threatened by Soviet military power.

Canada, then, regarded NATO not only as an important supplement to her membership in the Commonwealth and the U.N. but as an effective guarantee of the continuance of both her North American and her European associations. In return she accepted, as did the United States, the most binding military commitment in her history. Her role in relation to Europe had immensely broadened. In relation to the rest of the world, however, it had not as yet changed significantly.

The eight years following the adoption of the NATO pact provided a full and at times a severe test of the Canadian-American partnership in continental and in world affairs that had been fashioned in the previous decade. Rapid growth in each country led to an increase in the number and magnitude of bilateral contacts of all kinds; the task of managing North American affairs became more complicated and more demanding. Of equal consequence was the fact that the two nations had to learn to develop policies, not only for Europe where their common interest was obvious, but also for other parts of the world, particularly the Far East and the Middle East, in respect to which there was no background of similar outlook. Lastly, this new atmosphere of intimate cooperation had to be maintained after each country had seen the defeat of a political party long in power and the accession of a new administration or government apparently pledged to a certain change of emphasis in its country's foreign policy; on the Canadian side this political change did not come until 1957.

The period began with the Korean War and ended with the Suez crisis; in between came the strenuous effort of the Eisenhower administration to reorganize and enlarge the alliance against world communism and at the same time to find a new military strategy for the global struggle. It is against the background of these immense events that the course of Canadian-American affairs in these years must be seen. Canada's neighbor was no longer simply a rich and powerful country; it was a world force of a new magnitude. Living beside such a force might be exhilarating; it was also exhausting, even, at times, alarming.

The Korean War, which broke out with shattering ferocity in June 1950, required Canada to concern itself with the Far East to an extent that was entirely new. The United States had had trading contacts with Asia reaching back to the 1780's, had acquired island possessions in the Pacific, had developed a sense of obligation respecting the territorial integrity of China, and had fought a long and often savage war with Japan, where Americans had remained to organize a vast school in democracy. Canada, on the other hand, had always looked the other way, toward Europe; apart from missionary activities, contacts with Asia had been few and trade little, and Canada had taken only a minor part in the Pacific War of 1941-1945. The two countries had adopted similar measures to exclude Oriental immigrants, and both of them had uprooted Japanese residents during the war; otherwise, they had little in common in their attitudes toward the Far East. When the Chinese Civil War ended in victory for the communist forces in 1949, the Canadian government indicated that diplomatic recognition would follow, when it was clear that the Peking regime was in effective control of the country. There was little grasp in Canada of the traumatic effect upon the American mind of the accession in China of an anti-American government. Indeed, there was often a strong feeling of bewilderment to learn that some Americans felt that other Americans were responsible for so vast an outcome many thousands of miles away. Thus, Canada's psychological preparation for the Korean War was considerably different from that of its neighbor.

In the first stages of the Korean crisis, Canada's role was, necessarily, a passive one, because it was not a member of the Security Council and had no forces in the Far East. There was general approval of the Council's resolutions calling, first, for a cessation of hostilities and then, two days later, for the members of the U.N. to come to the assistance of the Republic of Korea. Canada had no direct national interest in the region, and there was some disposition to feel that the United States had acted in advance of a mandate from the Council. In particular, there was uneasiness over President Truman's order to the Seventh Fleet to provide protection to Taiwan, which seemed to involve the U.N. action in the American controversy over China policy. But such reservations were minor in the face of the general view that the president's support of Korea was courageous and deserved full Canadian support. It was widely believed that the very survival of the U.N. was at stake and that Canada must now help to demonstrate that the world organization could be effective. In short, Canada must take its part in a collective policy action to repel the aggressive attack upon South Korea. This action did not have larger objectives. Following the allocation of naval and air transport units to the U.N. command, the Canadian government announced in August that it would raise a special force, in the form of an infantry brigade, to be put at the disposal of the U.N. for use in Korea or, if necessary, elsewhere. The government hoped that this step would encourage other countries to similar action, to the end that the U.N. would be provided with a force in being to back up its efforts to keep the peace.

But long before Canadian troops appeared on the Korean battlefront (in February 1951) the "police action" had threatened to grow into a major war involving all the great powers. In September 1950 the original goal of the action had been accomplished when General MacArthur's counteroffensive, including the brilliant Inchon landing, had defeated the North Korean Army and pushed it back beyond the thirty-eighth parallel. There was then a pause during which warnings were heard from the Chinese communists that they would not remain aloof if the offensive was carried toward their border. Nevertheless, the second goal of the U.N. – "the establishment of a unified, independent, and democratic government in the sovereign State of Korea" – was still to be attained. In October the U.N. Assembly approved of the crossing of the parallel, and in a short time MacArthur's troops were approaching the Yalu River. Few western leaders, including apparently the U.S. (and U.N.) commander, had taken the Chinese threat seriously, but before the end of the month U.N. forces were already in contact with units of the Chinese army. By the end of November the complexion of the war had entirely changed, as the U.N. forces struggled to avoid a military debacle in northern Korea. American reaction to these dramatic events was as intense as it was divided. Because the United States was carrying nearly all the burden of the war, which was now producing heavy casualties, there was a strong desire that the troops in the field should be supported in every possible way. President Truman went so far as to indicate that the use of the atomic bomb was under consideration. Other Americans, following General MacArthur's lead, argued that the Chinese "privileged sanctuary" beyond the Yalu must be attacked. The world was suddenly a long way from a limited "police action." Nevertheless, after hard fighting at the beginning of 1951 the line was stabilized roughly along the thirty-eighth parallel, and, with the failure of Chinese spring offensives, the conflict turned into a stalemate. In June of that year began the ceasefire talks which would stretch out exasperatingly over the next two years.

On the official level, Canadian-American relations remained good throughout the course of the Korean War. While striving to follow up or open up whatever possibilities for negotiations that might exist, the Canadian government consistently supported and defended American policy. In the realm of public discussion and debate, however, the tone was often highly critical. To many Canadians, it was by no means clear that the policy of keeping to a limited war was going to prevail; pronouncements by many Americans in high places were considered dangerous and provocative, especially where they related to carrying the war into Manchuria or supporting the ambitions of Chiang Kai-Shek for the invasion of mainland China (to use the contemporary phrase). That is, Canadians were more concerned with what the United States might do than with what it was actually doing. In turn, opinion in many American quarters was not slow to reject these strictures, when there was any awareness of them. There was a widespread feeling that the allies of the United States, including the neighbor to the north, were readier with advice and criticism than they were with military contributions. It was against this background that the Canadian secretary of state for external affairs, Lester B. Pearson, asserted, in a speech of April 10, 1951, that although relations with the United States were growing steadily closer, they would not always be smooth and easy. And he went on : "There will be difficulties and frictions. These, however, will be easier to settle if the United States realizes that while we are most anxious to work with her and support her in the leadership she is giving to the free world, we are not willing to be merely an echo of somebody else's voice. It would be easier also if it were recognized by the United States at this time that we in Canada have had our own experience of tragedy and suffering and loss in war. In our turn, we should be careful not to transfer the suspicions and touchiness and hesitations of yesteryear from London to Washington. . . . We must convince the United States by action rather than merely by word that we are, in fact, pulling our weight on this international team. But this does not mean that we should be told that until we do one twelfth or one sixteenth or some other fraction as much as they are doing in any particular enterprise, we are defaulting. It would also help if the United States took more notice of what we *do* do, and, indeed, occasionally of what we say. It is disconcerting, for example, that about the only time the American people seem to be aware of our existence, in contrast, say to the existence of a Latin American republic, is when we do something that they do not like, or do not do something which they would like." These remarks coming just before the dismissal of General MacArthur, were indeed noticed, and for a few days the undefended border was enlivened by the passage of a goodly number of verbal brickbats in both directions. It was henceforth abundantly clear that far more was involved in Canadian-American relations than the adjustment of bilateral affairs.

The early 1950's were a time of sore frustration for the United States as it adjusted to a burdensome and infinitely complicated role in world affairs. Great efforts were made which seemed to bring little success and little recognition. Although official spokesmen frequently warned that the country and its allies were engaged in a struggle, waged on many levels and many fronts, that might go on for a generation or more, they were speaking to a people whose dominant trait was not generally thought to be patience. For their vast expenditures of blood and treasure, Americans expected tangible results. When these were not forthcoming there was often anger, alarm, or even an almost pathological suspicion. The public temper was not improved by the fact that one political party had been in power for twenty years, and one wing of the opposition was in full cry against the "Truman-Acheson" foreign policy. There were periodic "great debates," which did not cease when the Republicans finally won the 1952 elections under Eisenhower. Senator Joseph McCarthy of Wisconsin appeared to be attracting a wide following by his charges of "twenty years of treason" and by his harassment of prominent members of the new administration. That administration, while firmly committed to a responsible and restrained conduct of policy, sometimes seemed to be reluctant to confront its critics, even the most abusive of them, while it was also looking for more effective, and at the same time cheaper, means of gaining the objectives of American policy. Controversy swirled, and Canadians, who were almost as close to it as Americans, sometimes wondered whether anti-intellectual, militarist, and "go-it-alone" tendencies would gain the upper hand in American life.

These years saw a steady succession of incidents, often individually of relatively minor significance, that helped to sharpen the tone of the Canadian-American discourse; reference to one of them must suffice here. At the beginning of 1954, when Canadian opinion was already disturbed by the efforts of a U.S. Senate subcommittee to extend its investigative activities north of the border, the secretary of state, John Foster Dulles, made an important statement of policy. The new administration, he declared, had determined to scrap the policy of containment of the previous half dozen years; it was unbearably expensive and led to the fighting of unsuccessful local wars all round the perimeter of the communist world. In place of reacting at the edges, the United States would henceforth strike massively at the center. Instead of relying upon ground troops, the president and his advisers had taken the "basic decision ... to depend primarily upon a great capacity to retaliate, instantly, by means and at places of their own choosing." It thus appeared that an important change in strategy had been made without any consultation with the allies of the United States, inside or outside NATO. The new doctrine unleashed another "great debate" reaching into many countries, not least Canada. The most authoritative Canadian response came from Lester Pearson, in a speech at the National Press Club in Washington (March 15), in which he referred to a Canadian feeling that their destiny might "be decided, not by ourselves, but across our border 'by means and at places *not* of our choosing,' to adapt a famous phrase. This accounts for much of the uneasiness that enters into the minds of Canadians as they look south, and realize that they are quite unable to escape the consequences of what you do — or don't do. It induces on our part an 'agonizing reappraisal' of the glory and the grandeur of independence!" The uneasiness of Canadians and others in the alliance died down when subsequent statements by the secretary of state pretty well interpreted the doctrine of massive retaliation out of existence.

The incident suggested that Canada had a part to play in the alliance as both a frank critic and a firm friend. In the second capacity, Prime Minister St. Laurent used the occasion of a visit to the Far East at this same time to state to the Indian Parliament that the United States was the most unselfish major power in history and that the Canadian-American relation was proof that no country need fear the consequences of close association with the United States. Shortly afterward, at the Geneva Conference on Indo-China, Pearson took the same line when he responded to communist charges by saying: "As the leader of the delegation of a country which is a neighbor of the most powerful state in the world, I can say with a conviction based on our national experience that the people of the United States are neither aggressive nor imperalist; and it is the people of the United States that freely elect their governments. . . . Our own experience of free partnership and co-operation shows the rest of the world how little it has to fear from this so-called 'aggressive imperialism' of the United States."

In other statements of this period Canadian government leaders tried to explain the course of their country in North American and world affairs. On the one hand it was stressed that Canada was irrevocably associated with the United States. There could be no question of neutrality for Canada if the United States were engaged in a major war, nor was it realistic to think of the Commonwealth or any grouping of "neutralist" nations as a Third Force, an idea that attracted many at the time. On the other hand, this association did not mean that Canada subscribed to, or was committed to, all aspects of American policy, for instance, those relating to Taiwan or the off-shore islands (Quemoy and Matsu). Yet, because Canada would be affected by the consequences of that policy, it had a right to comment or criticize. Such comments should be constructive and responsible, not carping and unbalanced. In such wise Canadians sought to adjust to the era of Eisenhower and Dulles, although the secretary of state continued to have a bad press in Canada. Many Canadians, perhaps most, instinctively felt that relations with the United States were better when the Democrats were in power in Washington, but the president was well liked and most of his senior advisers were respected. Besides, the Democrats regained control of Congress in the 1954 midterm elections, a result which Canadians, probably oversimply, took to be an assurance against undesirable trade and other economic legislation. The decline of "McCarthyism" removed another irritant. By 1955 there was less asperity in the Canadian-American interchange than in the years immediately preceding.

American voters in 1952 had concluded that it was time for a change, but Canadian voters were slower to follow suit. The Liberal party, which had been in power since 1935, continued its unbroken record of political success. After Mackenzie King ended his record tenure as prime minister, Louis St. Laurent led the party to a smashing electoral success in 1949 and then in 1953 added another victory to the long string. The Liberal party seemed to be so unbeatable that Canadian politics took on an almost suffocating dullness, in contrast to the lively scene in the United States. Indeed, in these years, Canadians seemed to follow American politics more closely than their own.

Of many advantages enjoyed by the Liberals, not the least was the personality of the prime minister. Half Irish, half French-Canadian and perfectly bilingual, St. Laurent was at the same time a courteous gentleman and a firm and competent administrator. Although sufficiently attractive to the general public to be known popularly as "Uncle Louie" he was also a strong and effective leader. On the other hand, the leading opposition party, now known as the Progressive Conservatives, was led by George Drew, who was unable to build up much confidence outside his native Ontario. Also, non-Liberal votes were shared with the Co-operative Commonwealth Federation and the Social Credit party. With half or less than half of the popular vote, the middle-of-the-road Liberals could win large majorities in the House of Commons. They had passed enough social legislation to attract much support among voters of a vaguely leftist tinge, their competent administration gained the confidence of the business community, and their hold on Quebec remained solid. Moreover, the economy was expanding rapidly, the employment level was high, and there were no downturns in the business cycle. It was perhaps not surprising that some Liberal leaders appeared to give the impression that they had a God-given right to rule Canada indefinitely.

Some signs of this attitude appeared in 1956 in connection with the notorious pipeline affair. In its origins this enterprise was in the best Canadian tradition, that of government assistance in the building of transcontinental transport and communications facilities. Just as such assistance had been necessary to build railroads, airlines, and a broadcasting network, so it was needed

to ensure the movement of natural gas from Alberta and Saskatchewan fields to the large eastern markets. Nor was it unprecedented that American capital and technological skill should play
a part. Accordingly, early in 1956, the government made an
arrangement with Trans-Canada Pipe Lines Limited, an Ameri-
can-financed company, by which it would build a pipeline
eastward from the Manitoba-Ontario border and would lend to
the company ninety percent of the cost of building the line in the
west. Although the terms appeared to be overgenerous, it was
considered that they were essential to the early completion of
this expensive but vital national project.

The legislation embodying this plan was prepared and introduced by the man who was generally regarded as the ablest
member of the government, at least in his own field of economic
development. Clarence Decatur Howe, an American by birth
and a graduate of the Massachusetts Institute of Technology, had
been a member of the government for twenty years; during the
war and postwar years he had been the organizing and driving
genius behind Canada's rapid industrial expansion. But he had
never shown much patience with parliamentary processes. In his
zeal for action he had often pushed his projects ahead with little
apparent regard for the feelings of the members of the Commons.
Now, in 1956, he was determined that his pipeline bill be given
early passage in order that full use might be made of the
approaching construction season. At the first sign of delaying
tactics by the opposition parties Howe insisted that closure be
applied, and the bill was carried through all stages under this
limitation on debate, an unprecedented procedure in Canadian
history. The House was in a constant uproar, as the opposition
charged the government with a ruthless disregard of the rights of
Parliament and with promoting a scheme for the further enrichment of a group of Texas millionaires. The bill was passed and
work on the pipeline began, but a considerable section of the
Canadian voting public was alienated in the process. The incident also sharpened nationalist sensitivities as changes were

rung on the theme of American economic domination of Canada. To many, the Liberals appeared not only as a submissive partner of the United States in foreign affairs but as a meek handmaiden of American interests in the economic realm.

Nationalist concern also focused on the possible implications of continental defense measures. At the beginning of the 1950's it was decided that radar warning fences must be constructed to give advance notice in the event of a Soviet manned-bomber attack. The first of these—the Pinetree line, stretching roughly along the international border and jointly financed—was substantially in place by 1954. Before this time, however, it had been agreed that Canada would build and pay for a second line—the Mid-Canada, along the fifty-fifth parallel—and that the United States would take responsibility for a far more costly Arctic system—the Distant Early Warning (DEW) line. The DEW line was truly a mammoth project, but the United States undertook it as a "crash" program, leading to immense activity in the far north. Although the agreement itself carefully safeguarded Canadian interests, there were soon stories and rumors to the effect that the American military were in effective control of the north of the continent. By 1957, as the lines were completed and Canadian personnel took over most of the tasks of operation, this concern tended to disappear.

Other issues of the 1950's, which confirmed Pearson's remark that Canadian-American relations inevitably involved "difficulties and frictions," must be reserved for topical treatment in later chapters. At this point we must return to the major theme of the impact of world affairs on the relations of the two countries, in this instance, the Suez crisis at the end of 1956.

Like the Far East before the Korean War, the Middle East before the Suez crisis was an area with which Canada had hitherto been little concerned. For a half dozen years it had been represented on the U.N. truce-supervision organization, which was trying to prevent hostilities on the border between Israel and its Arab neighbors, but Canada's direct interest in the region was limited. There was a certain instinctive tendency to be sympathetic to Great Britain's concern to ensure the flow of oil from the Middle East and to protect her "lifeline" from the Mediterranean to the Indian Ocean. There was also a strong inclination to be critical of Colonel Nasser's moves to take over the Suez Canal and to be dubious about the role played by Secretary of State John Foster Dulles in the complicated and protracted negotiations of the summer of 1956. But many topics were competing for attention at this time, not least of them the American electoral campaign. In consequence, the attack on Egypt, at the end of October 1956, by Israel and then by Great Britain and France, burst like a thunderclap upon the Canadian public, coinciding as it did with the terrible events in Hungary.

The crisis was, of course, the worst possible kind for Canada, because it involved a clear rift between Britain and France on the one hand and the United States on the other and the possibility of having to be in opposition to one or the other. For several days the Canadian government was silent, and then, on November 4, Prime Minister St. Laurent restricted himself to a statement regretting "that at a time when the United Nations Security Council was seized of the matter the United Kingdom and France felt it necessary to intervene with force on their own responsibility." The Progressive Conservative opposition, which felt that Great Britain had been more sinned against than sinning, set up a barrage of criticism against the government's aloof attitude, which stung St. Laurent into saying that he had been "scandalized" by the actions of the "supermen of Europe" and Pearson into asserting that Canada would no longer be "a colonial chore-boy running around shouting 'ready, aye ready.' " He went on, however, to say that instead of "gratuitous condemnation," there was a real need for positive action to bring the western allies together again. Press reaction, as in the United States and Great Britain, was sharply divided, but although, many criticisms of the British action were voiced, the tone was often more of sorrow rather than anger, "almost tearful," as the

London *Economist* put it, "like finding a beloved uncle arrested for rape."

While the acrimonius debate continued, L. B. Pearson was playing a leading part in the intense diplomatic activity going on behind the scenes at U.N. headquarters. After consultations with Prime Minister Nehru of India, the Canadian secretary of state for external affairs succeeded in winning assembly approval for his proposal that a United Nations Emergency Force should be formed to police the zone of conflict. It was perhaps the most brilliant demonstration in Canadian history of the exercise of the role of "interpreter," now played on a much wider stage; Canada sought not only to reconcile British and American differences but to diminish friction between the older members of the Common-wealth and its newer Asian members. It may have been a "one night stand" in view of the improbability of another similar combination of circumstances, but it was a valuable contribution at a dangerous time. UNEF was formed, including Canadian units, and it played an essential role until disbanded in 1967. Pearson's efforts were recognized by the award of the Nobel Peace Prize in 1957.

The U.N. settlement did not end the debate, which persisted for many weeks in the Canadian press as proof of how intensely public opinion had been gripped by the crisis. In English-speaking Canada especially, there was a strong tendency to blame American policy in general, and John Foster Dulles in particular, and to find all possible excuses for the British Govern-ment's action. One analyst of the Canadian reaction has des-cribed the criticisms of the United States as "a form of tensional outlet on almost a national scale." Spokesmen for the govern-ment tried to point out that members of the western coalition could no longer successfully undertake independent actions, involving the use of power, unless they had at least the tacit support of the United States. This was still hard doctrine for many Canadians to swallow, and there was a considerable incli-nation to rebuke the Liberals for having "meekly followed the unrealistic position of the United States of America," to use the words of a Progressive Conservative amendment in the House of Commons. Such sentiment had some effect in influencing the outcome of the 1957 Canadian federal election.

One final incident should be noticed, as sharp and emotional as it was brief. At this time a subcommittee of the U.S. Senate named Herbert Norman, Canadian ambassador to Egypt and a noted scholar, as a man who had had connections with the communist movement, despite the fact that he had been cleared by his own government. The Canadian government could protest to the state department, but the department had no control over the actions of Senators. When the news was flashed, early in 1957, that Norman had committed suicide in Cairo, the Canadian public immediately concluded that he had been hounded to death by the senatorial "witch-hunt," and a wave of indignation swept over the country, more intensely anti-American, according to seasoned observers, than anything that had been seen in fifty years. One leading newspaper referred to "that precious friend-ship" as "the most one-sided love affair in international history" after President Eisenhower had used noncommittal language in commenting on the incident. Many in Canada felt that their government could have acted more effectively throughout the affair.

Thus, by the time of the political campaign preceding the June 10, 1957, federal election Canadian-American relations were flavored by a certain tartness. It would not be accurate to say that "anti-Americanism" had a controlling effect upon the outcome of the election. All Canadian parties warmly advocated close and friendly relations with the United States. As in American elections, voters were influenced by local and domestic issues more than by larger questions. Of overriding concern for many of them was the fact that the Liberals had been in office for twenty-two consecutive years and that at long last it was indeed "time for a change." Many voters did not believe that the Liber-als could or should actually be beaten, but that they should be chastened by a strengthening of the opposition. Nevertheless, there was some undercurrent of feeling that the government had tended to be pliant in its relations with the United States, and this feeling probably influenced some votes.

The results of the election surprised observers, including the pollsters. Indeed, many people, whatever their political preferences, were cheered to find that some element of unpredictability still remained in the voters, as Americans had discovered in the presidential election of 1948. The Liberals suffered heavy losses, including the defeat of C. D. Howe and eight other cabinet ministers. They came out of the elections with fewer seats that the Progressive Conservatives, who made astounding gains in the west, where they had never been strong before, and who also did very well in Ontario. Yet the minor parties (C.C.F. and Social Credit) and independent candidates had won nearly fifty seats, with the result that the Progressive Conservatives, under their new leader, John Diefenbaker, would not have a clear majority in the new parliament. The electorate had rebuked the Liberals, but had not given its full confidence to the main opposition party. For the first time in a long generation Canada faced the prospect of minority government. It was clear that the electorate would soon have to be consulted again.

17 A Troubled Passage, 1957-1967

The decade after 1957 found Canadians in an uncertain and occasionally in a troubled mood. Some of the high promise of the postwar period appeared to be going sour. The economy, always extremely vulnerable to outside influences, was sharply buffeted by unemployment and by a threat to the dollar before recovery resumed. National unity was so severely strained that many dispassionate observers believed that the country was in danger of breaking up or of turning into a weak and ineffective confederation. Federal politics were marked by wild and erratic swings, ranging from minority government through a period of almost one-party rule back to minority government, and exhibiting a quarreling Parliament and a management of affairs that was often hesitant and incompetent. On the international scene hopes for a respected and effective role as a "middle power" were frequently disappointed as world alignments rapidly altered and the implications of the alliance with the United States were pondered. Finally, despite vigorous efforts to encourage the growth of a Canadian sense of identity and to limit the impact of American influences, there was a widespread feeling that these efforts were both ineffective and lacking in public support. Many another country would gladly have exchanged its own worries for these that were preoccupying Canadians; moreover, in the latter 1960's the problems were in better perspective than they had been a few years earlier. Nevertheless, because such questions will have a fundamental effect on the future of Canada, they deserve to be briefly outlined here before receiving fuller topical treatment in the concluding chapters.

In federal politics, the period had begun with a crushing reversal of the fortunes of the major parties. The Progressive Conservatives, after being out of power for twenty-two consecutive years, had won the largest number of seats in 1957, although, as we have seen, they did not have a majority in the House of Commons; in fact, they had received fewer popular votes than the Liberals. It was soon apparent, however, that there was a growing disposition in the country to give the new men in office in Ottawa a genuine opportunity to govern. The prime minister, John Diefenbaker, was capable of an orotund eloquence that struck some sophisticated city-dwellers as rather old-fashioned but which nevertheless had for a time a wide appeal. His call for a strengthening of trade and other ties with Great Britain and the Commonwealth and a lessening of dependence upon the United States struck a responsive chord, as did his glowing "vision" of a brilliant future for Canada in the North. By the time a second election was held in 1958, less than a year later, something very close to a band-wagon psychology was building up, which was focused more upon Mr. Diefenbaker than upon his party. Indeed, some observers professed to see a kind of "presidential" element coming into Canadian politics, as people voted according to their view of the merits of the party leaders rather than for the party or the local candidate. Moreover, the Liberals were in some disarray, not yet consolidated behind their new leader, Lester Pearson, and out of office in every provincial government except Newfoundland. Above all, there was the feeling that effective government must be restored by giving one party a clear majority. This was done; but perhaps the voters overcorrected. At any rate, Diefenbaker was given the largest parliamentary majority in Canadian history: two hundred and eight seats in a house of two hundred and sixty-five. The Liberals were reduced to forty-nine members, the C.C.F. to a remnant of eight, and Social Credit wiped out altogether. No leader had ever been given a stronger mandate; even with normal attrition, the Conservatives might expect to remain in power for many years to come. Yet seldom has a government fallen from the heights as quickly as this one.

One explanation for the fall derives from the long years of opposition that had gone before. Like the Republicans in the United States after 1953, the Conservatives found it hard to adjust to the responsibilities of office; instinctively, they were more at home when attacking a government than when administering one. Moreover, they had difficulty in retaining support in the populous central region of the country, especially in Quebec. In 1958 the Conservatives picked up fifty out of seventy-five seats in that province, the first time they had gained a majority of Quebec's seats since 1887, but it was not long before they were in trouble. Despite a number of gestures toward French Canada, including adjustments in federal-provincial financing, appointment of General Georges Vanier as governor general, provision of simultaneous translation in Parliament, and some changes respecting bilingualism, and despite the adoption of policies on nuclear weapons and American investment that were potentially popular in Quebec, the Conservatives steadily lost ground. This was partly because Quebec itself was changing so rapidly that the Conservatives always seemed to be one step behind. Moreover, many of the fifty seats won in 1958 were in constituencies where French-Canadian nationalist sentiment was running strong; votes that had been cast against a strong central government could not be retained by the Conservatives once they themselves were firmly in power. Most important, perhaps, was the fact that the Conservative leadership had been without Quebec support for so long that it had decided that the party must learn to do without it and had made calculations for winning elections without it. To be sure, the party did get fifty seats in 1958, but it did not need them to stay in power. Accordingly, the leaders acted, or seemed to act, as if the Quebec seats did not matter, a tendency that was accentuated by the rather indifferent quality of the Conservative members from Quebec.

The situation in Ontario was better, but it, too, deteriorated steadily. An increase of unemployment alarmed many voters among the industrial workers, and urban dwellers generally gained the impression that the government was not very responsive to their problems. Of particular significance to a Conservative party was the fact that the government's conduct of affairs steadily lost it the confidence of influential business and financial groups; the drop in their contributions to the party's campaign chests would prove to be a powerful blow. Indeed, as time went on, the impression spread that Diefenbaker, a prairie lawyer himself, was leading a Canadian version of a populist party, with its surest support in the West and, to a lesser extent, in the Maritime Provinces. These two regions, often slighted by earlier governments, deserved the increased attention which they now received. But when the politically powerful central provinces felt alienated, there were danger signals ahead.

Many factors influenced this shifting of the political balance in the years after 1958, but two of them are of particular importance in the context of Canadian-American relations. One of these is the large question of foreign and defense policy, and the other is the almost equally large theme of trade and financial policy.

The Diefenbaker government had no intention of making any substantial changes in the external policies which it inherited. Despite an occasional charge in the heat of campaigning that the Liberals had been too meek toward the Americans and despite a genuine desire for closer relations with the United Kingdom, the Conservatives were fully committed to the Canadian-American alliance and fully prepared to support the United States as the leader of the western powers in world affairs. Nevertheless, for a variety of reasons, some beyond its own control, the Diefenbaker government was to have more difficulty in its relations with Canada's giant neighbor than any other Canadian government of recent times.

Of all the problems, continental defense was for a time the most baffling and intractable. It had been so for several years, as Canada sought to find a role that was worthy of her position as an independent country and that was also within her means. The problem entered a new phase when, in August 1957, the new Conservative government in one of its first major acts joined with the United States in the formation of the North American Air Defense Command (NORAD). In the final agreement, made some nine months later, the two countries agreed to set up an "integrated command" which would have operational control over Canadian and United States air defenses. Headquarters of

NORAD were set up at Colorado Springs, with an American in command and a Canadian as his deputy. The arrangement made for a closer blending of defense strategy and tactics than had ever been achieved during the Second World War. From the beginning a great deal of uneasiness was voiced in Canada, inside and outside the House of Commons, as to whether Canada could ever be anything but a cipher in such an organization. A Canadian–United States Defense Committee, at the cabinet level, was set up as an assurance of close consultation, but Canadian criticism of NORAD did not end. Many were convinced that Canada no longer had any effective voice, civil or military, in decisions relating to air defense, a feeling that was strengthened after much of the country was linked to the Semi-Automatic Ground Environment System (SAGE).

A still greater shock came shortly afterward, in 1959, when the Canadian government decided that it had to scrap the program for building the Arrow (CF–105), an interceptor aircraft on which several hundred million dollars had already been spent. This program, the pride of Canada's small but excellent aircraft industry, had originated some years earlier in an effort to give Canada a limited but genuine role in the production of defense weaponry. When it became apparent, however, that neither the United States nor any other NATO country intended to buy the aircraft, on the ground that it was unsuitable, there was no choice but to close down the program abruptly. A highly skilled team of designers, engineers, and technicians was soon scattered, most of them gravitating to California. In place of the Arrow the Canadian government decided to buy American-made interceptors and missiles (Bomarcs), having concluded that "the independent development of major military systems by Canada" was no longer possible in the new era.

Canada was not the only country being driven to this conclusion, as the example of Great Britain would later show. Nevertheless, the incident was a brutal shock to Canada's pride, and it led to a sharp outcry against the United States, often described as irrational, because the United States was not responsible for the failure of the program, but wounded feelings are seldom assuaged by rational arguments. The important need, however, was to find another way in which Canada could participate in defense production, and this need was recognized in Washington. The result was the negotiation of the Defense Production Sharing Program of 1960, which made it possible for Canadian industries to compete on the same terms as American industries for defense contracts. A good deal of business subsequently rolled in, but it became clear that henceforth Canada would be essentially a helper in these great projects.

One effect of the various controversies over defense policy was a distinct increase of neutralist sentiment in Canada — not a new phenomenon. Throughout the 1950's there had been advocates of the idea that Canada could make its best contribution to world peace by getting out of military alliances and by working with such countries as India for the reconciliation of cold-war differences. A strong impetus behind such feeling had been opposition to certain aspects of American foreign policy — that it placed too much emphasis upon military considerations, that it was unduly rigid respecting the recognition of the communist regime in China, and so on — but by 1960-1961 a sense of futility over Canada's defense role was a further stimulus to neutralism. And other factors played their part. The revelation that a U–2 "spy plane" had been sent across the Soviet Union not long before a projected summit conference in 1960 was thought by some to show that the United States was pursuing a confused if not a provocative course. Many Canadians did not share the growing American concern over the existence of the Castro regime in Cuba, and the abortive "Bay of Pigs" invasion of April 1961 was the subject of much criticism. This strand of opinion was clearly expressed later in the same year when a newly formed political party, the New Democratic Party (which absorbed the old C.C.F.), advocated that Canada leave NORAD and that she should stay in NATO only as long as that organization did not join the "nuclear club."

Neutralist sentiment never claimed more than minority support, because most Canadians did not see any practical alternative to the close military and political association with the United States and western Europe. Such certainly was the view of the Diefenbaker government. Indeed, the prime minister, as in a noted U.N. speech of 1960, excelled as an oratorical critic of the evils of communism. Nevertheless, relations with the government in Washington were not so smooth as they had sometimes been. Part of the explanation appears to have been a bit of bad luck. In May 1961, early in his administration, President Kennedy visited Ottawa, intent upon urging Canada to join the Organization of American States and to increase her aid to India. After one of the meetings an American working paper was inadvertently left behind, and it was passed to Mr. Diefenbaker. It contained a penciled notation, in the president's handwriting, making a somewhat exasperated reference to the prime minister. Easy personal associations did not flower out of such a beginning. Nor did Diefenbaker take it kindly, a year later, when the president singled out the leader of the opposition, L. B. Pearson, for a private talk, on the occasion of a Nobel Prize dinner at the White House. More serious was the fact that there was growing irritation in Washington over the refusal of the Canadian government to take a definite stand on the question of accepting nuclear warheads for Bomarc missiles, a matter that was left hanging for several years.

But before this question became one of public knowledge and public debate, controversies over economic policy occupied the center of the stage for several months. These controversies, although not new, became sharper with the rise of unemployment and the general stagnation that marked the last part of 1959 and the following year. It gradually became obvious that there were two widely separated points of view about actions that should be taken to correct this unfortunate condition. One group of spokesmen, including professional economists, labor union leaders, and commercial bankers, argued for a change of monetary and fiscal policy that would lower the Canadian interest rate.

With the Canadian rate higher than the American, Canadian borrowers were obtaining funds in the United States markets and then converting their borrowings into Canadian funds to carry out projects in Canada. This action increased the demand for Canadian dollars, which were at a premium relative to American dollars during this period. But with the Canadian dollar at a premium, exports declined, imports rose, and unemployment resulted. On the other side of the controversy was the governor of the Bank of Canada, James Coyne, whose views were also supported in some newspapers. He argued that short-term unemployment was less serious than the question of foreign control of the Canadian economy. He advocated measures that would stem the inflow of American capital (which was being sharply stimulated by the "tight money" policy of the Bank), reduce consumer spending, and increase savings to be invested in Canadian enterprises. If necessary, tariffs should be raised to protect exposed sectors of the economy.

For many months, while the debate raged, it was not clear whether the government favored one side or the other. In December 1960, the minister of finance's supplementary budget seemed to indicate support of Coyne, because it contained a measure aimed at reducing the capital inflow. Nevertheless, Coyne continued to sound warnings against inflation that might come from driving down interest rates and against relying upon outside capital. Despite the government's apparent support of his position, it became obvious early in 1961 that the minister of finance, Donald Fleming, felt embarrassed by Coyne's continued pronouncements, which were providing political ammunition to the opposition. Coyne stopped making speeches, but the tension between him and Fleming became sharper until it grew into an open quarrel, with the minister of finance demanding the resignation of the governor of the Bank and being met by a flat refusal. In the upshot, the debate over economic policy became sidetracked as the country witnessed what has been called "one of the most incredible public brawls in Canadian political history." Coyne eventually resigned, but not before the government gave the impression of acting in both a vindictive and a blundering manner.

A brooding uneasiness continued to pervade the economic scene in the following year. Although there was an upturn in the business cycle, many observers felt that it might prove to be temporary. Budgetary deficits and a deficit in the balance of payments alarmed the financial community, which was clearly losing confidence in the government. There was much uncertainty about Canada's current and future trade position. Diefenbaker voiced strong opposition to Great Britain's entry into the European Common Market, but had no concrete alternative proposals for increasing Commonwealth trade. He succeeded in infuriating the British government as no Canadian prime minister has done in modern times. Nor did the Canadian government respond positively to President Kennedy's plans for expanding world trade, when these were advanced early in 1962. Admittedly, it was extremely difficult for Canada to find a satisfactory policy for dealing with such giants as the United States and the Common Market, but the Conservative government's approach seemed to be both negative and floundering. By the spring of 1962, just as an election was being called, it was clear that confidence in the Canadian dollar was waning. The government was having increasing difficulty in maintaining it at a discount of about five cents on the American dollar,* and at the beginning of May, after the campaign had started, Fleming gave up the attempt to maintain a floating rate, and pegged the dollar at ninety-two and a half cents in terms of the U.S. dollar. This was a sound financial move, but coming when it did, and after repeated denials that the step would be taken, it was made to appear as another instance of bungling and mismanagement, and a blow to Canadian prestige.

---

*The Canadian dollar had been at a premium in relation to the American dollar during most of the previous decade.

The stage was thus set for a campaign that had some similarities to the American election of 1960 when John Kennedy accused the Republican administration of indecisive leadership, of allowing the country's prestige to decline, and of letting the economy stagnate. In fact the Liberals used Theodore H. White's *The Making of the President 1960* as a kind of textbook from which to cull pointers on the way to win elections in the North America of the 1960's. There was much talk about the need to "get the economy moving again," for more imaginative policies, and for drawing on the best brains in the country.

These tactics were partly successful for the Liberals, who doubled the number of their seats (from forty-nine to one hundred) while the Conservatives saw their contingent almost cut in half (from two hundred and eight to one hundred and sixteen). But the country again had a minority government. Each of the smaller parties had made gains, with the New Democrats going from eight to nineteen and Social Credit achieving the most astounding result, going from zero to thirty. The Conservatives had lost the confidence of the majority of the voters, but the Liberals had not gained it. The results were thus as close as those in the 1960 American election, but the parliamentary system did not give the government as secure a grant of power as the president received after a hair's-breadth result.

During the election campaign the Canadian dollar was under steady and mounting pressure. Speculators were betting that the exchange rate could not be maintained at ninety-two and a half cents. Gold and foreign-exchange reserves went down alarmingly as strenuous efforts were made to restore confidence. The return of a minority government was the final blow, and a week after the election the prime minister was driven to the necessity of announcing drastic "austerity" measures aimed at reducing imports, conserving foreign exchange, and reducing government expenditures. In addition, the government secured very large credits from outside sources, mainly from the United States. The crisis was ended, but many observers were profoundly discouraged by the episode. A step away from freer trade had been taken, the government's freedom to use fiscal policy to encourage economic growth had been limited, and, above all, although the United States had been most generous and understanding at the height of the emergency, the terms of the settlement involved yet another servitude to the rich and powerful neighbor. However, buoyant economic conditions in the following months made it possible to concentrate on increasing prosperity rather than on the national implications of the exchange crisis. It became preferable to argue that the two economies were "interdependent."

With the easing of the financial crisis, the defense issue again took the spotlight. It had received relatively little attention in the election campaign partly because the government's position was so foggy that it was difficult to attack and partly because the main opposition group, the Liberals, were equally undecided and uncertain. Some four years had gone by since the government had agreed with the United States to accept Bomarc missiles, and in the interval other arrangements had been made to procure American-made interceptors, strike-reconnaissance aircraft, and Honest John rockets for the use of Canada's NORAD and NATO forces. These weapons were fully effective only if they were equipped with nuclear warheads or ammunition. In 1961-1962 two Bomarc sites were constructed in Ontario and Quebec. Nevertheless, by the end of 1962 a decision had still not been taken to provide these weapons with nuclear armament. From time to time Diefenbaker stated that if war came the nuclear armament would be acquired immediately, but it was not hard to make the reply that the nature of modern war would leave no time for such a step. American authorities maintained an outward silence on the subject, but stories frequently emanated from Washington indicating bafflement, if not impatience, at Canadian indecision.

It was also clear, both before and after the 1962 election, that a tug-of-war was going on within the Canadian cabinet. On the one hand, Minister of National Defence Douglas Harkness believed that Canadian forces should have the most effective equipment for any combat role that they might have to assume, either in North America or in Europe. Canada could not be a weak link in the western alliance. On the other hand, Secretary of State for External Affairs Howard Green opposed any step that would appear to enlarge the "nuclear club" at a time when intensive disarmament discussions were under way. Possibly Canada could play a useful and constructive role in these discussions, but its political and moral position would be undercut if it became a "nuclear power." It was clear that Green, who was the oldest and closest political friend of the prime minister, had Diefenbaker's ear.

There were other considerations. A good deal of military opinion, voiced mainly by retired officers, held that it was an utter farce for a country like Canada to spend money on a nuclear role: far better to make a distinctive and useful contribution by building up effective and well-equipped conventional forces. Much scorn was also heaped on the Bomarc by many commentators who took delight in quoting American officials on the uselessness of this weapon, especially against missiles. A great deal of debate also centered on the question of the custody of the weapons. American law required that this remain in American hands, a fact that seemed to many Canadians to promise a kind of satellite status for their country, a feeling that was by no means removed by American assurances that a "two-key" procedure could be worked out.

Many other points were made on both sides of a debate which was still unresolved when the great crisis over the Soviet missile bases in Cuba suddenly erupted in October 1962, widely regarded as the most dangerous United States–Soviet confrontation since the end of the Second World War. The crisis helped to bring the Canadian defense dilemma to a head. There was some criticism of President Kennedy's conduct of the affair on the ground that he acted hastily and without adequate consultation with his allies, including Canada. But this was a minority view. The prevailing response was highly favorable to the president, who was henceforth seen as a fearless world leader, restrained, iron-nerved, and resourceful. Kennedy had always been very popular with the Canadian public, but from now on his position was very nearly unchallengeable. One result was to produce a feeling that somehow Canada had not backed the president sufficiently during the crisis. Although Diefenbaker made his explanations, many did not find them convincing. The Canadian people were looking more to the president than to their own prime minister.

The last stages of the controversy came rapidly and with high drama. The year 1963 opened with an Ottawa press conference given by the retiring NATO commander, General Lauris Norstad, who stated that it was his understanding that Canada had committed itself to acquire nuclear warheads, and a few days later, in Washington, he indicated that NATO would suffer if Canada's forces remained nonnuclear. Less than a week later, on January 12, the Liberal leader, Lester Pearson, finally made up his mind on the subject by stating that, because a commitment had been made to accept nuclear warheads for defensive tactical weapons, it must be honored. In a parliamentary debate later in the month, Diefenbaker denied that Canada was evading its responsibilities. He said that Canada would cooperate with its allies, "but she will not be a pawn nor be pushed around by other nations to do those things which, in the opinion of the Canadian people, are not in keeping with her sovereignty." Moreover, with rapid changes in strategic thinking taking place, this was no time to adopt hardened positions. Finally, he revealed that negotiations had "been going on quite forcibly . . . for two or three months . . . so that . . . in case of need nuclear warheads will be made readily available."

This speech was apparently the last straw, as far as the American government was concerned. It drew from the state department on January 30, a statement, released to the press at the same time that it was delivered to Canadian authorities, which contained the bluntest rebuke to a Canadian prime minister ever made by the United States government. In icy language of the kind usually reserved for communications with communist countries, the statement declared that "the Canadian Government has not as yet proposed any arrangement sufficiently practical to contribute effectively to North American defense," and it directly contradicted certain assertions made by the prime minister. The statement was clearly an implementation of a point made more than once by President Kennedy in the previous year: while it was bearing the burdens of world leadership, the United States had a right to expect, and to take steps to secure, the active cooperation of its allies.

In this instance, the state department's pronouncement was highly effective. To be sure, there was a loud verbal reaction in Canada, in which all political parties joined, against what Diefenbaker called "an unwarranted intrusion" in Canadian affairs, but there was also an immediate crisis within the ranks of the government. Many factors entered into this crisis apart from the defense issue, because there had been growing dissatisfaction with the prime minister on many counts. In the weekend following January 30, an attempt was made by several members of the cabinet to force Diefenbaker's resignation, but it failed; instead the minister of national defence, Douglas Harkness, resigned. On February 5, the opposition parties united behind a want-of-confidence motion, and the minority Conservative government was defeated in the House of Commons, the second time that this had happened since Confederation in 1867. For the fourth time in six years the country faced a general election. And there was more drama to come, although most of it took place behind closed doors. The cabinet was still intent upon deposing the prime minister, who was now more than ever regarded as a political liability, in order that the party could be re-formed to present a united front to the voters. The confrontation took place in a Conservative party caucus, at which one cabinet minister spoke against Diefenbaker's "anti-nuclear and anti-American attitude" and others voiced their discontent in various ways. But

Diefenbaker, the most skillful and tenacious political in-fighter of his generation in Canadian politics, had the back-benchers solidly behind him, and he both routed and humiliated the rebels. Two more ministers soon resigned, and three others decided not to run again. With leading Conservative newspapers deserting him and the business and financial community in open opposition, Mr. Diefenbaker moved into the campaign asserting that everyone was against him but the people and that the Liberals were getting their orders from across the border.

In fact, however, "anti-Americanism" played a much smaller part in the campaign than many people expected. For one thing, it was quite impossible to run against President Kennedy, given his popularity in Canada. Nor, despite the fact that it had precipi-tated the election, did the defense question wholly dominate the political jousting. There was too much opposition to nuclear weapons in the country, particularly in Quebec, where the Liber-als had to make gains, for Pearson to give heavy stress to this issue. Instead, the Liberal campaign pitch was on the need for stable government, the restoration of confidence, and the strengthening of national unity. In view of the defections from the Conservative cause, the Liberals believed that this ap-proach would gain them the victory. Nevertheless, the results of the April 8, 1963, election proved to be much closer than had seemed possible at the beginning of the campaign. Conservative strength held firm on the Prairies and to a lesser extent in the Maritimes. Social Credit support in Quebec fell away somewhat, but this group still managed to take twenty-four seats. In con-sequence, although the Liberals were able to make impressive gains in Ontario and Quebec, they could pick up only a few new seats elsewhere. Their one hundred and twenty-nine seats thus fell just short of a clear majority in a House of two hundred and sixty-five members, and the weary voters could wonder whether the politicians would soon be among them again. As it turned out, however, the minor parties, soon to be three instead of two after a split among the Social Crediters, had no desire to precipitate an early election nor, after a time, did the Conservatives. The Liberal government which Lester Pearson formed after the April election in 1963 thus had a precarious, and yet a durable, existence. In 1965 a misguided attempt to secure a working majority led to a result little different from that of 1963.

At the time of writing, it is too soon to attempt an assessment of this government. An interim balance sheet would show, first, that those who voted Liberal in 1963 in expectation of a return to the competent and efficient administration of the King–St. Laurent era were often disappointed. The Pearson regime was marked, at least in its first three years, by crisis after crisis brought on by haste, sloppiness, and inexperience, not to use the stronger terms preferred by the political opposition. Many observers were also worried by the government's apparent readiness to give way to the demands of the provinces, especially of Quebec, and thus to weaken the central power. On the other hand, those who supported the Liberals in the belief that they would bring about smoother relations with the United States seemed to be justified. The acrimonious defense issue soon disappeared from the headlines. The Bomarcs got their nuclear warheads, but because these weapons were now completely obsolete and because Canadian geography was of rapidly diminishing consequence in American defense calculations, this question lost its importance. Prime Minister Pearson established good personal relations with President Kennedy and, later, for a time at least, with President Johnson. Political and economic cooperation became easier and more intimate, and critics of the Liberals charged that they had taken the easy path that would end in full absorption by the United States. Others felt that the government was unduly nationalistic. Thus Canadians reached the centenary of Confederation still wondering whether the country could be held together and increasingly uncertain whether modern technology and national independence were mutually compatible. But such debates are not truly agonizing in an affluent society.

IV

CANADIAN

ISSUES

AND

PROBLEMS

In no other aspect of life is the American impact on Canada so powerful, continuous, and visible as in the economic realm. Canada is more intimately associated with the American economy than with any other in the world; this association is closer than any one country has had with another in recorded history. Instinctively, many Canadians feel that there must be something dangerous, at least potentially, in such a relationship. This feeling is reinforced by the memory of national policies worked out in the second half of the nineteenth century which seemed to give Canada control over its own economic life, and in a nationalistic mood it is easy to forget that to a large extent these policies were forced upon the country by American protectionism. Their aim was to expand the Canadian economy and at the same time to protect it from penetration from the south. These policies were intended to induce the economy to grow along an east-west axis by developing manufacturing plants in the central provinces to supply the domestic market, by promoting the settlement of the west where wheat could be grown for overseas export, and by building railroads to move products and people back and forth across the country. Because the economy did grow to a large extent along an east-west axis in the years down through the First World War and in fact enjoyed one burst of prosperity before and during that war, it was possible to believe that the national policies, rather than world conditions, had been responsible for that growth and, more than that, to maintain that national distinctiveness depended upon the continuance of the east-west axis. Although it was often pointed out that this economic strategy entailed heavy burdens in the form of transportation and other charges and in the fostering of inefficient enterprises, and that these burdens were very inequitably shared by the various parts of Canada, the reply nevertheless came that these burdens represented the cost of remaining Canadian. The disadvantaged regions were given subsidies from time to time within a framework of patchwork, crazy-quilt, federal-provincial financing, and a large section of the transportation system required constant public support; but the national policies continued to be defended and maintained.

In the last generation, however, the pull of the United States has increasingly distorted the relative simplicity of the older east-west economy. As early as the beginning of the 1920's there was more American than British capital invested in Canada and, a matter of greater importance, it was of a different kind. British investment in Canada, like British investment in the United States in an earlier period, was predominantly in bond money or mortgage money; it did not bring control of business or industry, and in time it was paid off or liquidated. From the beginning, however, American capital was mainly in the form of direct investment for the purpose of acquiring and developing properties and enterprises in Canada. Such investment did not eventually diminish or disappear; on the contrary, it grew steadily, and in certain periods very rapidly. To a considerable extent, American investment represented not so much the desire to secure a profitable return on money as the desire to find favorable opportunities for the exercise of entrepreneurial talent. Very often American companies were concerned to apply technology and organization to the development of Canadian natural resources, with these in turn to be shipped as raw materials for finishing in American plants or to be semiprocessed in Canada before shipping. A second main interest was to reach the Canadian market, otherwise closed by the presence of the protective tariff; this market (and after 1932 the Commonwealth preferential market) could be reached by the device of building branch plants behind the tariff. Thus, one of the national policies, ironically enough, was a strong stimulus to the rise of American-controlled industry in Canada.

While Canadians continued to pay lip service to the desirability of a transcontinental economy, they nevertheless warmly welcomed the growing intimacy with the United States. New natural resources, notably forest products and minerals, were acquiring a position of leading importance, and the main market for them was to the south. Every effort was made to secure American capital and American technical and managerial skill for the development of these resources. Moreover, as Canadian businessmen made their own efforts to diversify and expand the economy, their imports of American goods, particularly machinery, steadily rose. Many factors encouraged the growing continental integration: the rapid growth of the automotive, electronics, and other new industries, in which the United States was the great leader, the relative industrial decline of Great Britain, the American move away from protectionism after 1934, the exposure to American advertising, which led Canadians to want American brands and designs, and the close Canadian-American economic cooperation during the Second World War. For these and other reasons the volume of trade between the two countries grew enormously in the twenty years between the latter 1930's and the latter 1950's; Canadian exports to the United States tripled, and Canadian imports from the United States more than quadrupled. The combined trade between the two countries was by far the greatest bilateral exchange that the world had ever seen. Each was the best customer of the other in a trade that was clearly mutually beneficial.

Nevertheless, because of the great difference in size between the two economies, Canada was much more aware of this trade than was the United States. Canadian exports to the United States had come to comprise sixty percent of all her exports, amounting to twelve per cent of her gross national product, while seventy per cent of her imports came from the United States, a much larger dollar value than the exports, yet amounting to about one percent of the American G.N.P. American trade with Canada, although the largest with any single country, was still not much more than twenty percent of all American trade. Canada thus appeared to have fallen into a state of heavy dependence upon the American market, while Americans seemed to be hardly conscious of the large sales that they were making to the north.

Before the end of the 1950's Canadians were beginning to worry publicly about many features of their economic association with the United States. One concern centered on the nature of the export trade. About three quarters of Canadian exports were in the form of raw or semiprocessed materials, with the most profitable final stages of production being done in the United States and providing employment for American workers. Some of the finished products came back as imports, to be bought by Canadian consumers. Although there was a certain inevitability in this procedure, resulting from the size and efficiency of American industry, Canadians nevertheless pointed to the structure of the U.S. tariff, with its low rates on raw materials and its high rates on finished goods, as an indication that American policy was deliberately keeping the Canadian economy at a primitive level. Some Canadians even took up the old cry that they were hewers of wood and drawers of water, forgetting that the leading export industries relied much more upon a highly efficient and intensive application of advanced technology than they did upon the extensive use of unskilled labor.

A second concern had to do with uncertainties in the American market. Despite the fact that the United States was heavily and in some respects increasingly dependent upon Canadian resources, it usually had alternative sources of supply, both domestic and foreign. It was the domestic that caused Canadians the main trouble, for domestic producers could exert political pressure upon the administration and upon Congress to secure cutbacks in imports. Sometimes limitation was effected by means of tariff changes, but more usually by the imposition of quotas or the alteration of customs regulations. Canadian producers relying mainly on the American market could thus be deeply affected by even a slight change in the political balance at Washington. As a rule, the great primary-resource exports were not touched, although lead and zinc, newsprint, oil and gas, and lumber were some of the products that at one time or another were subject to some sort of limitation. More usually, the ax fell on such items as dairy and fish products and grains, a reflection of the sharp sensitivity of American producers to food and agricultural imports. It should be noted that Canadian representations regarding these restrictions usually received a sympathetic and often a responsive hearing in Washington and that in recent years these restrictions have been fewer in number and importance. It should also be noted that although Canadians often deplored their reliance upon the American market, they were quick to react to any measures that would limit their access to it. For many items there was no alternative that looked very promising.

In making representations to Washington and to American audiences Canadian government and business spokesmen had one strong argument which they never tired of making in scores, if not hundreds, of speeches and messages. It was that in merchandise exchange with the United States Canada bought much more than she was able to sell. She bought more from the United States than did all of Latin America or western Europe. In the 1950's and 1960's Canada ran an annual current-accounts deficit with the United States which was frequently well over a billion dollars. What would Americans think, ran the Canadian refrain, if their country ran a deficit with one country that was the American equivalent of over twenty billion dollars a year? As Americans came to be increasingly concerned with their own balance-of-payments problem, they were naturally sympathetic to the Canadian case, particularly when it could be pointed out that Canadians, through their American dollar payments of various kinds, were helping, not hurting, the American payments balance. Thus Canadians developed the feeling that they had not only an economic but a kind of moral right to a large place in the American market, a view that gained a good deal of acceptance in the United States, particularly by the executive branch.

Given an annual current-accounts deficit of such mammoth size Canada had been able to avoid an overall balance-of-payments deficit (except in one or two years) only by the import of large amounts of American capital. And in fact the years of largest trade deficits were normally also the years of largest American investment in Canada, preventing any real balance-of-payments problem. After 1950 there was only one year of sharp pressure on the Canadian currency — 1962 — and most experts have attributed that crisis to faulty fiscal and monetary policy coinciding with an election campaign. In general, American investment has kept the Canadian dollar so strong that it has frequently shown a tendency to appreciate in value, and since 1962 there has sometimes been doubt whether it was pegged at too low a rate.

But Canadians refuse to be happy about this situation. On the contrary, the high level of American investment in the years after the Second World War has raised another large cluster of worries that has often received highly vocal expression. Many citizens were alarmed to learn that Canada had accumulated the largest foreign indebtedness of any country in the world. What would happen when the obligations fell due, or if the capital were suddenly withdrawn? Was it not immoral, or at least irresponsible, to rely so heavily upon outsiders for the development of the economy? These viewers-with-alarm were not comforted when told that the indebtedness actually bore a smaller relationship to total Canadian assets than it had in the 1920's or that there was no reason to think that the investment would dry up or retreat, unless Canadians took measures to force this result.

A more vivid concern arose from the knowledge that important sectors of the economy had fallen under foreign ownership and control, a result of the American form of direct investment. The recital was lengthy, and it was often repeated. Over half of all Canadian manufacturing plants were owned from the outside: over ninety-five percent of the auto industry, ninety percent of the rubber industry, eighty percent of the chemical industry, seventy percent of the oil, gas, and electrical apparatus industries. The great resource industries were not immune; forty-three percent of the pulp and paper and fifty-two percent of the mining industry were foreign owned. As a leading Canadian businessman pointed out, such a concentration of foreign investment had never been equaled in any other country except where there was a colonial relationship or some dependency status. In fact, some Canadians argued that these last phrases actually described Canada's position: an economic satellite, a branch-plant economy, and a miniature replica of the American industrial giant.

Beyond the general concern over the size of American investment and the extent of American control over strategic sectors of the economy, there were specific complaints about the conduct of American firms in Canada. The great majority of these companies — several thousand of them — were wholly owned by the parent companies in the United States and did not offer stock for sale to Canadian investors. These subsidiaries were said to be restricted in their freedom to seek out foreign or United States markets, to make their own decisions regarding purchases of supplies and materials, and to carry on research in Canada. It was believed that insufficient efforts were made to hire and promote Canadians to senior positions and that American executives, perhaps assigned temporarily in Canada, took little interest in the communities where they resided. Objective surveys indicated that these and other criticisms were often exaggerated or that some of the practices in question were not confined to American subsidiaries; nevertheless, there was sufficient public sentiment on the subject to cause many American firms to engage in programs of "Canadianization."

Moreover, the Canadian government, after repeated expressions of disquiet by its spokesmen over the amount of American ownership in Canada, sought to take action. The most notable attempt came in the budget of 1963 when the minister of finance, Walter Gordon, announced that a suitable objective to work toward would be a twenty-five percent Canadian equity interest in foreign-owned firms, and he proposed tax changes to encourage the achievement of this result. A more drastic measure, announced at the same time, was aimed at preventing nonresident takeovers of established Canadian firms. But this first attempt by Gordon to realize his goals proved to be a dismal fiasco. Under intense criticism from many quarters, he found it necessary to water down his proposals looking to increased Canadian ownership and to withdraw his anti-takeover tax as administratively unworkable. Tension was heightened a few weeks later when President Kennedy sent a special message to Congress proposing an interest-equalization tax to discourage foreign borrowing in the American financial market, in order to protect the American balance-of-payments position. Immediately, there was "consternation in the financial markets of Canada," as Gordon's successor Mitchell Sharp, later put it, because whatever the concern over American direct investment in Canada (unaffected by the president's proposal), there was a continuing need for a flow of American capital into Canada to finance its current-accounts deficit with the United States. Urgent representations from Ottawa were successful, and the United States agreed to exempt new issues of Canadian securities from the tax. For its part Canada agreed that borrowing would be restrained if it led to an increase in Canada's foreign-exchanges reserves. Later, in 1965, when President Johnson announced his various "guideline" programs to limit United States investment abroad and to bring back funds, Canada was again in large part exempted. These incidents dramatically revealed the magnitude and intimacy of Canadian-American financial ties, although some Canadian observers interpreted them as proof of a unique economic dependence: Canada, they asserted, was clamoring for preferences within the American Empire as she had done within the British Empire in earlier years.

But despite Canada's earnest wish for unrestricted access to American capital, the concern over American ownership of Canadian industry also remained. While he was minister of finance, Gordon continued to encourage and promote the achievement of his goal of a twenty-five percent Canadian ownership in American firms to the end that "a Canadian point of view" would be available when company policy decisions were made. To many Canadian observers his program was both misguided and certain to be ineffective. A twenty-five percent ownership would not bring an authentic Canadian voice to an American-owned firm, and it would have the bad effect of siphoning Canadian capital away from new enterprises that would serve to expand the economy. And some analysts argued that there were good economic reasons, not harmful to Canada, why American firms wanted to maintain full ownership of their subsidiaries.

In such terms the rather inconclusive debate over American investment in Canada continues, as it is likely to do for a long time to come. It is perfectly clear that Canada could discourage the inflow, and reverse its direction, by adopting various restrictive and discriminatory measures, for which there is ample precedent elsewhere. As has been noted, Mexico enjoyed a prolonged respite from American investment after its nationalization of foreign oil properties in 1938. But it is also perfectly clear that Canadian authorities have no intention of adopting such measures, even relatively mild ones. One main deterrent is found in the provincial governments, which welcome United States direct investment as a stimulant to natural resources development and which want unrestricted access to the New York money market.

Nevertheless, some kinds of penetration encounter much sharper resistance than others do. Rumors of American financial interest in the press or in radio and television produce swift reaction. Most notable in recent years was the controversy raised by the purchase, in 1963, of the small Dutch-owned Mercantile Bank of Canada by the First National City Bank of New York (Citibank). Canadian officials had long taken the view that Canada's ability to maintain an independent monetary and economic policy, limited though it was, would be destroyed entirely if large American banks were active within the country. Accordingly, the minister of finance introduced an amendment to the Bank Act to limit the further growth of the Mercantile Bank as

long as it remained American owned. In turn, the chairman of
Citibank, James S. Rockefeller, criticized the amendment as
retroactive, and the U.S. state department sent a note to Ottawa
calling it discriminatory. In Congress there was talk of retaliation
against Canadian banks doing business in the United States. The
Canadian government stood firm on the amendment but, early in
1967, agreed to a change in the date of its application to allow
the Mercantile Bank five years' grace before it must sell seventy-
five percent of its shares to Canadians.

On the whole, the signs point to increased integration between
the two economies. A few years ago, when the concept of a
developing northern frontier captured the Canadian imagination,
many thought that this vast region, remote from the United States
and rich in resources, would provide the foundation for a new,
exciting expansion, firmly under Canadian control. It has since
become clear, however, that these northern resources, mainly
mineral, are the very ones that are most in demand in the United
States and that most depend for their exploitation upon inputs of
American capital and technology. Every advance into the Canadian north has strengthened the trend toward continental
economic integration.

More recently, there have been indications of further integration in the domain of secondary industry. Historically, the Canadian manufacturing capacity was built up behind the protective tariff for the purpose of supplying the domestic market. It
has been assumed that, without this protection, most manufacturing plants in Canada could not compete against imports
coming from larger and more efficient American plants or from
European and Asian plants having lower labor costs. Corre-
spondingly, it was not to be expected that high-cost Canadian
manufactured goods could find a very large export market, either
in the United States or elsewhere; in fact they have had a relatively modest place in the figures of items shipped from Canada.
Moreover, as long as the most efficient Canadian production for
export was in the primary-resource field, and as long as Canadian-based manufacturers were relatively sure of the domestic

market, there was little attempt to increase the export of manufactured goods, particularly on the part of American subsidiaries, which existed to exploit the Canadian market.

Nevertheless, the picture has begun to change somewhat. In recent years the protective tariff has been under heavier attack than ever before in Canadian history. It is frequently emphasized that protection lowers the standard of living by costing consumers at least a billion dollars a year, that it pays a premium to economic inefficiency, and that it is inconsistent with the need for economic growth which depends upon access to much larger markets. Historians have even begun to argue that earlier development was achieved in spite of rather than because of the old national policies. A related line of argument has been directed against the highly centralized organization of the Canadian economy, in which most important enterprises sought to be transcontinental under Montreal or Toronto direction. Just as the United States achieved extraordinarily rapid growth in the nineteenth century by stressing decentralized and regional direction of economic activity, so Canada in the latter part of the twentieth century can expand more rapidly by encouraging rather than restraining regional and provincial ambitions for development.

In addition, careful studies indicate that conditions in central Canada, in several lines at least, allow for manufacturing that can be sufficiently efficient to sustain a considerable and growing export trade, given favorable factors in respect of foreign tariffs, the rate of exchange of Canadian currency, and the size and number of Canadian plants. As long ago as 1944 the plunge was taken for one industry, agricultural implements, when the United States and Canada made a free-exchange agreement. The experience of this agreement has not been altogether happy for Canada, because there has been some tendency for the industry to move out of the country; nevertheless, the two-way movement, if not even, has been large and flourishing.

From time to time there has been much speculation on the possiblity of further agreements of this kind, sometimes inspired by the example of the European Economic Community. But the main stimulus has come from the need to find more jobs. Studies conducted by Canadian authorities have revealed that the work force is increasing at an unprecedented rate, faster indeed than in any other industrialized country including the United States. Projections indicated that about twice as many new jobs would have to be provided in the half dozen years down to 1970 as in the previous period of the same length. Moreover, Canadians do not differ from other people of the contemporary era in expecting that the government will take steps to ensure continued economic growth and a rising standard of living. These considerations all point to the need for a very sizable enlargement in the export of manufactured and processed goods, because although most of the new jobs would be in the innumerable service occupations, these in turn would depend upon an enlarged industrial base. The great resource industries need to increase the amount of processing beyond the present scale, and secondary industry must move more actively into foreign markets. Such markets may be found throughout the world, but for many lines the American market provides the only feasible opportunity for considerable expansion. Hence, much economic thought has been concentrating on the necessity for lowering Canadian and American tariffs, even for selective free trade, as well as for the liberalization of world trade generally. If the worldwide effort should run into obstacles, the pressure for freer Canadian-American trade would increase.

Canadians are under no illusions regarding the dangers that such moves might bring. Free trade, even of the most selective kind, might wipe out or cripple industries that have been painfully and slowly built up over the years, and might concentrate industry in central Canada even more than is now the case. Moreover, closer economic integration would mean that basic policies, whether monetary, tax, social, or antitrust, would have to be continental; in effect, they would have to be made in

Washington, for the tail could not wag the dog. How long could Canada retain any real political independence under such conditions? Canadians would much prefer a multilateral approach, looking to a progressive lowering of world trade barriers.

Nevertheless, the insistent pressure for industrial growth has kept the idea of selective free trade with the United States to the fore, leading to an important agreement early in 1965, affecting the automobile industry. This agreement is the most striking move away from traditional national policies ever taken in Canadian history, and the prime minister stated that it might well be the forerunner of others to come. Each country undertook to abolish the tariff on vehicles and parts imported from the other, while the Canadian government stipulated that car manufacturers in Canada would be eligible to make such free imports only if they maintained their production, and its Canadian content, to 1964 levels or better. Thus, in this agreement there was no danger that the Canadian car industry would die out (although some Canadian parts manufacturers might suffer), but there was the distinct probability that in time the industry would undergo intensive reorganization. A high degree of specialization would be necessary if Canadian-made vehicles were to be sold successfully in the United States. Instead of an industry based upon the assembling of two dozen or more models for the small Canadian market, it might become one in which Canadian-based factories concentrated on a few models for the continental market, with all other vehicles sold in Canada coming from American factories. After two years of the agreement Canada had sharply increased its export of automotive products to the United States, with American exports to Canada up by a smaller percentage, but in each country organized labor was suspicious of the pact.

It is too soon to see all the implications of the automobile agreement. Nor can it provide an exact pattern for later developments, because no other industry is organized in the same way. But it does seem probable that the key word in subsequent changes will be specialization. It is not to be expected that, under their present organization, parent companies in the United States will encourage competition with their own operations by countenancing exports from their Canadian subsidiaries into the American market. It has been suggested, however, that companies could reorganize their production in order to concentrate certain lines in Canada and thus make use of advantageous conditions relating to location, materials, and labor. Again, the taxpayers, in the interests of an enlarged industrial base, would have to underwrite some of the costs of retraining. Such a base would be more efficient and more productive than the present one, but it would also be much more fully integrated into the continental economy. There could be no retreat from such steps, and Canadians are understandably apprehensive about the consequences for the independence of their country. It is, however, argued that integration is proceeding in any event, and that it is better for it to be accompanied by firm agreements that improve access to the American market.

There is no prospect of across-the-board free trade between the two countries. Highly complicated farm policies, particularly in the United States, and the political power of agricultural groups would prevent the free exchange of commodities in this area. Other interests, such as certain mineral producers in the United States and textile manufacturers in Canada, would also oppose free-trade schemes. Nevertheless, influential spokesmen in each country frequently join to propose free-trade arrangements, some bilateral, some North Atlantic, and some still broader in scope. Much will depend upon the willingness of large American corporations to ensure to Canadian-based industry a viable role in enlarged markets. Canadian observers also emphasize that much will equally depend upon the ability of Canada to conserve certain advantages relating to exchange rates and materials and to maintain and improve price and wage stability.

Reference to wages leads to some concluding remarks on the place of organized labor in Canadian-American relations. In this realm, as in so many others mentioned in earlier pages, the association is intimate and of long standing, in many instances going back a century or more. About three quarters of Canada's organized workers belong to "international unions," that is, unions that have their headquarters in the United States. There is no parallel for this situation anywhere else in the world. Canadian unions would certainly not be so strong as they are today if they had not had the example and sometimes the active assistance of their American brothers.

It is also true that this close association has been a cause of frequent controversy in Canada. Because American membership in the international unions is so much larger than the Canadian, it has been charged that the Canadian locals are little more than colonial appendages. More than once politicians and business spokesmen on the northern side of the border have beaten the drums against "foreign agitators" who were disturbing the Canadian Eden. It has been argued that the large international unions determine Canadian labor policy, goad Canadian unions into making impossible wage demands, take their dues, and even call strikes from the American headquarters.

In fact, however, there is little truth in these accusations. Some of them come from sources that are basically antiunion in outlook; if the American tie did not provide an opportunity for criticism, some other would be found. More often, the criticisms are based on misunderstanding or lack of information. If investigations in the United States reveal the existence of malpractices in unions, it is assumed that these must extend to the Canadian affiliates, which are, however, fully autonomous and live under a distinct legislative framework. Moreover, strikes are not called by international headquarters; they are called by the locals. Headquarters is more likely to oppose than to encourage the calling of a strike, because a prolonged stoppage will mean the expenditure of large amounts of strike pay. Much more union money has flowed into Canada than out. Furthermore, the social and political outlook of Canadian labor is often quite different from that of American labor. In particular, Canadian unions have been much readier to engage in open political activity, as in their sponsorship of the New Democratic party in 1961. When American labor leaders objected to this activity, their views were bluntly rejected in Canada, notably by the steel union. There is little doubt that Canadian unions are more independent of their American counterparts than is Canadian business of American capital, technology, and skill. Because of similarities in the social and economic scene, Canadian unionists often talk and act like American unionists; undoubtedly they would do so even if there were no formal affiliation.

Still, genuine difficulties may arise, affecting the governments as well as the large labor federations of the two countries. The most notorious instance in recent years has arisen in the area of Great Lakes and coastal shipping. In 1949 the old American Federation of Labor intervened in Canada to destroy the Canadian Seaman's Union, on the grounds that it was communist-dominated and that it was engaging in double unionism. With Canadian assistance, some of it reluctant, the Seafarers International Union became dominant on the Lakes. But the SIU in Canada fell afoul of the Canadian Labor Congress, and in 1959 was expelled from it on charges of raiding and engaging in corrupt and undemocratic practices. The Canadian Maritime Union was established in an attempt to replace the SIU in Canada, while the SIU continued to be a member in good standing of the AFL-CIO in the United States. Then followed a savage battle on the Lakes as the SIU in both countries tried to break the CMU. The Canadian federal government set up an Inquiry Commission, and its revelations of SIU malpractices led to the drastic action of placing all the maritime unions under government trustees for the purpose of uprooting the corrupt leadership of the Canadian SIU. This action was supported by the CLC, but it was strongly opposed by the president of the AFL-CIO, who did not want to offend the American SIU leaders and who sought to put pressure on the American Government to object to the Canadian step. In fact, the American secretary of labor did indicate his displeasure, and the Canadian government in turn officially protested to Washington against harassment of Canadian shipping. The struggle illustrated that labor disputes can affect Canadian-American relations, but it also illustrated that the CLC and Canadian unions are anything but satellites of the American labor movement. The CLC has emerged even more autonomous of the AFL-CIO; equally, the international union ties remain close and enduring.

By the beginning of the 1960's it was apparent that French Canadians, especially those living in Quebec, were becoming increasingly dissatisfied with their status and condition in the country and insistent that major readjustments should be made. In 1963 the federal government was sufficiently impressed by this dissatisfaction to appoint a royal commission consisting of ten members, drawn from both language groups and from all sections of the country, and empowered to "inquire into and report upon the existing state of bilingualism and biculturalism in Canada and to recommend what steps should be taken to develop the Canadian Confederation on the basis of an equal partnership between the two founding races, taking into account the contribution made by the other ethnic groups to the cultural enrichment of Canada. . . ." After a year and a half of studies and hearings the commissioners issued early in 1965 a preliminary report in which they argued that "Canada is in the most critical period of its history" since 1867, and that it had reached a "crisis . . . when decisions must be taken and developments must occur leading to its break-up, or to a new set of conditions for its future existence." After this sharp warning, the commissioners returned to their inquiries, with a final report expected two or three years later. This report, with the voluminous research studies accompanying it, promises to be one of the most wide-ranging investigations ever undertaken of the problems relating to the coexistence of two or more languages.

Even without the report, however, it is possible to make some general observations about the topics with which it will deal. One point worth stressing at the outset is that, although French-speaking and English-speaking Canadians have lived side by side for two centuries and more, they have never really known one another and their relations are still inhibited by a large number of misconceptions and by a remarkable lack of elementary factual information. As the majority group, which is being asked to change some aspects of the political and constitutional framework of Canadian Confederation, English-speaking

Canadians have a particular need to grasp some aspects of the French-Canadian point of view.

In this respect it is important to appreciate the French Canadian's sense of a long history on the continent. French has been spoken in Quebec without a break since 1608, and the Acadian branch is a little older. The French Canadian does not see his nationality as starting in 1867, let alone any more recent date, but in the early seventeenth century. Nearly all French Canadians today are descended from people who had reached North America before the middle of the eighteenth century, most of them before the beginning of that century. Their political tie with France was broken in 1760, nearly a generation before Americans broke theirs with the mother country, and long before most English-speaking Canadians ceased to look across the sea. They are a minority in Canada as a whole, and in North America, but they have always been a majority in their homeland along the St. Lawrence. Nor have they been confined to that homeland; large and important settlements of people of French-Canadian origin exist in many other parts of North America.

As a coherent community, functioning in Quebec for more than three hundred years, French Canadians have developed and administered a large number of distinctive institutions and associations, to which they have given tenacious loyalty. This intricately organized and widely ramifying network of institutions and associations keeps the French Canadian fully aware of his historical origins and of his identity as a member of a unique collectivity. From the beginning the Roman Catholic Church has been the central institution in this network, partly because nearly all French Canadians have been faithful adherents of that church and partly because political and economic circumstances allowed, or forced, the Church to play a role which is unexampled in North American history. Its involvement in education, in organizing social services, in supporting voluntary associations, and even in directing and influencing political and economic activities has been pervasive and enduring. With good reason, the French Canadian sees the Church as the fundamental factor that has ensured the survival of his collectivity or "nation" in North America. In consequence, his relationship to it has been of a rare intimacy. In addition to church membership, nearly all French Canadians have direct and personal family ties with the Church, because the clergy have always been recruited from all levels of society. Today, because of the extension of the role of the state and because of other factors, it is no longer necessary, or desirable, that the Church should play so all-embracing a role as it did in the past, and French Canadians are increasingly turning to additional means and agencies to foster their survival and development. This transition has its painful, and sometimes its contentious, side, but it is not accompanied by the anticlericalism that has often been exhibited in other Catholic communities. The Church continues to be a central institution. Indeed, because the clergy are increasingly responding to modern trends, it is itself sometimes a leading force for change and progress.

It is impossible in a brief space to list and describe all the other institutions and associations that have given French Canada its distinctive characteristics. Important among them, however, is the civil law, formed out of the old French law, the Napoleonic code, and some other elements, and codified in 1866, with occasional changes since. It exists side by side with the common law of English origin, and each has been influenced by the other. In addition to an extensive and distinctive school and university system, which in the past has been closely related to the Church, one could also make a long list of other bodies and associations (*corps intermédiaires*) between the individual and the state: cooperatives, credit unions (*caisses populaires*), labor unions, leisure organizations, welfare associations, hospitals, patriotic and fraternal orders, as well as newspapers, periodicals, and radio and television stations. There are two important points to note about this elaborate network of corps intermédiaires (in which the Church and the schools are to be included). First, they have been, and still are for the most part, completely separate from the equivalent bodies of the English-speaking community, Catholic as well as non-Catholic. In the areas where these bodies operate, there has been a voluntary segregation, which is only now breaking down to a very limited extent. Second, to an extent which is not true in the English-speaking community, the leaders of the corps intermédiaires have been the real leaders of French-Canadian society, and it has been difficult, if not impossible, for initiatives to be taken, even by the government, without their approval. Even the extensive urbanization of recent years has not done much to reduce the importance of these bodies, although French-Canadian advocates of drastic change sometimes denounce their influence as reactionary.

But the areas in which these bodies function do not encompass all of life. In particular, they do not in any direct sense include more than a fraction of the political and economic worlds. Thus, we must see how the French Canadian has tried to act in these two vital spheres.

Until recently, French Canadians, unlike Americans or their English-speaking compatriots, have rarely looked to government for extensive or positive action, at either the provincial or the federal level. To be sure, Confederation in 1867 gave them control of the provincial government of Quebec, but for a long time after that date neither they nor other Canadians thought of the provincial governments as very potent bodies. This view continued to be held even after judicial decisions strengthened the provinces in relation to the federal government. The provincial government of Quebec, like that of the other provinces, had very limited revenues and was heavily dependent upon the federal government for subsidies. The Quebec government, less powerful in many ways than any one of several large business corporations operating in the province, was not thought of as an instrument for developing and expanding the French-Canadian entity. Nor were most French Canadians, before about 1960, prepared to entrust large responsibilities to this government, even if it had been capable of exercising them. And partly because the government was relatively weak, ineffective, and not engaged in significant enterprises, it often became a plaything of the politicians, whose main concern was the distribution of patronage to the party faithful. Effective economic power was in the hands of English-speaking elements, Canadian and American, and the main concern of these interests was to develop and maintain suitable relations with provincial political leaders, in order that business might be undisturbed and unimpeded. Indeed, French-Canadian critics of the system developed the theory of the Negro King (*le roi nègre*): that the real rulers used a French-Canadian leader to govern the province for them, just as colonial powers in Africa used to install a chieftain to keep order by any means which he cared to use. It was scarcely an atmosphere in which vigorous democratic government could flourish.

But although the provincial government (before the 1960's) made little attempt to develop its positive functions, it did seek in various ways to protect the interests of the French-Canadian people. It tried, without success, to defend the rights of French-speaking minorities in the other provinces, and, more effectively, its spokesmen developed and acted upon a theory of provincial rights which had some analogies with American states-rights doctrines. Quebec was by no means the only province to assert itself against the federal government, but it was persistent and inflexible in its demand for autonomy. This opposition to what was regarded as unconstitutional encroachment by the federal government became stronger from the 1920's onward as the central government began to move more actively into the fields of social and economic legislation. Negativism was so tenacious during Maurice Duplessis' second and longer period in office (1944-1959) that the province seemed to have placed itself under a veritable state of siege. As well as resisting federal encroachment the Quebec government also took certain actions in the half century before 1960 to strengthen the French-Canadian personality in the province. Legislation was passed to ensure the greater use of French, to provide for a provincial holiday (June 24), and to adopt a provincial flag; and in the 1950's a wide-ranging provincial royal commission set forth elaborate arguments asserting Quebec's special place in the Canadian Confederation.

In federal politics French Canadians were, of course, in a minority and could never hope to determine major national policies. On more than one occasion it was made clear that in major controversies the will of the English-speaking majority would prevail, as during the conscription crises of the two World Wars. Nevertheless, except during such direct confrontations, French Canadians often appeared to be influential at Ottawa. Normally, they held several seats in the cabinet and other high posts in the government. It was also a common practice for the leader of each major political party to have a Quebec "lieutenant" when the leader was not himself a French Canadian (as he has been on two occasions). More important, perhaps, has been the tendency of Quebec voters to concentrate their support behind one political party, instead of dividing it between two or more. A solid bloc of Quebec members was an important political fact, especially to a party in power that depended upon their support. The dangerous possibility in this strategy was that English-speaking support might concentrate behind another party, thus leaving the French Canadians helpless.

It is widely believed in English-speaking Canada that Quebec, by concentrating its strength, has often been able to control the course of federal policy. The cry of "French rule" has been heard from time to time. In fact, however, French Canadians have rarely sat in the inner circles of power. Although they have contributed two prime ministers, they have not as a rule held the most important posts in the cabinet; for example, there has never been a French-Canadian minister of finance, and they have been very sparsely represented in the upper reaches of the bureaucracy. The main functions of the Quebec "lieutenant," when there has been one, and of Quebec cabinet ministers have been to look out for the province's interests, to explain its opinion trends, and to defend federal policies before their own people. Otherwise, they have tended to be rather silent when major decisions have been under discussion.

Turning from political life to economic development, we should note first that, although French Canadians had been actively engaged in commercial activities before 1760, they gradually gave way before English-speaking entrepreneurs who controlled most of the large business enterprises. English-speaking observers dismissed the habitants as unprogressive and backward, while French-Canadian spokesmen, like American Jeffersonians, exalted the virtues of the rural life. In time, however, the pressure of population upon available land forced change, and the younger people began to move away to the New England mills, nearer than the remote Canadian West. This exodus alarmed many Quebec leaders, especially in the Church, and they organized a campaign to colonize the difficult country north of the St. Lawrence valley, a campaign that continued well into the twentieth century.

By the 1890's, however, it was apparent that another and more productive outlet was available, through the development of Quebec's natural resources, particularly its forests and mines, and through the encouragement of industrial growth. Inevitably, because French Canadians lacked the necessary capital and technical skills, such enterprises were controlled and operated by English-speaking outsiders, from Canada and the United States. Nevertheless, both the politicians and the clergy welcomed and encouraged this influx; it meant jobs, revenues, and at least a partial stopping of the population drain out of the province, even at the cost of greatly increased English-speaking domination of the Quebec economy. With every census after 1900 it was clear that Quebec was ceasing to be an agricultural community. Its people were engaged in the great primary-resource industries and they were also flocking to the cities, especially Montreal, to make the province by the 1950's the most urbanized in the country next to Ontario. To an overwhelming extent they were working for English-speaking employers, and even in communities that were ninety-five percent French-speaking, they had little chance of advancement unless they spoke English. Many French Canadians began to refer to themselves as the "nine to fives": speaking English at work and French at home. Provincial governments, particularly that of Duplessis, enthusiastically supported the English-speaking business interest, even to the extent of using the police against French-Canadian strikers.

Such, in brief, were some of the salient facts about the Quebec of the latter 1950's. The issue of survival (*survivance*), which for so long had been the major theme of French-Canadian writing and oratory, was no longer in doubt. French Canada, at least in the homeland of Quebec, was a large and durable community, adequately organized to maintain its identity. By putting their main nineteenth- and early-twentieth-century effort behind the protection of traditional values rather than into scientific and commercial activity, French Canadians had fallen behind in the race for material progress, but they had made sure of group survival. The naive view, once held by some observers, that urbanization and industrialization would assimilate French Canadians to the English-speaking majority of North America was proved to be false; they were not going the way of the Franco-Americans in New England. But was it not true that they were "condemned to survive," a people without effective control over their own lives and inadequately equipped to compete in the modern world? On the surface the province seemed to be relatively quiet in the last years of the Duplessis regime, an inward-looking people, isolated on an English-speaking continent, grimly holding onto their language, their faith, and their institutions. English-speaking Canada was quite unaware that any fundamental change was occurring in Quebec: it knew only that Duplessis was a rather dictatorial and uncooperative character and hoped that his successor would get along better with the rest of the country.

In fact, however, there was mounting discontent and disillusionment in Quebec, even though it rarely received adequate voice. The educational system, despite its emphasis on traditional studies, was turning out many competent and well-trained young people who saw little opportunity for challenging and rewarding employment unless they ceased, in effect, to be French Canadians. The industrial workers, now increasingly unionized, believed that Duplessis and his system were at the beck and call of the English-speaking capitalists. Members of the intellectual community, lay and clerical, were increasingly indignant at the prevalence of bossism, patronage, and electoral frauds in Quebec's political life. The spread of a television network across the province gave the population a view of the outside world and an opportunity to see authority challenged in vigorous commentary and debate. The province was undergoing a rapid social and economic transformation while the traditional political and institutional structure remained outwardly intact. Potentially, it was an explosive situation.

The signal for change came with the death of the old leader, Duplessis, in 1959. At first, almost incredibly, it appeared that Duplessis' party, the Union Nationale, would itself be the instrument of reform and renovation, because the new premier, Paul Sauvé, inaugurated a brisk program of housecleaning. But in a few months Sauvé died suddenly, and it was soon obvious that there was no real momentum left in the party in power. An election in 1960 finally turned the Union Nationale out of office and brought in the Liberals, led by Jean Lesage. English-speaking Canadians heaved a sigh of relief at the ending of the Duplessis era, expecting that Quebec's negativism and obstructionism would give way to cooperation with the rest of the country. The new premier and several of his colleagues had had parliamentary and executive experience at Ottawa; others in the new team had come from the universities and from journalism, after years of trenchant criticism of *duplessisme*. It seemed reasonable to think that such men would join with other Canadians to build a stronger and more united country. The years from 1960 to 1966, while the Lesage government was in office, were a distinct shock for English-speaking Canada.

The new Quebec government, which strengthened its position after an election in 1962, inaugurated and, at times tried to keep up with, a phenomenon that has commonly been called "the quiet revolution" (*la révolution tranquille*). After the long years of authoritarianism, censorship, severe restraint, and discipline, there was, almost suddenly, the sense of a new freedom in which existing traditions could be questioned, exciting plans could be made, and high hopes entertained. The common denominator of all designs, both radical and moderate, was the determination that in the new Quebec the French personality or the "French fact" (*le fait français*) must be strengthened and given opportunity for fuller expression (*épanouissement*). It gradually became clear that in the welter of programs and strategies there were two general schools of thought, which often merged and overlapped, and both of which could reside in a single breast.

The one school, which was relatively small in numbers but which received much publicity, asserted that Quebec must achieve independence, either in the outright political sense or through such a cutting of its ties with the rest of the country that it would acquire de facto control of its own affairs. It was argued that Quebec could never protect itself in Confederation, because the centralizing tendencies of the federal government were inexorable and a constant support to anglicizing forces. Bilingualism in Canada was a farce, and to those who said that separatism would mean abandoning the French-Canadian minorities in the other provinces it was replied that these minorities were already doomed by the pressures of assimilation. Where French Canadians did have a majority — in Quebec — they must consolidate their position before they, too, succumbed to these pressures, even now ominously at work. In answer to the view that Quebec was too closely tied to the rest of the country for separatism to be practicable, the separatists said that Canada itself was tied in a thousand ways to the United States, and yet politically separate; independence would not mean a wall but decent and friendly relations between two distinct peoples, far better than the current bickering within Confederation. Quebec had the essentials of a viable state: it was larger than most European countries, it was richer and more highly developed than any of the new nations of the 1950's and 1960's, and its people formed a cohesive nation with a long and distinctive history. Independence represented the only means by which French Canadians could live dignified lives in North America. To many people, particularly of the younger generation, arguments of this kind were unanswerable.

A second school of thought rejected separatism as both impossible and undesirable. It would almost certainly depress the standard of living, and French Canadians were too North American in outlook to remain contented if their hopes for joining the affluent society were disappointed. It would not keep out anglicizing forces, because Quebec would be just as exposed to American and English-Canadian influences as she was within Confederation. The weakening of economic ties with the rest of Canada would expose Quebec to domination from other quarters. Independence would mean forsaking the French-Canadian minorities, in the other provinces, who, contrary to the separatists, had the will and the opportunity to survive, if they had help from Quebec. Worst of all, for many, an independent Quebec would be on the defensive and turned in upon itself: it might become racist in outlook, develop a right-wing authoritarianism — in short, return to the state-of-siege mentality.

On the whole, the Lesage government adhered to the second school of thought. It resolved to strengthen le fait français, from within the Confederation framework, by embarking upon a bold program of modernizing and developing Quebec's political, social, and economic institutions. The essential premise of the government was that the powers of the provincial government were sufficient, or could be made sufficient, to direct and to stimulate the proposed changes. Hence, the government and its supporters had to carry on a double campaign: to map out and implement new measures within the province, and to press for enlarged powers and revenues in discussions and negotiations with the federal government and the other provinces. Without the second, the first was impossible.

Among the reform projects, one of the most urgent, yet most difficult, was to destroy the paternalism and patronage that had so long been characteristic of Quebec party politics; many partisans had no desire for a change in the rules of the game, especially because the provincial Liberals had been out of power for so long. Nevertheless, the provincial leaders, who separated their party from the federal Liberals in the process, made tangible progress, and to some extent their actions were copied by the Union Nationale. Party organization became more democratic, and patronage, while not dead, became a shadow of its former self. In the realm of economic policy, the government set itself some very ambitious goals. Because the economy was overwhelmingly in English-speaking hands, the government sought to enlarge the public and semipublic sector, in which French Canadians could more readily participate. To a large extent, the impetus here came from the need to provide opportunities for an expanding middle class of well-trained French Canadians who wanted to use their skills in their own language. One Quebec economist stated, "If we can offer graduates interesting jobs, they will be too busy to be separatists." In this respect the nationalization of a portion of the hydroelectric power industry was a symbolic act. In general, however, the government was not committed to an extensive program of public ownership because it did not want to discourage the entry of foreign capital. Instead, it sought to supplement the activities of private industry by encouraging enterprises that had hitherto been lacking or weak. In particular, the government projected, too ambitiously, as it turned out, an extensive iron and steel complex, which private industry had shown no signs of bringing into Quebec. Also, it began to nudge the mining and pulp and paper industries in directions that would make for a more integrated provincial economy. These and other actions were aimed at the goal of a substantially increased French-Canadian participation in Quebec's economic life, but it cannot be said that any of them had more than minimal success.

To some observers the Quebec government's program appeared to be assertive nationalism, and doubtless many French Canadians supported it for that very reason. Yet the program required such a sharp break with past habits and practices that it was often much more painful for French Canadians than it was for any who might be indirectly affected. Modernization meant the discarding or the disintegration of many small economic units, which had been carefully protected by the previous regime, despite the fact that they had been hopelessly inefficient. Such units had been a means of preserving some crumbs for French-Canadian individuals and families in a society where the large economic units were controlled from the outside. But these small units had to be superseded if Quebec were to be competitive on the larger economic scene. Thus, in a very real sense, the program of modernization met with more opposition, or inertia, from within Quebec than it did from the outside.

For the same reason, modernization faced its greatest challenge and its greatest task in the realm of education, the central problem of the new Quebec. The structure which had been built up over the years had many undeniable merits. Not only was it an effective means of handing down the values and traditions of the French-Canadian people from one generation to the next, but, at its best, it turned out graduates who were as highly qualified as any to be found elsewhere. These graduates became the natural leaders of Quebec, especially in politics, law, and the Church. It had long been apparent, however, that the system, although competent to produce an elite of a certain kind, was inadequate for the needs of the people as a whole. It was abundantly clear that French Canadians were not receiving sufficient training to equip them for life in a modern industrial society. Indeed, year by year, they had been falling steadily behind the rest of Canada and North America as a whole, even while the system was defended as necessary to French-Canadian survival.

After some understandable hesitation, the Lesage government began a frontal attack on the structure, preparing the way by the appointment of a royal commission which was empowered to make a thorough study. Within the Quebec context, the commission's recommendations were almost revolutionary. They would mean an end of the dominant influence of the Roman Catholic Church over the school system. The schools would continue to be denominational, but they would be under a Department of Education—a departure for Quebec. The teaching of religion would receive less emphasis, and much more attention would be given to the skills needed for twentieth-century industrial life. The new system would be under highly centralized direction.

The implementation of these recommendations will be the work of a generation and more. It will also be costly, and it will require active and continuing public support. French Canadians have to be convinced that the educational system can be renovated and expanded without the loss of features that have helped to retain their distinctive collective personality. Needless to say, some spokesmen for the traditional system have seen the proposed changes as a subtle engine of assimilation; nevertheless, some of the strongest support for change has come from the Roman Catholic hierarchy. Confidence has also been maintained by the provincial government's firm insistence that control of education must remain in provincial hands. Unlike provincial and state authorities elsewhere in North America, Quebec cannot allow itself to waver on this point under the spell of prospective federal funds. It must find its own sources of revenue to support the gigantic educational expansion. Hence, the educational problem lies at the root of the insistence upon a reordering of the federal system.

A related source of confidence derives from the royal commission's argument that educational modernization must involve no discrimination against the use of the French language. Quite the contrary. The recommendations call for intensive effort to improve the quality of French-language teaching and for continuous demonstration that French is a working language in the modern world, in North America as elsewhere. It is pointed out that a language is condemned to death if it is merely used at home or on selected and protected ethnic occasions; if it is to survive, it must be the instrument of scientific, technical, and commercial training, and students must have assurance that French-language training will be usable in subsequent employment.

Concern over the future of French on a continent where most people speak English, or soon learn it, has led many Quebec spokesmen to insist that the provincial government must take stronger measures to protect the language. Some have argued that the teaching of English to French Canadians must be postponed to the secondary level, in order that children should first acquire a thorough grounding in the maternal tongue. Others have called for unilingualism: a declaration of government policy that French is the only official language in Quebec. The Lesage government resisted such demands by arguing that government edicts in this area would be ineffective and that Quebec would not benefit if language barriers were erected along its borders; instead, French Canadians must themselves demonstrate a clear will to improve the position of their language. Government leaders have, however, asserted that French must be regarded as the "language of priority" in Quebec, and a number of specific steps have been taken to strengthen its position and improve its quality.

On the constitutional front, the Lesage government proved to be a tough and at times an ingenious advocate of provincial autonomy. It demanded changes in taxation policy to provide Quebec with increased revenues. It not only withdrew from a large number of joint federal-provincial programs, but it secured equivalent financial compensation following withdrawal.

For its part, the federal government recoiled before these insistent demands and sought to find formulas of compromise.

This approach was particularly evident for about three years after 1963, when Lester Pearson's Liberal government came into office at Ottawa. This government not only shared a party affiliation with that of Lesage, and thus was somewhat more disposed than otherwise to search for harmony, but it was also dependent upon Quebec for political support. More important than these considerations, however, was the Pearson government's assumption that in the context of Quebec's evolving intellectual climate the Lesage position was a moderate one; to rebuff it might mean that more extreme elements would prevail in Quebec, leading to greater strains on national unity. Hence, the Pearson government agreed to Quebec's proposal for "opting out" of joint programs, with financial compensation, accepted other forms of financial decentralization, and in general appeared to defer to the Quebec point of view. The phrase "cooperative federalism" came into vogue. Federal-provincial conferences and consultations, at a great variety of levels, were held more frequently than ever before. In fact, in many respects the federal government appeared to be harassed and on the defensive, not only in relation to Quebec but also to some other provinces, particularly British Columbia. Many Canadians feared that centrifugal tendencies were tearing the country apart and argued that the country could not survive without a strong and positive federal government.

On the other hand, many spokesmen in Quebec vigorously asserted that Pearson's cooperative federalism was a subterfuge and a sham, more likely to hinder than to assist French Canada in realizing its goal. In their view Quebec would always be hobbled and restricted as long as it was regarded as one province among ten within the Canadian federal structure. Real power would always remain in the hands of the English-speaking majority and the danger of assimilation would always be present. A satisfactory answer could only be based upon an acceptance of the view that Canada consisted not of one nation but of two. Quebec, as the homeland of the French-Canadian people, had never been a province like the others—even the British North America Act of

1867 recognized this fact in several of its clauses — and now it was essential to give explicit constitutional recognition to the existence of two nations by recognizing Quebec as an "associate state" or by according it a "special status" within Confederation.

Concern over Quebec's place in Confederation also delayed a settlement of the old question of "repatriating" the British North America Act. For many years it had been regarded as anomalous that Canada, a fully independent country, should have its written constitution cast in the form of a British statute, which could not be amended except by formal application to the British Parliament. Even though in this matter the British Parliament always acted automatically upon Canadian request, and never without it, it was generally agreed that the procedure was antiquated and that the Act of 1867, and its various amendments of later years, should be repealed by the British Parliament and re-enacted within Canada. Needless to say, the British Parliament was ready to take these statutes off its books whenever it should be requested to do so by Canada.

But the stumbling block lay in the inability of Canadian authorities to agree on an amending formula once the British North America Act became a wholly Canadian document. For some forty years, from the 1920's into the 1960's, there were fruitless discussions between the federal and provincial governments on the subject. Finally, however, in 1964, agreement was reached when all governments gave their support to the so-called Fulton-Favreau Formula, which safeguarded existing rights through the provision that no amendment affecting the powers of the provinces or the use of the French and English languages could be enacted without the consent of all the provinces and of the federal government. Amendments on some other subjects required the approval of two thirds of the provinces representing at least fifty percent of the population of Canada, whereas, with several exceptions, the Parliament of Canada could, without reference to the provinces, amend the constitution in matters relating solely to the structure of the federal government. In addition, flexibility was provided for by a device allowing provinces to delegate powers to the federal government. It was a complicated arrangement, but, as was often pointed out, Canada was a complicated country to govern. Whatever the problems, the constitution would at last be domiciled in Canada, and in future times Canadians could proceed to change it according to their needs.

In 1965, however, it gradually became apparent that there was strong opposition to the Formula, despite the fact that the federal cabinet and every provincial cabinet had approved it. The opposition parties at Ottawa denounced the plan as one that was unworkable because of the rigid amendment provisions and as one that would balkanize the country. Many legal and editorial voices were also raised in criticism. Of prime importance, however, was the fact that Premier Lesage was unable, despite intensive effort, to convince the people of Quebec that they should support the Formula. It turned out that while French Canadians were concerned, as in the past, to prevent changes that would affect entrenched rights, they were now also concerned to secure new powers to support the future development of their "collectivity" or "nation." The meager rights accorded by the British North America Act were now considered to be quite inadequate. The leader of the provincial opposition, Daniel Johnson, attacked the Formula as a "strait-jacket" that would forever prevent Quebec from securing the needed powers. The British North America Act, said Johnson, was a relic of the colonial past. It should be allowed to die in London, and Canadians should proceed to write a new constitution based on the coexistence of two nations with equal rights, and with guarantees for both French and English minorities. Jean Lesage was forced to withdraw support for the Formula, and his defeat at the hands of Daniel Johnson in the June 1966 provincial election ensured that it would not be revived. It was obvious that some other approach to Canada's constitutional problems would have to be found. Some argued for a parliamentary committee on which all parties would be represented, while others advocated a broadly-based constitutional conference. Whatever the procedure, the debate has increasingly centered around two conceptions. According to one of these, Quebec would have a special status—added powers and revenues—but the other provinces would seek no new powers; indeed, they might delegate more of their powers to Ottawa, with the latter becoming the effective government of English-speaking Canada. According to the other conception, renewed emphasis would be placed upon the federal nature of Canadian government, but Quebec would not have a special status; *all* the provinces would acquire the powers and revenues needed to cope with their greatly expanded responsibilities.

The provincial election of June 1966 marked the end of a phase of the quiet revolution, which, indeed, had been slowing down in the last two years of the Lesage government. There has been a certain reassertion on the part of the traditional elements of Quebec society, especially in the rural areas; not only did these elements feel that the changes of the 1960's threatened some of the basic values of the "collectivity," particularly in the educational field, but they also had little sense of participating in any of the material benefits resulting from the new policies. Quite the contrary: they worried about higher taxes going to pay good salaries to a new race of functionaries, bureaucrats, and teachers. Sentiment of this kind changed enough seats to return the Union Nationale to office in June 1966.

Yet there could be no question of returning to the Duplessis era. The Union Nationale party had been considerably reformed and renovated in recent years. Its leaders were prepared to accept and continue the modern techniques introduced in the 1960's. There was indication, however, of a conservative aim to hold down government expenses and to postpone new social and economic programs. Some observers have also discerned in Premier Johnson and his associates an affinity for the social theory known as corporatism, which has had a recurring popularity among conservative Roman Catholics since Pius XI's "Quadragesimo Anno" (1931), but the strong opposition of Quebec's labor unions makes unlikely any real move in this direction.

In the year following the Quebec election of June 1966 relations between Quebec and the federal government were somewhat smoother than had been expected. Although some of his public pronouncements called for drastic and immediate changes in the constitutional and fiscal status quo, Premier Johnson proved to be cool and pragmatic in federal-provincial negotiations. Moreover, for long periods of time he was so fully occupied with internal problems that he had little time to devote to larger questions. Equally important was the fact that, for the first time in several years, influential French Canadians began to stress that Quebec had an essential stake in Confederation and that it would suffer drastically if it loosened its ties with the rest of Canada. They also argued that, from an economic standpoint, Quebec was still weak and in need of outside capital: there should be a moratorium on constitutional speculation which might scare away investment. But it is by no means certain that such prudential arguments have much influence among French Canadians, particularly the younger ones, who insist that the right to live their lives in French should take priority over all other considerations.

The gulf between the two language groups was dramatically revealed in the various reactions to the visit of the French president, General Charles de Gaulle, to Quebec in July 1967. One of several dozen heads of state invited to Canada in conjunction with the Centennial celebrations, General de Gaulle did not restrict himself to the vague diplomatic generalities usual to such occasions. Instead, from the moment of his arrival in Quebec, he voiced eloquent encouragement for French-Canadian nationalist aspirations, stressed the ties between France and Quebec, and, most startlingly, declaimed "Vive le Québec libre," a slogan associated with Quebec separatists. In turn, the Canadian prime minister declared that the general's statements were "unacceptable" to the government of Canada, and de Gaulle returned home without going to Ottawa.

For a few days most English-speaking Canadians gave themselves over to an orgy of indignation: resentment against foreign "meddling," dislike of de Gaulle, and irritation at the fervent enthusiasm of Quebec's greeting to him were vigorously expressed. It was a notable display of nationalism in English-speaking Canada.

In French-speaking Canada reactions were more complex. Outside Quebec, where separatism is greatly feared by French Canadians, opposition toward de Gaulle's statements was general. Within Quebec opinion depended in part upon political loyalties. Yet it was also clear that nearly all Quebec French Canadians, including those who criticized particular statements, had been deeply moved by de Gaulle's visit. For reasons that were often rather obscure to outsiders, the visit gave them a quickened sense of pride and a renewed determination that Quebec must be recognized as a distinct entity, conducting its affairs in the French language. For a few days at least the stifling "claustrophobia" of living on an English-speaking continent had been somewhat relieved. Once again, as on countless earlier occasions, the reactions of the English-speaking and French-speaking communities had been sharply divergent. And although some French Canadians pointedly reminded de Gaulle that their destiny was to live on this continent, his visit also strengthened Quebec's determination to make "le fait français" a growing reality in North America.

One of the most persistent themes of recent Canadian writing and public discussion has been the nature, the desirability, or even the existence, of a national outlook. What is distinctive, in a positive sense, in the Canadian outlook? Should there be a conscious attempt to foster and develop national symbols? How would a heightened nationalism affect the relations between the two language groups? Or should there be two nationalisms within one federal state? Is a vigorous Canadian nationalism doomed by American cultural pressures? These and similar questions have been raised so often that outside observers have sometimes asserted that the country is seized by a kind of introspective hypochondria, extraordinary for a people who are favored in so many ways. Books and articles with such titles as "Lament for a Nation" and "Death of a Nation" are gravely debated and considered to be of ominous portent. This debate cannot be understood unless we recall some of the historical background.

In only a limited sense can Canadians look back to a common early history. In the first place there is the diverse origin of the Canadian population: French-speaking settlers brought under British rule after France's defeat in 1760, several small and disconnected maritime communities to the east, loyalists who had been on the losing side in the American Revolution, immigrants from the British Isles and later from many European countries, to mention only the main components in a general way. Moreover, these various British North American provinces, physically separated by distance and poor communications, knew and appeared to care relatively little about one another. Growth in colonial times was gradual, indeed often painfully slow, and it was usually peaceful, not marked by many dramatic and stirring events of the kind that draw people together in a sense of joint endeavor.

When some of the colonies did come together in 1867 to form Confederation, they were impelled by a need to solve certain concrete and practical problems rather than by a conscious desire to build a new nationality in North America, though that aspiration was not entirely absent. Nor was there any impulse to turn away from the Old World; on the contrary, economic, defense, and emotional ties with Great Britain remained close and vital. The contrast with the development of the United States is striking, for the latter's history is marked by a sharp and violent break with Europe, by the fiery trial of civil war, and by the vivid sense of a distinctive way of life and of a shared ideology.

Canadian Confederation was not followed by any sudden flowering of national consciousness. The "Canada First" movement of the 1870's was short-lived and oriented solely toward the English-speaking community. It was followed by bitter quarrels in which English-speaking Canadians showed their determination to prevent French-Canadian institutions from having any effective or expanding role in the West. The two language groups were also divided in their response to the call of Empire, with English-speaking Canadians manifesting an intense, at time a racial, pride in membership in the British Empire which for most of them was as real and as vital as their feeling for Canada; they had an ardent sense of *British* nationality. They had little desire for distinctively Canadian symbols or emblems that might obscure the tie with the Crown and the mother country. French Canadians could not share this strong imperial sentiment, but they too had a strong over-the-seas allegiance in their ultramontane devotion to the Vatican. For neither group could Canada be the sole focus of loyalty. The strongest common bond felt by Canadians was a negative one — determination not to be absorbed by the United States — yet even this determination was qualified by the fact that every year thousands of Canadians went off to live in the republic to the south.

In the early years of the present century, however, the implications of the imperial tie forced to the fore the question of a distinctive Canadian nationalism. Participation in the Boer War and, far more important, in the First World War unloosed a vigorous debate over where a Canadian's primary focus of loyalty should be. French Canadians accused their English-speaking compatriots of having a colonial mentality, while the latter insisted upon full and unreserved support of the Empire in peril. Nevertheless, out of the gigantic war effort of 1914-1918 came a deeper national self-consciousness, which was reflected in many ways in the following years. In addition to Canadian membership in the League of Nations and the postwar push for "Dominion status," a long list can be compiled of new national associations and organizations that originated in the 1920's. Yet, on the whole, these developments did not bring English-speaking and French-speaking Canadians any closer together than they had been before. Nationalist evolution in the two groups was parallel, not fused.

The Second World War saw a further quickening in the development of Canadian nationalism. In 1939 Canadians had some sense of making a deliberate decision to go to war in order to defend the national interest, in contrast to the almost automatic response in 1914 to come to the aid of England. Moreover, in the second war, the Canadian forces — air, land, and naval — fought under their own organization and command to a much greater extent than they had in 1914-1918. At home, the pace of industrial expansion was so rapid that Canada became a major factor in the allied war effort. By 1945 Canadians saw themselves as a "middle power," with an important role to play in the United Nations, in economic reconstruction, and in the councils of the so-called North Atlantic Triangle, a concept that was very popular in Canada at that time. The war and immediate postwar years saw such events as the raising of the most important legations to the rank of embassies, the passing of a Canadian Citizenship Act, membership in NATO, the ending of appeals to the Judicial Committee of the Privy Council, and the rounding out of Confederation through the admission of Newfoundland as the tenth province, all seen by Canadians as signposts of a healthy evolution, both internal and external. As recently as the later 1930's a large number of Canadians had found rather daring the assertion that their first loyalty should be to Canada rather than to the Commonwealth; a decade later, few Canadians were willing to accord primacy to the larger entity.

But the growing self-consciousness accompanying these events led many Canadians to worry aloud about several factors which, it was urged, threatened to stifle, if not destroy, Canada's national development. Most of these factors were related to the new association with the United States, which had emerged during and after the Second World War. Before 1940 the majority of Canadians had long had the sense, through membership in the Empire, of being part of the great world, indeed, a sense of sharing in Great Power status, which was sometimes contrasted with the narrow isolationism of the United States. Now most of this had to change before declining British and rising American power. The very year of greatest sentimental outpouring toward the mother country — 1940 and "There'll Always Be an England" — saw Canada and the United States join in a permanent arrangement for continental defense. The intense pressure for expanded war output linked the two economies more closely than ever before. There was a greater consciousness of the impact of American cultural influences. This impact was not new, but in the emerging era of the mass media it was much more visible than ever before, and it was not effectively offset by a sense of closeness to British civilization, as to some extent had been true in the past. By the end of the 1940's, and increasingly thereafter, there was growing agreement that a major effort must be made to protect Canadian life from American pressures, an effort in which the Canadian federal government must play a prominent part.

In preparing to play this role the federal government set out to secure information through the time-honored device of the royal commission, which had so often been used to study national problems. The first such commission, under the chairmanship of Vincent Massey, was asked to investigate the state of the arts, of letters, and of the sciences. In 1951 it reported that the American cultural impact on Canada was so great that it threatened to "stifle rather than stimulate our own creative effort," and it concluded that federal expenditure on the country's cultural defenses was equally important as money spent on its military defenses: "the two cannot be separated."

A few years later, a royal commission on broadcasting warned sharply about the dangers to "a Canadian identity" coming "from a tidal wave of American cultural activity." It argued that as Canadians had used the power of government in the past "to compensate for our disabilities of geography, sparse population and vast distances," so they must "apply this system to broadcasting" by providing "quite substantial amounts of money" for strengthening and extending the government-owned Canadian Broadcasting Corporation, because the private system would always be heavily dependent on imported American radio and television programs.

And in 1961 another royal commission, this time on publications, asserted that the United States had built up "the world's most penetrating and effective apparatus for the transmission of ideas" and that "Canada, more than any other country, is naked to that force." In particular, the commission noted "the veritable deluge" of American periodicals coming into Canada—three out of every four magazines read by Canadians were imported from the United States—and recommended steps that might make it possible for Canadian periodicals to compete more effectively with their larger and more affluent American contemporaries.

Finally, on the economic front, still another royal commission had earlier emphasized the rapid growth and heavy concentration of American investment and ownership in Canada, and had also highlighted the fact that seventy percent of Canadian labor union members belonged to organizations with headquarters in the United States. The commission asserted that there was a real possibility that the continuing integration of the two economies would lead eventually to the loss of Canada's political independence.

These royal commission reports were only the most considered and the most official expressions of a widely held point of view—that there was a broad role for the federal government to play in fostering Canadian nationalism and in protecting it from the eroding effects of American cultural and economic waves. Thus, concern over American influence was a significant, although by no means the only, factor making for an enlargement of the functions of the federal government. Many of the country's most influential political, intellectual, and business leaders strongly supported programs and policies looking toward a larger and more positive role for the federal government in order to strengthen "the Canadian identity." The aftermath has been a wide-ranging and rather inconclusive debate over Canadian nationalism.

The sharpest objections to a broader role for the federal government came from French-speaking spokesmen in Quebec. Their objections did not arise out of any opposition to the goal of limiting American cultural and economic penetration; that they shared with the rest of the country. French Canadians, however, saw the danger as one that did not emanate solely from the United States; it was continent-wide, coming generally from English-speaking North American civilization. To place more and more power in the hands of the Canadian federal government was to strengthen a government that was controlled by the country's English-speaking majority. This government, embarked upon a centralizing course, for whatever motives, could be a more immediate threat to the French-Canadian way of life than the real but less primary American pressures. Vivid memories of earlier cultural controversies between the two language groups convinced French Canadians that they must never agree to a reorientation of the Canadian polity of the kind advocated by English-speaking Canadian nationalists.

Beyond this basic objection, however, the response of French Canadians has been much more varied than is sometimes realized. Some, as we have seen, have argued that the solution lies in separation, in political independence for Quebec from the rest of Canada, as the only certain means of protecting and developing the "French fact" in North America. At the other end of the political spectrum are the opponents of a distinctive French-Canadian nationalism who favor looking to Ottawa as much as to Quebec; with characteristically French mordancy, the term *"fédéraste"* has been hurled at this group. Others, while calling for resistance to what they term Ottawa's centralizing tendencies, have been otherwise reasonably content with the status quo in Quebec. Still others, the most influential in recent years, have battled on a broader front by striving for reform and modernization within Quebec and by insisting at the same time on recognition of the right of French Canadians to function in their own language everywhere in the country.

These French Canadians, and indeed nearly all others who envisage a continuing political association with the rest of Canada, seek constitutional changes which will recognize the legal existence of "two majorities" with guarantees of equal rights for the English-language minority in Quebec and the French-language minorities in the other provinces. Some authorities look to a revision of the Canadian Bill of Rights that would protect not only the rights of individuals, as at present, but also the rights of groups (*droits collectifs*). It is argued that if such rights, especially those relating to language, acquired a firm constitutional base, on which appeal could be made to the courts, French Canadians would see less necessity to build a fortress-province to ensure survival.

While many French Canadians debate whether their country is Quebec or Canada, and certainly oppose what is sometimes called "pan-Canadian" nationalism, they are increasingly hostile to many of the old British forms and symbols. Rationally or not, they see these as visible testimony of the 1760 conquest and of English-speaking dominance. On such matters as a distinctively Canadian flag and national anthem there has been overwhelming Quebec support coupled with either amusement or exasperation at the reluctance of many English-speaking Canadians to adopt these changes. It is also probable that most French Canadians would prefer to have a head of state who is a permanent resident of Canada, although most of them at present see little point in openly challenging the attachment to the monarchy existing among English-speaking Canadians. It should be emphasized, perhaps, that while a preference for a republican constitution is probably fairly widespread among French Canadians, and by no means absent among English-speaking Canadians, there is little or no sentiment for adopting the presidential-congressional system of the United States. Canadian advocates of a republic would keep the cabinet structure, with the prime minister as the head of government; the head of state would be an elected or appointed president, perhaps on the Italian model.

The sharpness and vehemence of the broadsides from Quebec have forced many English-speaking Canadians to re-examine their positions in this debate. Reactions have been both varied and shifting, and only a few of the main ones can be sketched here.

One fairly drastic change has been in the attitudes of the English-speaking population within Quebec, numbering about a million. These people, who on the whole have a much higher standard of living than the French-Canadian majority in the province, have often appeared to be a rather aloof enclave. But various factors, including concern over the rise of separatism and more points of contact with a modernized French-Canadian community, have led English-speaking Quebeckers to show increasing sympathy for French-Canadian demands for political and constitutional change. The rights enjoyed by the minority in Quebec are often held up as a model to be imitated in the other provinces.

Similarly, in the neighboring province of Ontario there has been some change. A substantial French-Canadian minority of over half a million gives the question some pertinence, and the decline of anti-Catholic feeling removes a main source of past hostility. Moreover, Ontario has been just as strong as Quebec—sometimes stronger—in resisting the power of the federal government, and this fact often makes for a bond between the two largest provinces. But much of English-speaking Ontario, especially in the smaller towns and in the countryside, has changed very little in its attitude toward Quebec.

Of the eastern and western provinces, only New Brunswick and Manitoba feel much direct contact with "the French-Canadian problem." In both provinces French-speaking minorities have gained some additional recognition for the use of the French language, and majority feeling may be somewhat more sympathetic than in the past. Elsewhere in these two regions, but especially in the three westernmost provinces, Quebec's claims appear to be absurd, untenable, and dangerous.

Looking more generally at the reactions of English-speaking Canadians, it is clear that relatively few of them are receptive to such terms as "two majorities" and "two cultures," let alone "two nations." They cannot see themselves as one of two distinct groups making up the people of Canada. "Why can't we all just be Canadians?" is a remark that is often uttered, rather plaintively. Usually it is hastily added that there is no wish to introduce into Canada anything like the American melting-pot. Instead, the preferred term in Canada is "mosaic," by which it is meant that there can be unity in diversity. Canadians, whether of British, French, or other origin (and about a quarter of them are neither British nor French by background), must be free to practice their own religions, preserve whatever special customs they have, and, in general, not be forced to conform to any single pattern of outlook or conduct. As good democrats, also, they should be prepared to abide by majority decisions on matters of common concern to the whole country. The idea that French Canadians, as the descendants of the first Canadians, should have constitutional guarantees for the use of their language throughout Canada and that as a group they should have some form of political equality with the majority is either mystifying or repugnant to most English-speaking Canadians.

Thus it might seem that Quebec's resurgence has only confirmed English-speaking Canadians in their view that a common nationality, buttressed by a strong federal government, is essential to the survival of Canada. Not only is such a government necessary for domestic purposes — to ensure economic justice as between geographic regions and social classes — but also to guard against the influence of American business, finance, and cultural penetration.

Nevertheless, there has not been a great outpouring of assertive nationalism. Regionalism remains strong. As mentioned before, some of the provinces, notably Ontario and British Columbia, bargain with Ottawa as toughly as does Quebec for control of revenues raised within their borders; in recent years a minority federal government has often been harassed and on the defensive in its dealings with stable and confident provincial administrations. Provincial governments, actively engaged in resources development, have also opposed economic protectionism that might keep out investment. Thus, although generalized pronouncements on the need to resist American economic penetration are popular, their implementation is usually opposed by a variety of powerful forces.

Similarly, plans to resist American cultural penetration have had little success. Proposals to discourage the circulation of American magazines in Canada by withdrawing the right to tax deduction on the part of Canadian firms advertising in such magazines have not been implemented, for fear that the right to a free press might eventually be infringed. Canadians have also continued to be large consumers of American television programs, either through Canadian stations or through stations in nearby American cities, and have strongly objected to any changes that might limit such access. Although intellectual and artistic leaders frequently deplore the flood of American culture in Canada, the general public often appears to prefer the American product to the Canadian. It is a common remark, by no means universally accurate, that Canadian authors, artists, and performers are ignored at home until they have had a success in New York or Hollywood.

To the proposition that a sense of identity could and should be strengthened by means of new and distinctive forms and symbols most English-speaking Canadians have been either hesitant or hostile. Indeed, many, particularly in the older generation, profess to see a dark, underhanded campaign at work to remove all the symbols of the country's English heritage. When Prime Minister Pearson, in 1963-1964, proposed the adoption of a flag which did not contain the Union Jack he was met by strong and vehement opposition, and it was widely asserted that the measure was prompted by a desire to cater to Quebec opinion. The maple-leaf flag was adopted in the House of Commons only after closure was applied to halt a filibuster on the part of the Progressive Conservative opposition. In the waspish debate preceding this vote many English-speaking Canadians declared, with sincere and heartfelt emotion, that there could be no true national pride without pride in the country's past: far from being a badge of colonial inferiority, the Union Jack was an intimate and authentic part of Canada's history. Eventually, Pearson was forced to compromise by coupling the resolution for the new flag with another one proclaiming that the Union Jack also had official status as a symbol of Canada's membership in the Commonwealth and of its allegiance to the Queen.

The flag controversy was only in part a dispute between English-speaking and French-speaking Canada; it was also a dispute within the English-speaking group. People of the younger generation tended to support the new flag, as did citizens of non-British extraction. General acceptance and widespread display of the maple-leaf flag since its official adoption early in 1965 indicate that the country as a whole may be somewhat readier for changes of this kind than had been thought.

The question of the monarchy is, however, another matter. It is probable that there is much less sentimental attachment, particularly among young people, than there used to be, and probably little among those of non-British stock. Nevertheless, opinion leaders continue to insist that the tie with the Crown is a basic guarantee of Canada's independence. As one newspaper editorialist put it (Toronto *Globe and Mail*, October 21, October 26, 1966): "To cut ourselves off from the Crown would be to cut ourselves off from our past, and probably also from an independent future. . . . The monarchy strengthens our community with the bonds of a personal loyalty that is more powerful than respect for any flag or written declaration of independence. . . . Without the throne we are a republic attached to a republic with nothing to set us apart but our maple leaf and our vague search for traditions and symbols. If we take off the old and put on the new we are almost certain to find that the new is 'made in U.S.A.' "

On the other side, it is argued (Toronto *Daily Star*, October 22, 1966), that the monarchy "has become remote from Canadian life to the point of meaninglessness and irrelevancy. . . . The monarchy tends to keep Canada from growing up psychologically. . . . The monarchy also clouds our independent status in the eyes of other nations." Some people also believe that until formal sovereignty is vested in the Canadian people British Canadians will not fully acknowledge, and act on, the principle of the fundamental equality of citizens of all ethnic origins. But there are few critics of the monarchy in Canada who give the issue very high priority.

More recently there have been vigorous polemics concerning the government's plan to integrate the armed forces. Integration is supported on grounds of efficiency and economy, but one effect will also be to do away with uniforms and methods that are British in origin and style. The result would be an undifferentiated "Canadianized" service, the idea of which is bitterly resented by many who served in distinctive units, especially in the navy.

Thus, the Canadian mood in the 1950's and 1960's has often

been puzzled and doubtful. Many of the older certainties have gone. Less than a generation ago, a writer asking the question "Is Canada a Nation?" could confidently assert that "the British connection" was a vital bond of nationhood; few would do so today. Others, perhaps with some complacence, used to find satisfaction in celebrating the superiority of Canadian institutions and manners over American: a more stable and effective political system, better administration of justice, less isolationism toward the outside world, more tolerance, lower divorce figures, and so on. But in recent years Canadian self-satisfaction has been somewhat shaken by scandals in government, frequent elections followed by minority governments, the collapse of financial institutions, and worry over the "balkanization" of Canada. In addition, such phenomena as the powerful impact of the Kennedy name, the dramatic successes of the American space program, and a sense of involvement in the civil rights battle to the south have kept the attention of Canadians, particularly of the younger generation, strongly focused on the United States. This has been true even when the reaction is antagonistic, as toward the Vietnam policy. The significant events seem to be happening across the border. Within Canada many appear to feel that their country is a failure because it lacks dynamic leadership, because it does not have a clear-cut identity, and because it does not offer a distinctive national faith to live by.

To combat such wavering and pessimism other observers urge Canadians both to face current reality and to remain true to their traditions. As a middle-sized power Canada has no "rendezvous with destiny" in the American sense, nor should it crave one. Nor is the goal of an all-inclusive "pan-Canadian" nationalism either feasible or desirable. To strive for this goal in a society as diverse as Canada's is only to perpetuate old quarrels and, as one letter to the editor has put it (Toronto *Globe and Mail*, November 19, 1964), to "encourage mediocrity, sentimentality and chauvinism." On their side, French Canadians are being urged to break away from the older defensive attitudes, to participate more fully in the life of both the country and the continent, and also to strengthen their ties with French-speaking communities abroad.

In short, many observers in both groups are asserting that in the world of the latter twentieth century Canada's outlook should be international rather than national. On political, military, and even economic levels Canada has to a remarkable extent subordinated its own national independence in favor of close cooperation with its associates in the North Atlantic world, and such cooperation should be broadened to include other areas. For a country like Canada anything like real independence is obviously impossible. On the cultural and ideological levels the soundest strategy would also be to encourage diversity at home and to promote educational, travel, artistic, and other connections with the world beyond North America. Such connections would always, necessarily, be less intimate than those maintained with the United States, but the extent to which they existed would be the extent to which Canada continued to remain distinct from its great neighbor. This strategy, rather than emphasis upon a defensive nationalism, flows from Canada's historical development, from its present circumstances, and from the nature of the modern world. Canadians should not lament the absence of a passionate nationalism; without it, they are better equipped to fulfill themselves and to make useful contributions to peace and progress. It remains to be seen whether such an approach will be satisfying to the mass of Canadians and whether it is consistent with the containment of the centrifugal tendencies that are frequently visible in the country.

V

CANADA

AND THE

UNITED

STATES

The bilateral relations of the United States and Canada are often the subject of mutual congratulation. It is a standing joke that no Canadian-American occasion is complete, especially if it involves after-dinner speeches, unless there are references to a century and a half of peace and to the four thousand miles of undefended border. Spokesmen like to point out that the association between the two countries is a model without parallel elsewhere in the world and an example of good neighborliness which others could profitably emulate.

Nevertheless, there are aspects of the partnership not normally referred to on ceremonial occasions which deserve attention if its nature is to be understood. The most important of these is the most obvious: the disparity in population, wealth, and power. Moreover, the United States has a range of world interests and commitments that lead it to view almost any subject in a different perspective from that adopted by Canada, even when purely bilateral issues are in question. As a result, it is perhaps straining the meaning of the word to speak of a partnership between two such unequal countries.

In the second place, it is sometimes forgotten that cooperation between these two countries does not proceed on an easy and automatic basis. It requires more than good will and a certain North American similarity of outlook, even when these are abundantly present. The North American partnership functions as well as it does because each side makes a constant and continuous effort to make it work, an effort in which the exercise of restraint is a most important factor. In all its official dealings with Canada, the United States seeks scrupulously to treat its northern neighbor as an exact equal and to avoid any slightest suggestion of bringing its immense power to bear to influence negotiations. Like all generalizations, there are probably some exceptions to this one in recent years—for example, the state department's intervention in the nuclear arms debate in 1963, but even this incident suggested little more than momentary exasperation, and within two days Dean Rusk expressed "regret if our tone was wrong." For their part, Canadian authorities have had to develop a patient understanding of the complex workings of the American political system, and they have also concluded that in respect to most aspects of American policy it is better to avoid open criticism.

The most authoritative recent statement of the "Principles for Partnership" between the two countries was made in June 1965, in a report signed by A. D. P. Heeney, Canadian ambassador to the United States in 1953-1957 and 1959-1962, and by Livingston T. Merchant, U.S. ambassador to Canada in 1956-1958 and 1961-1962. These two experienced observers argued that "many problems between our two governments are susceptible of solution only through the quiet, private and patient examination of facts in the search for accommodation. It should be regarded as incumbent on both parties during this time-consuming process to avoid, so far as possible, the adoption of public positions which can contribute unnecessarily to public division and difference." They went on to state that "in the conduct and development of their unique bilateral relationship . . . the two countries must have regard for the wider responsibilities and interests of each in the world and their obligations under various treaties and other arrangements to which each is a party." In the United States there was little reaction to the report, but many Canadians bridled at the suggestion (which the authors intended to apply only to those in official positions) that public criticism of American policy should be avoided "so far as possible." It remains clear, however, that bilateral relations must always be seen in the larger context of the world policy of each country, particularly that of the United States.

Furthermore, the bilateral relationship works as well as it does only because an elaborate and complex machinery of commissions, committees, boards, and other joint bodies has been developed over the years to deal with the common concerns of the two countries. It thus follows that a vast range of questions arising in Canadian-American relations is to a large extent de-politicized through automatic referral to these numerous agencies, which, with their experienced and technically trained staffs, are well equipped to secure the information on which equitable solutions can be based. There are permanently constituted joint entities concerned with defense, with the boundary, with international waterways, and with fisheries. There are agreements making it possible for agencies in the one country to deal directly with their opposite numbers in the other country on such subjects as atomic energy, taxation, securities, customs, aviation, weather information, crime, conservation and recreation, agriculture, labor, immigration and naturalization, and radio and television. At a higher political level there are joint cabinet committees on defense and trade and economic affairs, as well as a Canada-United States interparliamentary group. All this is in addition to the enormous volume of work done in the embassies and consulates which each country maintains in the other. There is a regularly constituted procedure or apparatus for the conduct of almost every conceivable kind of Canadian-American business, making possible the smooth and quiet adjustment of the thousands of questions of common concern. The level of cooperation is so efficient and so constant that the general public is scarcely aware of its existence.

Nevertheless, despite this elaborate machinery and despite the long experience in accommodation and adjustment, there are still many issues that become matters of public debate and even of sharp dispute. Some of these issues have already been discussed in other contexts in previous chapters and need only to be recalled at this point. Of first importance is the fact that every American economic and financial policy of any significance has a direct and often an immediate impact upon Canada. Whether the impact is beneficial or harmful, Canadians are left with a sense of frustration because of their exposure and vulnerability, but this area of policy is one in which there are only limited possibilities for cooperation between two independent governments. When cooperative procedures are worked out, as in the automobile agreement, many Canadians are convinced that the net effect is to increase their dependence on the American economy. In short, no way has yet been found to de-politicize the larger financial and economic aspects of Canadian-American relations. Another major issue, previously referred to, is continental defense. Since 1963 this question has lost much of its emotional content, but Canadians are increasingly doubtful that their country plays, or can play, any real role in making the decisions at NORAD headquarters. In the era of long-range missiles and of satellites the concept of continental defense is beginning to lose its meaning, and many Canadians feel that their limited military resources should be allocated in other directions, like limited-war or peace-keeping forces. Equally, the United States is developing defense systems which do not require Canadian cooperation or access to Canadian territory and air space. A recent topic of discussion in the defense area has been Canada's rapidly growing export of military equipment to the United States since a defense production agreement was concluded in 1960. With characteristic ambivalence, Canadians welcome the attendant industrial prosperity, but worry about the growing integration with the American economy and about the material support given to American policies of which Canadians may disapprove.

Finally, there is a cluster of topics which are frequently discussed, at least in Canada, but which are not readily amenable to government action. The loss of population to the United States, particularly of people with advanced skills and education, is frequently lamented north of the border. Again, however, the Canadian attitude is ambivalent, because there is also criticism when American immigration legislation, as in 1965, limits the flow of population across the border. Other recurring themes in newspaper editorials are the circulation of American periodicals in Canada, the influence in Canada of American business corporations and American labor unions, comparative estimates of the standard of living in the two countries, and the problems of an emerging international megalopolis stretching from Detroit to Montreal on both sides of the border. On the Canadian side, the list could be extended almost indefinitely, because, as we have already noted, there is an American dimension to nearly every topic discussed in Canada.

Nevertheless, one issue is beginning to receive almost as much attention south of the border as it does in Canada, and it may prove to be the leading bilateral question of the coming generation—the exploitation and allocation of such natural resources as metals, oil, natural gas, hydroelectric power, and, above all, water. References are now commonly being made to "continental resources," but in fact debate centers on Canadian resources and the policies to be adopted to govern their export to the large American market. On the American side, long-range forecasts predicting the depletion of certain basic resources give the question a growing urgency, and on the Canadian side there are many contradictory crosscurrents and numerous uncertainties.

To a very considerable extent resources are already moved and managed along continental rather than national lines. For over a century central Canada has relied upon American coal, and this dependence is still very real in the era of the thermal production of electrical power. On the other hand, the Canadian forest and mining industries have for many years found their main markets in the United States, and, as we have seen, these industries are either heavily or predominantly under American control. The best example of the joint exploitation of resources is to be found in the power developments at Niagara Falls and along the St. Lawrence River above Montreal. It was American interest in St. Lawrence power as well as the American steel industry's need for Labrador iron ore that hastened the completion of the St. Lawrence Seaway in 1959 after interminable delays in the previous generation. One may also point to the intricate interlacing of the Canadian and American railroad, highway, airline, pipeline, and power-grid systems to show how resources, as well as a great variety of other products, move according to continental patterns.

Nevertheless, Canadians have always viewed this trend with mixed feelings. On the one hand, they have been anxious to secure access to the rich American market and have protested vigorously when the United States has imposed quotas or other limitations on the import of such items as metals, oil, or natural gas. On the other hand, Canadians have also sought to provide for the east-west movement of commodities on transportation systems built wholly within Canadian territory; equally, they have tried to ensure that at least a proportion of the processing of raw materials should take place in Canada. Thus, while Canadian government leaders have assured Americans that "natural resources ... should be regarded as a common asset to be used for our common benefit" and that there was "little sense in barriers being imposed on the free flow of these resources across our borders,"* they have on other occasions strongly asserted that the satisfying of Canadian needs and development must take priority over all other considerations.

A good illustration of the contending forces is provided by recent controversies over the transmission of natural gas. By 1966 it was clear that the all-in-Canada thirty-inch pipeline from the west would soon be unable to serve adequately the growing market of southern Ontario and Quebec. The line could be twinned, but the price of deliveries in the Windsor-to-Montreal area would probably not be competitive with that from nearer American sources. Accordingly, Trans-Canada Pipe Lines Ltd. proposed to build a thousand-mile line (thirty-six inches in diameter) south of the Lakes to link Manitoba and Ontario by a shorter route than that to the north. But the Canadian government objected to this plan, which would place the major transmission line under the regulation of a foreign government, and it forced the company to revise its proposal to ensure that the main

---

* Paul Martin, secretary of state for external affairs, in an address to a joint session of the Canadian Public Relations Society and the Public Relations Society of America, Montreal, Nov. 9, 1964 (*Statements and Speeches*, Information Division, Department of External Affairs, Ottawa, No. 64/28).

facilities for supplying the eastern market would remain north of the border. (The government's failure to impose a flat veto on a line through the United States was denounced by some Canadians as another example of "creeping continentalism.") In turn, however, Trans-Canada's revised scheme ran into intense opposition from competing American natural-gas interests, which opposed any significant increase in Canadian exports by means of such a line and which sought to preserve or expand their own markets in southern Ontario and Quebec. After lengthy hearings, however, the U.S. Federal Power Commission approved Trans-Canada's application, in June 1967, on the ground that the proposed line would contribute to U.S. national security by providing ready access to additional supplies from Canadian reserves in the event of an emergency.

But the most complex and most persistent of all these bilateral resource problems are the ones relating to water. As one observer has put it, "Falling water is to twentieth-century North American diplomacy what fisheries were to the nineteenth century's."* The nature of the problem can be illustrated by reference to two major questions, the development of the Columbia River and the possibilty of exporting Canadian fresh water to the United States.

The mighty Columbia River, starting from its headwaters in southeastern British Columbia, flows first in a northwesterly direction and then southward until it crosses the forty-ninth parallel into the state of Washington, eventually to reach the Pacific Ocean. It is more than twelve hundred miles in total length, about one third in Canada and two thirds in the United States. Its headwaters are only a few thousand feet west of the Kootenay River which flows *south* into Montana (as the Kootenai) before it returns, through Idaho, into British Columbia to become linked by lakes with the Columbia River. Although the Columbia and its tributaries have had many uses over the years, by the 1930's hydroelectric-power development overshadowed

---

*J. G. Eayrs, "Sharing a Continent: The Hard Issues," in *The United States and Canada*, ed. J. S. Dickey (Englewood, N.J., 1964), p. 82.

all others. It was in this decade that the Grand Coulee Dam was built, to be followed by the McNary, the Bonneville, the Chief Joseph, and others, all in the United States. In the 1940's it was evident that the power potential on the American section of the river was within sight of being fully developed, yet the demand for cheap power in the Pacific northwestern states was still growing rapidly. There appeared to be little possibility of extensive further expansion unless storage dams were built on the upper Columbia, within Canada, to even out the year-round flow of water and thus make the American dams more efficient. Accordingly the question was submitted to the International Joint Commission in 1944 for study and recommendations.

On the Canadian side, there was a good deal of confusion and uncertainty. Because natural resources were under provincial jurisdiction, the government of British Columbia was directly concerned, but its outlook often differed from that of the federal authorities. Some of these advocated that Canada make its own plans for power development (and also irrigation) based upon diversion of the Kootenay into the Columbia and, possibly, of the Columbia into the Fraser. On the other hand, British Columbia spokesmen were increasingly in favor of selling their rights to Columbia power to the United States, arguing that the province's future needs should be met by developing the Peace River, far to the north. Eventually, the United States accepted a new concept, that of downstream benefits: half of the additional power generated in American dams as a result of storage facilities built in Canada would belong to the latter, and Canada would also receive payments for contributing to flood control along the American section of the river. After protracted negotiations in which, some Canadian spokesmen later alleged, the Canadian side was both divided and inadequately prepared, a treaty was finally concluded late in 1960 and signed by President Eisenhower and Prime Minister Diefenbaker in January 1961 just before the president went out of office.

A few weeks later the United States Senate approved the

treaty, with only one negative vote, but no action was taken by the Canadian Parliament. As months and then years went by, it became clear that there was sharp opposition to the treaty in Canada. On the one hand, the former chairman of the Canadian section of the International Joint Commission, General A. G. L. McNaughton, and other critics, argued that the treaty failed to protect Canadian interests because both the storage dams called for on the Canadian side and the projected Libby Dam on the Kootenai, in Montana, foreclosed the possibility of future large-scale power production on the Columbia system north of the forty-ninth parallel. McNaughton charged that the treaty amounted to "servitude in perpetuity of our vital rights and interests" and that it was worse than the Alaska Boundary award. But from a political point of view the most effective opposition to the treaty came from the government of British Columbia, which insisted that it did not need, or want, the power to which Canada would be entitled under the concept of downstream benefits. Instead of having this power transmitted for sale in the Vancouver area, the provincial government wished to sell it in the United States and thus realize a large cash return. This proposal, however, clashed with a long-standing Canadian policy against the export of large blocks of electrical energy on a long-term basis, as this technically would be. The resulting stalemate led to mounting impatience on the American side, which was ready either to buy or to transmit Canada's share of the power, but which above all wanted an early start on construction of the storage dams in Canada intended to prevent summer flood damage and to increase winter flow.

Eventually, the views of the government of British Columbia prevailed, and by January 1964 a new protocol to the treaty had been negotiated. By this protocol the United States agreed to buy Canada's downstream benefits in advance and to increase the payments relating to flood control. In September the Columbia River Treaty was finally ratified in Ottawa, a first lump-sum payment of just under $254,000,000 (U.S.) was made, and Presi-

dent Johnson and Prime Minister Pearson marked the occasion
by flying over the Columbia basin and meeting together at the
Peace Arch on the international border south of Vancouver, B.C.
A few days later the American payment, which, one Canadian
expert charged, was not large enough to cover the costs of
building the storage capacity, was in turn transferred to the
premier of British Columbia.

Thus, after more than twenty years of arduous and highly
technical negotiations, complicated by the nature of federalism,
the two countries joined in a vast program of regional development. Each side had sought strenuously and tenaciously to strike
the best possible bargain, but neither had lost sight of the fact
that the twists and turns of the Columbia river system made their
interests interdependent. Many Canadians remained convinced
that their country had taken certain short-term advantages at the
expense of long-term power development north of the international border. The negotiations also showed the difficulties of
reconciling the interests of two adjoining regions at different
stages of industrial development. Nevertheless, Canadians who
found shortcomings in the treaty had to blame their own divisions and shortsightedness more than any undue pressure coming from their powerful neighbor. From a procedural point of
view the Columbia River negotiations were a good example of
the workings of Canadian-American bilaterial relations.

A second question, that of exporting Canadian water to the
United States, is potentially of much vaster dimensions than
Columbia River development, although as yet discussions are
only at the exploratory stage. Every forecast indicates, however,
that it will become crucial as early as the 1970's; indeed, a
Canadian cabinet minister has predicted that American offers to
buy Canadian water will be the greatest issue confronting
Canada in the next several decades.

In the United States, industrial, agricultural, and municipal
use of water increased more than eight-fold between 1900 and
1960, and careful estimates have indicated that water needs

would double between 1960 and 1980. By that date demand might well exceed supply and would almost certainly do so soon afterward. In these circumstances there has been a growing tendency to look northward where it is calculated that Canada owns one quarter to one third of the world's supply of fresh liquid surface water, more than half of it flowing northward into Hudson Bay, the northern Pacific, or the Arctic Ocean, and largely untapped for any human use. Several Americans, including the United States secretary of the interior, Stewart Udall, have suggested that water should be considered a North American continental resource. The most ambitious plan for diversion has been put forward by a Los Angeles engineering firm in the form of the North American Water and Power Alliance (NAWAPA), by which some $100 billion would be spent, over thirty years, to divert northwestern water to be used in Canada, the United States, and Mexico for irrigation, power, and other purposes. Although NAWAPA has been extensively studied by Congress, it has not been endorsed by the administration. The latter has, however, shown an interest in plans to divert to the Great Lakes waters flowing into Hudson Bay.

As yet the Canadian reaction to these and other proposals has been either cool or negative. It is well understood that Canada could not remain indifferent in the event of a highly critical American water shortage; pressure to reach an agreement would probably become irresistible. It is also clear that if and when water becomes Canada's most valuable natural resource, it could be a mighty lever in economic arrangements with the United States. Hence, Canadian officials have been insistent that there is no continental water in Canada, only Canadian water.

Moreover, Canadian spokesmen, both official and unofficial, worry aloud about the implications of large-scale water exports. The decision to remove the earlier prohibition on electrical power exports is regarded as sensible in view of changes in transmission technology, the existence of a continental grid, and the increasing range of competing forms of energy. If later

Canadian needs made it necessary, the export of power could probably be cancelled. Not so with water. If extensive regions in the United States became dependent on water diverted from Canada, it would then be quite impossible to rescind the arrangements. Canadians therefore state that they must assess their own resources and calculate their own future needs before entering into any firm commitments. They also look to future development within the country, arguing that people should be brought into Canada to use the water instead of diverting it beyond the border; water is never surplus if it can be used to lure new industry, agriculture, and wealth to Canada. Some observers also believe that the United States is facing not so much a water shortage as a crisis in the use of water; to divert northern water might delay action on pollution and related problems.

Finally, discussions on water problems, as we have seen in the Columbia River negotiations, cannot be restricted to officials of the two federal governments. Provincial, state, and municipal jurisdictions, as well as corporate and other interests and pressure groups, all have to be taken in account. For instance, despite annual losses, estimated to be some $100 million, caused by fluctuations in water levels on the Great Lakes, no agreement has been reached on effective regulation. On the even larger issue of mammoth water diversion schemes, many Canadians are fearful that their voice may be divided and uninformed at a time when the federal authority is on the defensive in relation to the provinces. In the United States, however, the federal power appears to be growing in relation to the states, and it has at its disposal an unrivaled scientific expertise. In these circumstances Canadian authorities see American moves to expedite discussions on water as a form of pressure.

The water question is, however, only the latest illustration of the fact that the interdependence of these two countries in North America is growing and not declining. This fact will not necessarily make for easy and amicable relations in the future. The weaker country sees each evidence of closer ties as a possible threat to its identity and independence. The stronger country, relatively unaware of Canada as an entity and of the American impact on it, is primarily interested in the practical, smooth (and speedy) settlement of each issue as it arises, and as a rule it sees each issue as unconnected with the others. If the bilateral relationship is to continue to be constructive and fruitful, each country will have to redouble its efforts to make it work. Canadians will need to conquer a certain ultrasensitiveness and to concentrate on developing carefully thought out, expertly researched positions to bring to the negotiations. Americans will need to try harder to see the larger contours of Canadian-American relations and, at times at least, forego certain immediate advantages that might come from hard bargaining on individual issues in order to preserve and strengthen a relationship highly important to the United States.

Western Hemisphere. Before turning to the broader world scene we should first look briefly at Canada's part in hemisphere affairs, where her approach has been in striking contrast to that of her neighbor. From the early years of its history, the United States saw this hemisphere as the potential, if not the actual, home of a new political system, better than the one left behind in the Old World. For a long time, relations with the various political entities of the hemisphere and a resolve to prevent interference in its affairs by outside powers had the highest priority in American foreign policy. Canadians, on the other hand, did not think of the hemisphere as a unit having any coherent political significance, and they maintained that it was far more important to preserve old ties across the Atlantic with the countries of western Europe than to develop new ones with the regions beyond Florida and the Rio Grande.

In any real sense, the question of a Canadian policy toward Latin America did not come up until the period of the Second World War. Before that time energies had been too heavily committed to internal development and to issues involving Great Britain and the United States for much attention to be directed southward. Moreover, because of their membership in the British Empire, Canadians were more likely to be concerned with such places as the Crimea, the Sudan, or South Africa than with Cuba, Brazil, or Chile. And, because Canadians did not lay claim to a distinctive foreign policy, relating to distant regions, until well into the twentieth century, there was no way of giving formal expression to whatever attitudes they may have had with respect to Latin America.

Meanwhile, there had been important developments in the Latin American policy of the United States. On one level, it had joined with the countries to the south in developing procedures to improve cooperation in many areas of activity and to facilitate the peaceful settlement of disputes. Out of these efforts had come in 1889 the International Union of American Republics, with its permanent secretariat, later called the Pan American Union. On another level, the United States, now indisputably a world power, had effectively asserted its hegemony in the hemisphere by such actions as those recalled by the Olney Note, the Platt Amendment, the Panama Treaty, and the Roosevelt Corollary. Actions on this second level tended to dampen Latin American enthusiasm for what was coming to be called the Pan American movement. Nevertheless, despite "dollar diplomacy" and landings by U.S. Marines, the movement stayed alive, and, with the advent of the Good Neighbor policy in the 1930's, it acquired a new vitality. Although a chair had been reserved for Canada at the Pan American Union building in Washington as early as 1910, it was only in the new atmosphere of the 1930's that there began to be some public discussion of Canadian affiliation with the Pan American movement.

To some Canadians the idea was distinctly attractive. Membership in the Union would be a further proof of Canada's independent status in the family of nations and a demonstration that the leading strings to the mother country had been cut. In the 1930's it was frequently asserted that Canada must see itself as an American nation, not as an outpost of Empire; joining the Union would emphasize Canada's American character. Those who felt isolationist in the face of the war brewing in Europe also favored a hemispheric outlook. Finally, there was a marked sympathy among some French Canadians for closer ties with Americans of Latin and Catholic culture.

Nevertheless, the great majority of Canadians were either uninterested in the Pan American system or opposed to membership in it. Latin America was far away, there were few historical, economic, or cultural ties with it, and, above all, Canadians had no desire to join an association that appeared to be dominated by the United States. The Pan American system had come into being to regularize the relations between the Latin American republics and their powerful neighbor, the United States; it had no direct relevance to the situation or problems of Canada. As we know now, the question was purely academic because, until the early 1940's, the United States was opposed to Canadian membership: as a monarchical Dominion in the Empire-Commonwealth owing allegiance to the King across the sea, Canada was thought to be ineligible for association with independent republics. Some Canadian banks, life insurance companies, public utilities, and other business firms extended their activities to Latin America, as did Catholic and Protestant missionaries; otherwise there was little interest in the area.

In the last twenty-five to thirty years the Canadian connection with Latin America has deepened somewhat. Diplomatic relations have been established with all countries in the hemisphere, and there has been a considerable growth in trade, although it is still very small in the total Canadian figures. (One third of Canada's imports from the area consists of Venezuela oil.) Interest in Latin American history and culture has expanded considerably, and improved travel facilities have increased the number of Canadians who have some direct knowledge of the countries to the south.

But it is not the vitality of her ties with Latin America that now serves to spotlight attention on Canada's role in the hemisphere. Instead, the new focus stems from the evolution of the Pan American system and from the growing problem of aid to underdeveloped countries.

By 1948 the Pan American system had been transformed into a full-fledged regional security pact, the Organization of American States, with which was also associated a wide range of social, cultural, economic, and scientific activities. As the richest and most powerful member, the United States could never have anything but the leading role in the O.A.S.; nevertheless, the United States, to a greater extent than in earlier years, tried hard to work with the Latin American countries on a basis of equality and cooperation. For their part, the Latin Americans, despite some uneasiness over their close association with the Colossus of the North, determined to make the O.A.S. into an effective forum for consultation and cooperation.

As a result, both the United States and Latin America became openly and, almost insistently, favorable to Canadian membership in the O.A.S. Both sides saw that the Organization's claim to be a clearing house for the affairs of the hemisphere would be strengthened if the country with the hemisphere's largest territorial expanse should join. Complaints of Canada's "aloofness" were heard with some regularity and from widely separated sources. For its part, the United States was intensely aware of the magnitude of the tasks which had to be undertaken in its various Latin American programs and wished Canada to commit itself to a share in the responsibility. Many prominent American spokesmen, most notably President Kennedy in 1961, argued that O.A.S. membership would be the surest proof that Canada could give of its interest in Latin America. Perhaps the United States also hoped that the occasionally sharp bipolarity of its relations with Latin America within the O.A.S. would be eased by Canadian membership. For their part, the Latin American countries saw Canadian participation as a further offset to the power of the United States and as a promise of a strengthened attack upon social and economic problems. And, indeed, urging came from another source: it appears that the British government encouraged Canada to join in order to give the Commonwealth a voice in hemisphere discussions.

But social and economic problems in themselves forced attention upon Canada's relations with Latin America. As one of the prosperous countries of the northern hemisphere, Canada increasingly acknowledged a duty to provide assistance to the so-called underdeveloped countries, but most of her effort was directed toward southeast Asia and Africa, particularly to Commonwealth members. Somewhat belatedly, perhaps, Canadians have begun to realize that the needs of Latin America are both enormous and pressing and that they must make a much larger contribution in that region. The question has been whether an effective contribution required O.A.S. membership.

In response to these various factors and overtures the question of O.A.S. membership has frequently been broached in Canada during the last dozen years, although it has never been a topic of intense interest. For a time there was a disposition to evade the question on the ground that Canada's ability to function beyond its borders was fully taxed by United Nations and Commonwealth membership. More recently, prominent spokesmen of each major political party in Canada have from time to time announced strong, if rather vague, support of the general principle of O.A.S. membership and have predicted that Canada would certainly join the Organization sometime in the future; but this step, it was asserted, would have to wait until Canadian public opionion was clearly and positively favorable.

Meanwhile, arguments for and against O.A.S. membership are regularly reviewed in periodicals and other media. Those who support the step stress that Latin America, from being a distant region of minor significance to Canada, has become of vital and immediate importance because widespread social deterioration there could have a direct impact upon Canada. It is asserted, further, that Canada cannot make its most effective contribution to the amelioration of Latin American problems unless it assumes the responsibilities of O.A.S. membership: this Organization is not a tight military alliance under the domination of the United States but an effective and useful regional association, complementary to rather than competitive with the U.N. Even if the step were to be considered solely from the point of view of its impact upon relations with the United States, it could be argued that continued aloofness might prove to be a dangerous irritant, whereas membership would become one more means of conducting relations with the United States on a multilateral rather than a bilateral basis. Moreover, Canada, as a middle power with Commonwealth and European associations, would be able to play a role in Latin America which would be distinct from that of the United States. It is also noted that Trinidad and Tobago has joined the O.A.S. and that other Commonwealth-Caribbean countries have shown an interest in doing so; Canada should not bring up the rear. Finally, it would appear that most Canadians who have had any extensive personal or professional encounter with Latin America favor O.A.S. membership.

Spokesmen who oppose membership still occasionally refer to Canada's lack of close ties with Latin America, but increasingly it is acknowledged that the vast regions south of the United States are a crisis area that demands far more attention from Canada than it has received in the past. It is pointed out, however, that, without O.A.S. membership, Canada contributes to the Inter-American Development Bank and has an expanding program for assisting in the development of Commonwealth entities in the Caribbean. Nor is O.A.S. membership necessary for participation in a wide variety of inter-American scientific and cultural activities: Canada is a full member of the Inter-American Radio Office, the Inter-American Statistical Institute, the Pan-American Institute of Geography and History and sends delegates and observers to many other conferences and agencies. Further, it is argued that neither Canada nor the O.A.S. would gain prestige from the simple act of joining, because everything would depend on the nature and quality of Canada's subsequent participation.

On this point many Canadians have long expressed misgivings. They believe that, once in the O.A.S., Canada would have to side either with the United States or with a considerable bloc of populous Latin American countries voting against the United States. Either way, Canada would become unpopular without serving or protecting any essential national interest. There are enough problems in Canadian–United States relations without adding to them open and recorded differences respecting Latin American policy. There is also a lack of sympathy in Canada with what is thought to be an exclusivist attitude on the part of the United States toward Latin America, which discourages non-hemispheric interest in Latin American affairs. As a crisis area, Latin America is of legitimate concern to all parts of the world. Canadian membership in the O.A.S. might lend aid and comfort to the supposed American view that the outside world should keep its hands off the western hemisphere.

But more immediate objection to O.A.S. membership stems from opposition to the course of recent United States foreign policy, particularly that relating to Cuba and the Dominican Republic. Most Canadians (who had any view on the matter) believed that the United States either bypassed the O.A.S. or used it as an instrument of its own policy in dealing with Cuba in the early 1960's and with the Dominican Republic in 1965. The Canadian government saw no reason to sever diplomatic relations or end trade with Castro's Cuba; it would have been under considerable pressure to do these things from within the O.A.S., although such pressure can be resisted, as Mexico's example has shown. Even more sharply, Canadians felt that the O.A.S. had been humiliated when the United States intervened unilaterally in the Dominican Republic in 1965; this event dealt a strong blow to the growth of pro-O.A.S. feeling within Canada. It was widely asserted that the United States government used, or ignored, the O.A.S. according to its conception of American national interest. In the Canadian view, any supervisory or peacekeeping operations in the Latin American area should be under U.N., not O.A.S., auspices.

It nevertheless remains possible that such factors as a continued broadening of the scope of O.A.S. activities, further acceptance of the concept of regional organizations, and increased Canadian intercourse with Latin America may lead to the conclusion that more is to be gained than lost by applying for membership in the Organization of American States.

International Affairs. In recent years Canadians have frequently been puzzled over what role their country could, or should, play in world affairs. Earlier, before 1914, that role had been clear enough despite furious debate from time to time: the preservation of Canadian independence in North America and, when necessary, staunch support of Great Britain anywhere in the world. And later, between the two World Wars, there had also been broad agreement that Canada should insist upon recognition of its status as a full member of the family of nations but that it should also avoid becoming entangled in foreign affairs. In both periods, it was assumed that friendly relations with the United States were highly desirable, but there was little thought of the two countries coming together—either to agree or disagree—with respect to policies directed toward other parts of the world. Since 1945, however, Canadians, like the rest of the world, have had to cope with rapid and prodigious changes in the international state system, with the sudden and shattering accession of its neighbor to the rank of superpower, and in addition they have entered into an intimate military and diplomatic alliance with that neighbor. It has not always been easy to see what a Canadian role in world affairs should be in these circumstances.

In the almost quarter century since 1945 many suggestions have been put forward. One of the most durable of these has seen Canada as a "middle power," that is, Canada would perform functions, according to her power and capacity, which were somewhere between those of a great and of a small power. Canadians continue to find this vague term rather attractive and flattering (except when it has been interpreted to mean that Canada is geographically in the middle, between the United States and the Soviet Union!) but it is not clear that either great powers or small powers are ready to accord any special position to the so-called middle powers. In the dozen years after the end of the Second World War, when several leading countries of Europe and Asia were temporarily impotent and when vast regions of the world were still in a condition of colonial dependency, Canada was often a fairly conspicuous figure on the world scene. Relatively speaking, it was impossible to retain this position after the middle 1950's, and this fact has sometimes left Canadians with a certain sense of let-down.

It has also been argued that Canada should act as an "interpreter." Originally, this role meant smoothing and facilitating the conduct of Anglo-American relations; later, it was broadened to encompass much of western Europe on the one hand and North America on the other. In some minds the interpreting function should be concentrated on explaining the "old" Commonwealth to the "new," or the developed nations to the underdeveloped, and vice versa. These and other versions of the interpreting role implied that Canada and its spokesmen were above the bat- tle — disinterested, uniquely qualified to explain and reconcile opposing points of view, and duty-bound to bring cool words of reason to sweaty antagonists in the world arena. Yet this role had its limitations. Countries with issues to settle sometimes insisted upon settling them without Canadian assistance. In an increas- ingly complex world there was a growing number of problems about which Canadians were uninformed and from which they were remote both spatially and psychologically.

In some quarters it was argued that Canada could make its most constructive contribution to world affairs by adopting a neutral or nonaligned stance. This view implied severe criticism of the main lines of United States foreign policy, especially what was thought to be its rigid anticommunist emphasis and its reliance on military alliances, and it held that Canada should join with countries like India to induce the United States to modify dangerous policies. A related idea was that Canada should drasti- cally reduce its arms budget and greatly increase its contribution to foreign aid. But this point of view, while it had a considerable appeal in some intellectual and religious circles, never received widespread support. The public as a whole felt that Canada should take its stand with "the free world" against communism; in any event, it was heavily influenced by the American mass media to see world affairs in this light. Many respected analysts argued that Canada would have less influence in the world, not more, if it defected from the western alliance in favor of isolation, neutrality, and military weakness. Moreover, no Canadian gov- ernment of the period, whatever the private views of its members, was prepared to discover what pressure or retaliation from Washington might follow a policy of Canadian nonalignment.

The viewpoint which has prevailed, therefore, is that Canada should be a loyal and steadfast member of the western alliance, of which the United States is the leader. It should be prepared to pay the "dues" of membership in the form of military contributions, and while free to differ on points of emphasis it should never forsake its friends, especially the United States. But this role was less than satisfying to many Canadians, for after a century of evolution toward nationhood it seemed to offer little scope for independent action. Indeed, it was often charged that Canada had become little more than a "satellite" of its mighty neighbor, impelled, as in the Suez crisis, to desert such old friends as the United Kingdom and France. Moreover, did association with the United States in the NATO framework mean that Canada must invariably support American policies in other parts of the world, in Asia, Latin America, or the Middle East? Was it a "principle of partnership" that Canada should not differ publicly from American policy unless its own national interest was directly involved? Such questions as these have contributed to the Canadians' puzzlement.

Although the questions did not cease and, as will be noted at the end of this chapter, were being asked more insistently than ever in 1966-1967, it is possible to make some general statements about Canada's conduct of foreign policy within the framework of its close association with the United States.

An aspect on which emphasis has been placed relates to style. Canadians have tried hard to earn a reputation for competent and informed diplomacy as well as for a pragmatic, nondogmatic approach to problems. For the most part, Canadian spokesmen have avoided the temptation to coin ringing phrases, to assume dramatic ideological poses, and to score debating points against adversaries. Instead, they have spoken in vague, even platitudinous, generalities in public while striving to be skillful and well briefed in behind-the-scenes discussions and negotiations.

Whether or not Canadians have exhibited these qualities to any greater extent than have the representatives of other countries, they have earnestly believed that this style is essential for a country in Canada's position.

Turning from style to content, one of the favorite generalities of Canadian spokesmen has been that their foreign policy is firmly based upon support of the United Nations. Variations on this cliché are, of course, the stock in trade of most U.N. members, but Canadians express them with a peculiarly ardent sincerity. There is the memory of a long and continuous role, dating back to the founding in San Francisco when Canada seemed to be not much below the level of a great power. Unlike all of the great powers and many of the smaller ones, Canada has never felt restricted, threatened, or put on the defensive by U.N. debates or resolutions. Its citizens have rarely if ever seen the world organization in an unfavorable light, as have many Americans.

Instead, Canadians have seen it as a forum for constructive action. Canada has taken a full part in its many agencies and committees. It has ranked from second to fourth among all contributors to U.N. development, relief, and food programs. It gave support to the so-called "police action" in Korea and participated in nearly all the "peacekeeping" and truce supervision operations mounted since the late 1940's. Indeed, so much has been said about "peacekeeping" in the Canadian press that Canadians may be in some danger of thinking that they invented the idea and are mainly responsible for its success. Canadians have also usually given support to the principle that the U.N. should be inclusive in its membership policy. In 1955 the Canadian delegation helped to find a formula which led to the admission of several new members, from both east and west. In 1966 Canada supported a "two China" policy, but so far has not pushed the principle of universality to cover such divided countries as Germany, Korea, and Vietnam. In these and many other activities, Canada sees an opportunity to make an effective contribution to world order that is based on the value of the ideas it can put forward rather than the armed might which it wields.

For it is becoming clear in the 1960's that countries outside the small group of superpowers and great powers have an essential role to play in the newly emerging state system. Great powers that are saddled with vast responsibilities, extensive commitments, and ponderous military establishments are often very nearly immobilized in fixed diplomatic positions. They have too much at stake, both on their own account and that of their allies, to take a daring or experimental lead in proposals to alter the status quo. Thus, smaller powers have to send up the trial balloons and argue for change and adjustment. No smaller country can have a monopoly on work of this kind, but the more experienced, the more competent, and the more imaginative its representatives are, the more often they will be able to serve the needs of accommodation and adjustment. There is one danger in this work, which Canadians at least have not always avoided, and that is the unjustified sense that smaller countries function on a higher level of virtue than do the great powers. Nor is it always a fact that the proposals put forward by smaller powers have originated with them. But it is the fate of great powers in our era to have to put up with moralizing lectures from their weaker brethren and, often, to see others take the credit for ideas which they could not themselves advance.

Another reason for Canada's U.N. enthusiasm has often been mentioned. As a way of offsetting the intense but inevitable intimacy of bilateral Canadian-American relations, Canada welcomes opportunities for placing at least some of the discussions with her neighbor within a multilateral setting. (The same argument has been used to support NATO membership and to justify entry into the Organization of American States.) Thus U.N. membership lessens the glaring focus on relations with the United States and constantly reminds Canadians that they have duties and opportunities on the world stage that have little or even nothing to do with their neighbor.

When we turn to consider foreign policy as an instrument for preserving national security, it is apparent at once that, in the postwar period, membership in NATO has been the most basic factor in Canada's participation in world affairs. It is often asserted that Canadian leaders were the first to call publicly for such an alliance. Since 1949 Canada has always striven to play a full and faithful part in the Organization. Moreover, it is in respect to the North Atlantic area that Canada has found itself in fullest agreement with the cardinal features of American foreign policy. In this realm Canada has paid frequent tribute to the generosity and imaginativeness of American statesmanship and for the most part has loyally supported American leadership. In fact, Canada's concentration on the affairs of the North Atlantic world has been so intense and so sustained that there has often been much too little thought given to other areas in a rapidly changing world.

Despite general agreement, however, Canadian-American collaboration within NATO has not been without occasional friction. From the very beginning, a relatively small but articulate body of opinion, on the noncommunist left, has argued that NATO served no purpose but to intensify the tensions of the Cold War. A more widely held viewpoint accepted the need for NATO, but insisted that it should be more than simply an old-fashioned military alliance. Canada was largely responsible for the inclusion of Article Two in the treaty, which looked to economic cooperation; and on countless occasions since 1949 Canadian spokesmen have asserted that NATO must be thought of as "a stage in the evolution of a true Atlantic coalition between like-minded states who uphold the same basic ideals and values about human rights and dignity."* As in many other instances, this vision of NATO convinced Canadians that they had a nobler approach to international affairs than did the Americans who kept

---

*Paul Martin, secretary of state for external affairs, in an address to the Overseas Press Club of America, New York, May 28, 1963 (*Statements and Speeches*, Information Division, Department of External Affairs, Ottawa, No. 63/10).

their eyes firmly fixed on the question of deterring a possible Soviet attack.

There have also been Canadian misgivings with respect to various American proposals advanced over the years for making NATO more effective. The Eisenhower administration's emphasis upon nuclear weapons in the United States contribution to NATO defense and later plans to provide NATO with some form of nuclear deterrent usually had a bad press in Canada. There was also opposition in Canada to the "dumbbell" theory, popular in some Washington circles, by which Europe, having achieved unification, would be able to balance American power within NATO: such consolidation would allow no effective role for an independent Canada. As Lester Pearson once put it (1963), "We do not believe that continentalism, whether European or North American, it compatible with the Canadian interest."

More recently, Canadian voices have been added to those, in both the United States and Europe, who have argued that NATO has become obsolete because the danger of a Soviet military attack upon Europe is now slight. Although not expressing direct support for General de Gaulle's criticisms of the NATO structure, Canadian political leaders have asserted that the basic fault lies in that structure and not in the General's perversity. Indeed, in 1966 Canada's external affairs minister took the lead in opposing American efforts to build a united NATO front against the French, and her prime minister made a speech in Springfield, Illinois, indicating that France was right to be dissatisfied with an Atlantic alliance "dominated by America," and expressing agreement with de Gaulle's view that United States nuclear protection of Europe was no longer a credible deterrent. In short, Canada's support of American policy in Europe has not been of the blind and slavish variety, although it has been real and continuous.

In contrast to Europe, where the differences have been on points of emphasis, Asia is an area where prevailing American and Canadian viewpoints have been sharply divergent. In fact, since the late 1940's more harsh criticisms of United States Far Eastern policy have been made in Canada than of all other United States policies combined. At the official level an attitude of correctness has been observed, but the majority view in Canada has seldom been favorable on such subjects as General MacArthur's leadership during the Korean War, the refusal to recognize Communist China (despite a similar Canadian refusal) and United States opposition to the seating of the latter in the United Nations, John Foster Dulles's efforts to build a military alliance (SEATO) in southeast Asia, United States support of Chiang Kai Shek on Taiwan, United States policy respecting the offshore islands (Quemoy and Matsu), and the growing military role of the United States in Vietnam. The observer who is looking for Canadian-American differences can nowhere see them more clearly than in attitudes toward Asian policy.

In part, Canadian views on Far Eastern policy can be explained by an absence of long and intimate association with the area. There is nothing comparable in Canadian experience to an American concern that traces back from the war against Japan, to the Open Door Notes, to the annexation of the Philippines, to the 1853 expedition of Commodore Matthew C. Perry, and to a wide-ranging eighteenth-century trade. Most Canadians have never been able to sympathize with the view held by a great many Americans that the United States has vital interests to protect on the other side of the Pacific and an important role to play there. With their eyes firmly fixed on Europe, Canadians, since 1941, have frequently exhibited anxiety and alarm at the possibility that the United States would become so deeply committed across the Pacific that it would give inadequate attention to Atlantic and European questions.

In part, also, Canadian views respecting Asia are simply the north-of-the-border counterpart of an attitude which has been repeatedly and powerfully expressed within the United States since the end of the Second World War. Americans who argued that the United States should not fight a land war in Asia, that it should try harder to normalize relations with Communist China, and that it should reduce rather than enlarge its military, naval, and diplomatic commitments in Asia were advocating policies that were supported almost without debate in Canada. To adopt recent terminology, arising out of the Vietnam war, most Canadians have been on the side of the doves rather than the hawks.

The Vietnam conflict illustrates the impact of Far Eastern affairs upon Canadian-American relations. In one very limited sense, Canada has had a longer direct connection with the Vietnam problem than has the United States, because by the Geneva Agreement of 1954 Canada, along with India and Poland, was made a member of the International Commission for Supervision and Control in Vietnam, Laos, and Cambodia. Although the reports of Canadian members of this commission have frequently shown more sympathy with or understanding of the role of the United States than have those from the other two countries, the Canadian government has nevertheless consistently argued that membership on the commission precludes Canadian participation in the conflict. Indeed, the government has often emphasized that it does not take sides in the conflict in order to be available as an intermediary, acceptable to Washington and Hanoi alike, when negotiations may become possible. But, despite a certain appearance of impartiality, official policy has fully supported the United States. The prime minister and the secretary of state for external affairs have on several occasions explicitly endorsed the view that the United States is in South Vietnam to defend the latter against communist aggression: "Its motives were honorable; neither mean nor imperialistic," in Pearson's words. Moreover, Canada is closely associated with the American war effort by its export of materials under the Canadian-United States defense production agreement. In consequence, occasional proposals by Canadian leaders for a pause in the bombing of North Vietnam do not weigh very heavily on the other side of the balance.

Not surprisingly, the Canadian government's policy has had its vigorous critics. On the American side, the administration has accepted the view that Canada's role on the International Control Commission precludes a closer identification with the conflict, but it is probably also true that Washington officials are unconvinced by the Canadian distinction between support for American motives and objectives and intermittent criticism of methods, tactics, and strategy. Among Congress, the press, and the general public, those who strongly support the war often express resentment and antagonism over what appears to be Canada's failure to support the United States.

In Canada, the Vietnam issue has led to widespread questioning of the tradition of "quiet diplomacy," that is, going to almost any lengths to avoid open differences with the United States. Critics argue that Canada's behind-the-scenes representations have little or no influence on Washington and that the government should openly oppose and condemn the course and conduct of the United States in Vietnam. At the least, Canada should give voice to a kind of loyal liberal opposition for those in North America who want a different approach from that embodied in official Washington policy. Others go further by advocating a ban on the export from Canada of materials for use in the Vietnam conflict.

If past policy is any guide, however, it is unlikely that the Canadian government will risk a first-class row with the United States for the sake of a more explicit or more principled Vietnam policy. In answer to the critics of "quiet diplomacy" Prime Minister Lester Pearson asserted that to accuse "the United States of sole guilt and sole blame for what has happened [in Vietnam] and by doing so trying to impose a kind of moral sanction against the United States ... would ... cut, or certainly weaken, the lines of official communication between Ottawa and Washington on this subject and I cannot think any useful purpose would be achieved by doing that, especially if we felt we could use those lines of communication to give good advice to our friends."[*]

[*]From a speech delivered in the House of Commons, May 24, 1967 (*Statements and Speeches*, Information Division, Department of External Affairs, No. 67/20).

Despite, or perhaps because, of the North American intimacy, Canadian policy if often more distinct from Washington's than is that of other allies such as West Germany or Australia. At present, however, there is little indication that the majority of Canadians wish to push for a sharper separation. Even if such a separation should some time occur on Vietnam or another issue, it would have to be within the framework of the innumerable ties which Canada has with the world's most powerful country.

Appendix Facts about Canada

TABLE 1. POPULATION

	1966	1961
Newfoundland	493,396	457,853
Prince Edward Island	108,535	104,629
Nova Scotia	756,039	737,007
New Brunswick	616,788	597,936
Quebec	5,780,845	5,259,211
Ontario	6,960,870	6,236,092
Manitoba	963,066	921,686
Saskatchewan	955,344	925,181
Alberta	1,463,203	1,331,944
British Columbia	1,873,674	1,629,082
Yukon Territory	14,382	14,628
Northwest Territories	28,730	22,998
CANADA	20,014,880	18,238,247

Source: Census of Canada, 1961, 1966.

TABLE 2.   DISTRIBUTION OF THE POPULATION
             BY ETHNIC GROUP

	Number	Percent
British	7,996,669	43.8
English	4,195,175	23.0
Irish	1,753,351	9.6
Scottish	1,902,302	10.4
Other	145,841	0.8
Other European	9,657,195	53.0
Austrian	106,535	0.6
Belgian	61,382	0.3
Czech and Slovak	73,061	0.4
Danish	85,473	0.5
Finnish	59,436	0.3
French	5,540,346	30.4
German	1,049,599	5.8
Greek	56,475	0.3
Hungarian	126,220	0.7
Icelandic	30,623	0.2
Italian	450,351	2.5
Jewish	173,344	1.0
Lithuanian	27,629	0.2
Netherlands	429,679	2.4
Norwegian	148,681	0.8
Polish	323,517	1.8
Romanian	43,805	0.2
Russian	119,168	0.7
Swedish	121,757	0.7
Ukrainian	473,337	2.6
Yugoslavic	68,587	0.4
Other	88,190	0.5
Asiatic	121,753	0.7
Chinese	58,197	0.3
Japanese	29,157	0.2
Other	34,399	0.2
Other Origins	462,630	2.5
Native Indian and Eskimo	220,121	1.2
Negro	32,127	0.2
Other and not stated	210,382	1.2

Source: Census of Canada, 1961.

TABLE 3.   PRINCIPAL RELIGIOUS DENOMINATIONS

	Number	Percent
Adventist	25,999	0.1
Anglican Church of Canada	2,409,068	13.2
Baptist	593,553	3.3
Greek Orthodox	239,766	1.3
Jehovah's Witnesses	68,018	0.4
Jewish	254,368	1.4
Lutheran	662,744	3.6
Mennonite	152,452	0.8
Mormon	50,016	0.3
Pentecostal	143,877	0.8
Presbyterian	818,558	4.5
Roman Catholic	8,342,826	45.7
Salvation Army	92,054	0.5
Ukrainian (Greek) Catholic	189,653	1.0
United Church of Canada	3,664,008	20.1
Other	531,287	2.9
TOTAL	18,238,247	100.0

Source: Census of Canada, 1961.

TABLE 4. POPULATION SPEAKING ONE, BOTH, OR
NEITHER OF THE OFFICIAL LANGUAGES

Province or Territory	English only	French only	English and French	Neither English nor French
Newfoundland	450,945	522	5,299	1,087
Prince Edward Island	95,296	1,219	7,938	176
Nova Scotia	684,805	5,938	44,987	1,277
New Brunswick	370,922	112,054	113,495	1,465
Quebec	608,635	3,254,850	1,338,878	56,848
Ontario	5,548,766	95,236	493,270	98,820
Manitoba	825,955	7,954	68,368	19,409
Saskatchewan	865,821	3,853	42,074	13,433
Alberta	1,253,824	5,534	56,920	15,666
British Columbia	1,552,560	2,559	57,504	16,459
Yukon Territory	13,679	38	825	86
Northwest Territories	13,554	109	1,614	7,721
CANADA	12,284,762	3,489,866	2,231,172	232,447

Source: Census of Canada, 1961.

TABLE 5. LAND AND FRESHWATER AREAS

Province or Territory	Land (sq. miles)	Fresh water (sq. miles)	Total	Percent of total area
Newfoundland	143,045	13,140	156,185	4.1
Island of Newfoundland	41,164	2,195	43,359	1.1
Labrador	101,881	10,945	112,826	3.0
Prince Edward Island	2,184	—	2,184	0.1
Nova Scotia	20,402	1,023	21,425	0.6
New Brunswick	27,835	519	28,354	0.7
Quebec	523,860	71,000	594,860	15.4
Ontario	344,092	68,490	412,582	10.7
Manitoba	211,775	39,225	251,000	6.5
Saskatchewan	220,182	31,518	251,700	6.5
Alberta	248,800	6,485	255,285	6.6
British Columbia	359,279	6,976	366,255	9.5
Yukon Territory	205,346	1,730	207,076	5.4
Northwest Territories	1,253,438	51,465	1,304,903	33.9
CANADA	3,560,238	291,571	3,851,809	100.0

Source: *Canada Year Book, 1966.*

TABLE 6.   IMPORTS BY COUNTRIES — ($'000)

	1965	1966
Western Europe	1,335,646	1,429,912
Eastern Europe	44,588	56,566
Middle East	104,496	110,848
Other Africa	86,431	116,524
Other Asia	396,790	430,375
Oceania	72,273	83,968
South America	364,832	319,041
Central America and Antilles	183,185	183,557
United States of America	6,044,831	7,135,860
TOTAL	8,633,148[a]	9,866,841[b]

Source: Dominion Bureau of Statistics, External Trade Division.

[a]of this total, 991,838 comes from Commonwealth and preferential countries.

[b]of this total, 1,061,035 comes from Commonwealth and preferential countries.

TABLE 7.   IMPORTS BY SECTIONS FROM PRINCIPAL COUNTRIES, 1966 ($'000)

	All Countries	U.S.
Live animals	12,910	12,241
Food, feed, beverages, and tobacco	791,741	402,097
Crude materials, inedible	1,023,461	506,688
Fabricated materials, inedible	2,233,137	1,481,763
End products, inedible	5,483,420	4,451,648
Special transactions — trade	322,172	281,424
TOTAL	9,866,841	7,135,860

Source: Dominion Bureau of Statistics, External Trade Division.

TABLE 8.   IMPORTS BY COMMODITIES: SOME MAIN ITEMS, 1966 ($'000)

	All Countries	U.S.
Indian corn, shelled	31,554	31,548
Green coffee	64,877	8,704
Soya beans	52,438	52,436
Raw cotton	45,624	29,313
Iron ore	56,024	52,442
Alumina	52,341	13,684
Coal, bituminous and subbituminous	134,039	134,039
Crude Petroleum	299,001	—
Fuel Oil, heavy oil	52,124	9,993
Front end loaders	45,596	44,333
Combine reaper-threshers	44,543	42,833
Wheel tractors	130,043	108,624
Tractor parts and attachments	70,074	64,696
Automobiles		
Closed sedans, new	348,632	270,150
Trucks and chassis, commercial, new	51,931	51,931
Motor vehicle engines	97,860	92,181
Parts of motor vehicle engines	85,779	83,063
Parts and accessories for motor vehicles	829,021	815,298
Parts of aircraft engines	66,587	47,514
Aircraft assemblies, equipment and parts	83,350	75,301
Electronic computers and parts	93,495	83,126
Books and pamphlets	51,772	45,580
Shipments of less than $200 each	257,301	227,234
Settlers' effects	83,036	53,725
Tourist purchases exempt from duty	42,871	29,130

Source: Dominion Bureau of Statistics, External Trade Division.

TABLE 9.   DOMESTIC EXPORTS BY COUNTRIES (IN DOLLARS)

	1965	1966
Western Europe	2,038,662,614	2,038,154,138
Eastern Europe	313,293,635	398,414,830
Middle East	33,445,774	41,989,303
Other Africa	113,848,702	105,024,249
Other Asia	572,284,069	802,262,481
Oceania	179,985,923	161,595,085
South America	191,922,111	232,512,375
Central America and Antilles	238,328,672	259,856,395
United States	4,840,456,072	6,027,721,871
TOTAL	8,525,078,177	10,070,765,810

Source: Dominion Bureau of Statistics, External Trade Division.

TABLE 10.   EXPORTS, CANADA TO UNITED STATES, 1966
(IN DOLLARS)

Live animals	$ 68,951,450
Food, feed, beverages and tobacco	429,365,728
Crude materials, inedible	1,122,690,801
Fabricated materials, inedible	2,760,777,057
End products, inedible	1,625,975,331

Source: Dominion Bureau of Statistics, External Trade Division.

TABLE 11. PRODUCTION OF CERTAIN METALLIC MINERALS AND FUELS, 1963

	Gold '000 oz. T.	Silver "	Copper '000 T.	Iron '000 T.	Lead '000 T.	Zinc '000 T.	Coal '000 T.	Crude petroleum '000 Tons
Canada	4,003.1	29,932.0	452.6	30,143.6	201.2	473.7	10,575.7	38,327.2
United States	1,468.7	34,999.3	1,213.2	45,792.2	253.4	529.2	474,489.8	410,060.8

Source: *Canada Year Book, 1966.*

TABLE 12. GEOGRAPHICAL DISTRIBUTION OF THE BALANCE
ON CURRENT ACCOUNT BETWEEN CANADA AND
OTHER COUNTRIES, 1946-1964
(MILLIONS OF DOLLARS)

Year	United States	Britain	Other overseas countries	All countries
1946	−607	+500	+470	+363
1949	−601	+446	+332	+177
1952	−849	+388	+625	+164
1955	−1,035	+330	+ 7	−698
1958	−1,176	+104	− 59	−1,131
1961	−1,386	+187	+217	−982
1964	−1,655	+607	+615	−433

Source: *Canada Year Book, 1966.*

TABLE 13. FOREIGN CAPITAL INVESTED IN CANADA
(MILLIONS OF DOLLARS)

	1930	1945	1951	1959	1963
United States	4,660	4,990	7,259	15,826	20,488
Britain	2,766	1,750	1,778	3,199	3,331
Other countries	188	352	440	1,832	2,384

Source: *Canada Year Book, 1966.*

TABLE 14   CANADIAN LONG-TERM INVESTMENT ABROAD,
DECEMBER 31, 1963 ($'000)

Location of investment	Direct invest- ment	Portfolio investment		Govern- ment credits	Total invest- ment
		Stocks	Bonds		
United States	1,997	1,197	111	—	3,305
Britain	385	53	16	1,039	1,493
Other Commonwealth countries	366	13	29	29	437
Other foreign countries	397	259	119	217	992
TOTAL	3,145	1.522	275	1,285	6,227

Source: *Canada Year Book, 1966.*

TABLE 15.   PRICE OF THE U.S. DOLLAR, SELECTED MONTHS
AND YEARS, 1956-1966 (Canadian cents per U.S. dollar)

Month	1956	1958	1960	1962	1964	1966
Jan.	99.87	98.47	95.31	104.50	108.02	107.46
Mar.	99.87	97.73	95.09	104.94	108.05	107.62
May	99.18	96.69	97.81	108.23	108.09	107.67
July	98.18	96.00	97.84	107.89	108.13	107.48
Sept.	97.77	97.68	97.25	107.68	107.61	107.62
Nov.	96.44	96.83	97.67	107.68	107.39	108.20
Annual average	98.41	97.06	96.97	106.89	107.86	107.65

Source: *Canada Year Book, 1966.*

TABLE 16.   MEMBERS OF THE HOUSE OF COMMONS, 1966

131	Liberal
97	Progressive Conservative
21	New Democratic Party
9	Ralliement Créditiste
5	Social Credit
1	Progressive Conservative Independent
1	Independent

Source: *McGraw-Hill Directory and Almanac of Canada, 1967.*

Suggested Readings

For the most part, the following brief bibliography is confined to items published since 1960. Readers wishing a guide to earlier writing on Canada and Canadian-American relations will find useful book lists in G. W. Brown, ed., *Canada* (Berkeley and Los Angeles: University of California Press, 1950) and J. B. Brebner, *Canada: A Modern History* (Ann Arbor: The University of Michigan Press, 1960).

Because this book was prepared with American readers in mind, the general rule followed below is to cite the American place of publication and publisher; Canadian data are given for works not published in the United States.

Bibliographies

Canadiana (Ottawa: Queen's Printer), appearing monthly, lists all major publications of Canadian origin or interest, as noted by Canada's National Library. Several learned journals provide quarterly bibliographies; among the most important of these are the *Canadian Historical Review* and the *Canadian Journal of Economics and Political Science* (Toronto: University of Toronto Press), and *Canadian Literature* (Vancouver: University of British Columbia). In November 1966 the United States Information Service, U.S. Embassy, Ottawa, issued an extensive mimeographed *List of Selected Publications and Sources of Information* on Canadian-American Relations.

General Reference

Of numerous publications issued by the Dominion Bureau of Statistics (Ottawa: Queen's Printer) the most generally useful are the annual *Canada Year Book* and *Canada: Official Handbook of Present Conditions and Recent Progress.* In 1967 the latter appeared in an enlarged edition under the title *Canada: One Hundred Years 1867-1967.* Further statistical material is available in M. C. Urquhart, ed., *Historical Statistics of Canada, 1867–1960* (Toronto: Macmillan, 1965). Other annual reference works are the *Canadian Almanac and Directory* (Toronto: Copp Clark), *McGraw-Hill Directory and Almanac of Canada* (Toronto: McGraw-Hill, since 1966), *Canadian Who's Who* (Toronto: Trans-Canada Press) and *The Canadian Parliamentary Guide*, edited by Pierre G. Normandin (Ottawa). The *Encyclopedia Canadiana* (Ottawa: Grolier of Canada Limited, 1966, ten volumes) is similar in scope to the *Encyclopedia Americana*. In 1966 appeared the first volume of a long-range project, the *Dictionary of Canadian Biography/Dictionnaire biographique du Canada* (Toronto and Quebec: University of Toronto Press and Les Presses de l'Université Laval), Vol. I, 1000-1700, a work which will be a Canadian equivalent of the *Dictionary of American Biography* and the *Dictionary of National Biography*. In the meantime one may consult a shorter work, the *Macmillan Dictionary of Canadian Biography*, 3rd ed. (New York: St. Martin's Press, 1963), edited by W. Stewart Wallace. The *Canadian Annual Review* (Toronto: University of Toronto Press, since 1960) combines factual summary with interpretative comment. In a different form the *Canadian Annual Review of Public Affairs* (Toronto: The Annual Review Publishing Co.) was earlier published for the years 1902 to 1938.

The Land and the People

For those who like to begin by gaining some impression of what Canada looks like, there are many volumes of photographs. Roloff Beny, *To Every Thing There Is a Season* (Toronto: Longmans Canada, 1967) is perhaps the most sumptuous book to be inspired by the 1967 Centennial. Striking photographs of both the natural and the human scenery are also to be found in *Canada as Seen by the Camera of Yousuf Karsh and Described in the Words of John Fisher* (Toronto: Thomas Allen, 1960), *Canada*. Photographed by Peter Varley, introduction by Kildare Dobbs (Toronto: Macmillan, 1964), and *Canada, 20th Century*, by Guy Boulizon and Geoffrey Adams (Montreal: Beauchemin, 1965).

Although descriptive accounts often date rather quickly, one might mention Edward McCourt, *The Road across Canada* (Toronto: Macmillan, 1965), a motorist's chronicle of a journey on the Trans-Canada Highway from Newfoundland to British Columbia, and Gerald Clark, *Canada: The Uneasy Neighbor* (New York: David McKay, 1965), by one of Canada's leading journalists.

An atlas is especially useful in studying a country of Canada's vast territorial expanse. The *Oxford Regional Economic Atlas of the United States and Canada* (New York: Oxford University Press, 1967) provides urban plans, topographical maps of the continent by areas, special topic maps, and a gazeteer. The Canadian Department of Mines and Technical Surveys has published an *Atlas of Canada* (Ottawa: Queen's

Printer, 1957). Two historical treatments are D. G. G. Kerr, *An Historical Atlas of Canada* (Toronto: Nelson, 1960) and J. W. Chalmers, W. J. Eccles, and H. Fullard, *Philips' Historical Atlas of Canada* (London: George Philip, 1966).

Of numerous geographic accounts, two that concentrate on Canada are P. Camu, E. P. Weeks, and Z. W. Sametz, *Economic Geography of Canada* (New York: Macmillan, 1964) and John Warkentin, ed., *Canada: a Geographical Interpretation* (Toronto: Methuen Publications, 1967). Among many books on the continent as a whole are W. R. Mead and E. H. Brown, *The United States and Canada: A Regional Geography* (London: Hutchinson, 1962); P. F. Griffin, R. N. Young, and R. L. Chatham, *Anglo-America: A Regional Geography of the United States and Canada* (San Francisco: Fearon Publishers, 1962); A. J. Wright, *The United States and Canada: An Economic Geography* (New York: Appleton-Century-Crofts, 1956); and J. Wreford Watson, *North America: Its Countries and Regions* (London: Longmans, 1963).

Although Canada is pre-eminently a country of regions, there are not as many good regional studies as one would expect. Some provincial histories may be cited: W. L. Morton, *Manitoba: A History*, 2nd ed. (Toronto: University of Toronto Press, 1967); Margaret Ormsby, *British Columbia: A History* (Toronto: Macmillan, 1958); and John Chadwick, *Newfoundland: Island Into Province* (Toronto: Macmillan, 1967). In recent years several books have been devoted to the regions north of the fifty-fifth parallel, including R. A. J. Phillips, *Canada's North* (Toronto: Macmillan, 1967) and R. S. MacDonald, ed., *The Arctic Frontier* (Toronto: University of Toronto Press, 1966).

Among studies of the social structure of the Canadian population the outstanding work is John Porter, *The Vertical Mosaic: An Analysis of Social Class and Power in Canada* (Toronto: University of Toronto Press, 1965); its footnotes refer to most of the important literature on the subject down to its time of publication. Some textbook accounts are B. R. Blishen *et al.*, *Canadian Society* (Toronto: Macmillan, 1961); Richard Laskin, ed., *Social Problems: A Canadian Profile* (New York: McGraw-Hill, 1964); and S. D. Clark, *The Developing Canadian Community* (Toronto: University of Toronto Press, 1962). See also S. D. Clark, ed., *Urbanism and the Changing Canadian Society* (Toronto: University of Toronto Press, 1961) and Guy Sylvestre, ed., *Structures sociales du Canada français* (Toronto and Quebec: University of Toronto Press and Les Presses de l'Université Laval, 1966).

Cultural Life

There has been no space in this book for a discussion of cultural activity in Canada, but those interested in the subject can consult the following: C. F. Klinck *et al.*, eds., *Literary History of Canada* (Toronto: University of Toronto Press, 1965); Gérard Tougas, *History of French-Canadian Literature* (Toronto: Ryerson Press, 1966); Norah Story, ed., *The Oxford Companion to Canadian History and Literature* (Toronto: Oxford University Press, 1967); J. Russell Harper, *Painting in Canada* (Toronto and Quebec: University of Toronto Press and Les Presses de l'Université de Laval, 1966); Alan Gowans, *Building Canada: An Architectural History of Canadian Life* (New York: Oxford University Press, 1966); and Ernest MacMillan, *Music in Canada* (Toronto: University of Toronto Press, 1955). One of the well-known critic's less successful books was Edmund Wilson, *O Canada: An American's Notes on Canadian Culture* (New York: Farrar Straus, 1964).

Government and Politics

Only a few general treatments are listed here; works relating to particular periods or topics are cited below. The standard descriptive account is R. M. Dawson, revised by Norman Ward, *The Government of Canada*, 4th ed. (Toronto: University of Toronto Press, 1963). This book is one of many in the Canadian Government Series, published by the same press. J. E. Hodgetts and D. C. Corbett, *Canadian Public Administration* (Toronto: Macmillan, 1960) deals with a wide variety of topics, both theoretical and practical. Paul W. Fox, ed., *Politics: Canada*, rev. ed. (Toronto: McGraw-Hill, 1966) and H. G. Thorburn, *Party Politics in Canada* (Toronto: Prentice-Hall, 1963) are collections of readings, intended mainly for college students. R. M. Clark, ed., *Canadian Issues: Essays in Honour of Henry F. Angus* (Toronto: University of Toronto Press, 1961) and J. H. Aitchison, ed., *The Political Process in Canada: Essays in Honour of R. M. Dawson* (Toronto: University of Toronto Press, 1963) are collections of essays. Abraham Rotstein, ed., *The Prospect of Change: Proposals for Canada's Future* (New York: McGraw-Hill, 1965) has essays on politics as well as on economics, foreign policy, and cultural life. Canadian politics is not rich in revealing autobiographical memoirs, but *A Party Politician: The Memoirs of Chubby Power*, ed. Norman Ward (Toronto: Macmillan, 1966) should be mentioned.

Economic Life

Serious writing on the Canadian economy is much more extensive than that on Canadian politics; again, only the more general works are listed here. André Raynauld, *The Canadian Economic System* (Toronto: Macmillan, 1967) is an up-to-date analysis, and other general surveys are R. E. Caves and R. H. Holton, *The Canadian Economy: Prospect and Retrospect* (Cambridge, Mass.: Harvard University Press, 1959) and Ian Drummond, *The Canadian Economy: Organization and Development* (Homewood, Ill.: Richard D. Irwin, Inc., 1966). M. H. Watkins and D. F. Forster, eds., *Economics: Canada* (Toronto: McGraw-Hill, 1963) and J. J. Deutsch *et al.*, eds., *The Canadian Economy: Selected Readings*, rev. ed. (Toronto: Macmillan, 1966) draw together a wide variety of readings. T. N. Brewis *et al., Canadian Economic Policy*, rev. ed. (Toronto: Macmillan, 1965) is a collaborative work.

Because natural resources bulk especially large in the Canadian economy, one should note *Resources for Tomorrow*, issued by the Canadian Department of Northern Affairs and Natural Resources, 3 vols. (Ottawa: Queen's Printer, 1961, 1962); G. W. Wilson *et al., Canada: An Appraisal of Its Needs and Resources* (New York: Twentieth Century Fund, 1965); and Bernard Goodman, *Industrial Materials in Canadian American Relations* (Detroit: Wayne State University Press, 1961).

A standard historical treatment is W. T. Easterbrook and H. G. J. Aitken, *Canadian Economic History* (Toronto: Macmillan, 1956), soon to appear in a new edition. See also O. J. Firestone, *Canada's Economic Development, 1867-1953* (London: Bowes and Bowes, 1958).

Most works on the Canadian economy give prominence to the significance of American proximity. A study prepared for the Gordon Royal Commission on Canada's Economic Prospects is still of value: I. Brecher and S. S. Reisman, *Canada-United States Economic Relations* (Ottawa: Queen's Printer, 1957). H. G. J. Aitken has written, and edited, two useful books: *American Capital and Canadian Resources* (Cambridge, Mass.: Harvard University Press, 1961) and *The American Economic Impact on Canada* (Durham, N.C.: Duke University Press, 1959). The Canadian-American Committee, sponsored by the National Planning Association (U.S.A.) and the Private Planning Association of Canada, has published numerous short studies on economic relations between the two countries.

Canada's place in the North American, and the world, economy has provoked a good deal of spirited, even polemical, writing among economists in the last few years. See, for instance, Harry G. Johnson, *The Canadian Quandary: Economic Problems and Policies* (New York: McGraw-Hill, 1963) and J. H. Dales, *The Protective Tariff in Canada's Development* (Toronto: University of Toronto Press, 1967). On other topics see J. H. G. Crispo, *International Unionism in Canada: A Canadian-American Experiment* (Toronto: McGraw-Hill, 1966) and A. E. Safarian, *Foreign Ownership of Canadian Industry* (Toronto: McGraw-Hill, 1966).

Finally, on the present and the future, the federal government's Economic Council has since 1964 issued an *Annual Review* (Ottawa: Queen's Printer), and O. J. Firestone, *Problems of Economic Growth* (Ottawa: University of Ottawa Press, 1965) attempts economic projections for the period 1961-1991.

History of Canada — General

Of the longer one-volume general histories by professional historians one should note Donald Creighton, *A History of Canada: Dominion of the North* (Boston: Houghton Mifflin, 1958); W. L. Morton, *The Kingdom of Canada* (Indianapolis: Bobbs-Merrill, 1963); A. R. M. Lower, *Colony to Nation* (New York: Longmans, Green, 1958) and *Canadians in the Making* (Toronto: Longmans, 1958), the latter stressing social history; E. W. McInnis, *Canada: A Political and Social History* (New York: Rinehart, 1959) and J. B. Brebner's *Canada: A Modern History*, already mentioned.

Among books of an interpretative nature, Frank Underhill's *In Search of Canadian Liberalism* (Toronto: Macmillan, 1960) is social democratic in outlook, and G. P. de T. Glazebrook's *A History of Canadian Political Thought* (Toronto: McClelland and Stewart, 1966) is concerned with political activity and opinion rather than with formal speculation. K. A. MacKirdy, J. S. Moir, and Y. F. Zoltvany, eds., *Changing Perspectives in Canadian History: Selected Problems* (Toronto: J. M. Dent and Sons, 1967) provides brief extracts from a wide variety of Canadian historical writing. A brief introduction to the sources Canadian history is offered in the *Canadian Historical Documents Series*, 3 vols. (Toronto: Prentice-Hall, 1965, 1966).

An eighteen-volume history of Canada, *The Canadian Centenary Series* (Toronto: McClelland and Stewart, 1963–) is now being published, under the editorship of W. L. Morton and D. G. Creighton.

Mention should also be made of *The Carleton Library* (Toronto: McClelland and Stewart, 1963–), original and reprint paperback editions covering the fields of Canadian history, politics, law, economics, anthropology, sociology, geography, and journalism.

Canadian History before 1867

The first historian to bring the early history of Canada to the attention of a large reading public was Francis Parkman, in his *France and England in North America*, 9 vols. (Boston: Little Brown, 1865–1892); see also S. E. Morison's abridgement, *The Parkman Reader* (Boston: Little, Brown, 1955). Although Parkman has not been surpassed as a narrative historian, subsequent research and another century's perspective have done much to alter attitudes toward the French regime; see W. J. Eccles, *Canada under Louis XIV* (New York: Oxford University Press, 1964). A more traditional work, to 1763, is Gustave Lanctot, *A History of Canada*, 3 vols. (Cambridge, Mass.: Harvard University Press, 1963–1965); also, his *Canada and the American Revolution, 1774–1783* (Cambridge, Mass.: Harvard University Press, 1967).

The most recent general treatment of the post-Conquest generation is Hilda Neatby, *Quebec: The Revolutionary Age, 1760–1791* (Toronto: McClelland and Stewart, 1966). Fernand Ouellet's path-breaking *Histoire économique et sociale du Québec, 1760–1850* (Montreal: Fides, 1966) is to be translated into English. Helen Taft Manning's *The Revolt of French Canada, 1800–1835* (New York: St. Martin's Press, 1962) places Lower Canada in an imperial setting, and G. M. Craig, *Upper Canada: The Formative Years, 1784–1841)* (New York: Oxford University Press, 1963) examines American and British influences in that province. Probably the most influential work of the last generation has been Donald Creighton, *The Empire of the St. Lawrence* (Toronto: Macmillan, 1956; originally published in 1937 as *The Commercial Empire of the St. Lawrence, 1760–1850*).

Recent books on the War of 1812, from a Canadian point of view, are Morris Zaslow, ed., *The Defended Border: Upper Canada and the War of 1812* (Toronto: Macmillan, 1964) and J. Mackay Hitsman, *The Incredible War of 1812: A Military History* (Toronto: University of Toronto Press, 1965).

In the last few years the approach of Confederation in 1867 has been the subject of several excellent books, especially Donald Creighton,

The Road to Confederation: The Emergence of Canada, 1863–1867 (Boston: Houghton, Mifflin, 1865); P. B. Waite, *The Life and Times of Confederation, 1864–1867* (Toronto: University of Toronto Press, 1962); and W. L. Morton, *The Critical Years: The Union of British North America, 1857–1873* (Toronto: McClelland and Stewart, 1964).

On the eastern colonies, see W. S. MacNutt, *The Atlantic Provinces: The Emergence of Colonial Society, 1712–1857* (Toronto: McClelland and Stewart, 1965).

Canadian History since 1867

The most up-to-date and comprehensive account is J. M. S. Careless and R. Craig Brown, eds., *The Canadians, 1867–1967* (Toronto: Macmillan, 1967), in which thirty authors contribute essays on both chronological and topical themes.

Canada's role as a partner of Great Britain in overseas wars has been analyzed in the following books: Richard A. Preston, *Canada and "Imperial Defense" A Study of the Origins of the British Commonwealth's Defense Organization, 1867–1919* (Durham, N. C.: Duke University Press, 1967); Norman Penlington, *Canada and Imperialism, 1896–1899* (Toronto: University of Toronto Press, 1965); G. W. L. Nicholson, *Canadian Expeditionary Force, 1914-1919* (Ottawa: Queen's Printer, 1962); and the *Official History of the Canadian Army in the Second World War*, 3 vols. (Ottawa: Queen's Printer, 1955–1960), vols. I and III by C. P. Stacey and vol. II by G. W. L. Nicholson.

On a quite different theme, two books on recent voting patterns are John Meisel, *The Canadian General Election of 1957* (Toronto: University of Toronto Press, 1962) and Peter Regenstreif, *The Diefenbaker Interlude: Parties and Voting in Canada* (Toronto: Longmans, 1965).

Biography

Because much of the best work of Canadian historians in the last few years has been presented in the form of biographical studies, it is appropriate to make a separate list of some of the more important of these works. Men who held the post of prime minister have been the favorite subjects: Donald Creighton, *John A. Macdonald*, 2 vols. (Toronto: Macmillan, 1952, 1955), Joseph Schull, *Laurier: The First Canadian* (Toronto: Macmillan, 1965); the official biography of *William Lyon Mackenzie King* (Toronto: University of Toronto Press), vol. I (1874–1923) by R. M. Dawson (1958), vol. II (1924–1932) by Blair

Neatby (1963), and see Jack Pickersgill, *The Mackenzie King Record* (Toronto: University of Toronto Press, 1960); Roger Graham, *Arthur Meighen*, 3 vols. (Toronto: Clarke Irwin, 1960–1965); Peter Newman, *Renegade in Power: The Diefenbaker Years* (Toronto: McClelland and Stewart, 1963) and Bruce Hutchison, *Mr. Prime Minister, 1867–1964*, (Toronto: Longmans, 1964, condensed in 1967 as *Macdonald to Pearson*), the last two books by leading journalists.

Journalists have also been subjected to analysis, as in J. M. S. Careless, *Brown of the Globe*, 2 vols. (Toronto: Macmillan, 1959, 1963), and Ramsay Cook, *The Politics of John W. Dafoe and the "Free Press"* (Toronto: University of Toronto Press, 1963). Two books about men who never sat in the seats of power are G. F. G. Stanley, *Louis Riel* (Toronto: Ryerson Press, 1963), and Kenneth McNaught, *A Prophet in Politics: A Biography of J. S. Woodsworth* (Toronto: University of Toronto Press, 1959).

French Canada

Mason Wade, *The French Canadians, 1760–1945* (New York: Macmillan, 1955) is a comprehensive historical treatment, by a writer of American origin who also edited *Canadian Dualism: Studies of French-English Relations* (Toronto and Quebec: University of Toronto Press and les Presses de l'Université Laval, 1960), containing essays by some twenty authors.

Herbert F. Quinn, *The Union Nationale: A Study in Quebec Nationalism* (Toronto: University of Toronto Press, 1963) deals with the Duplessis era; two journalists' impressions of the "quiet revolution" are Peter Desbarats, *The State of Quebec* (Toronto: McClelland and Stewart, 1965) and Thomas Sloan, *Quebec: The Not-So-Quiet Revolution* (Toronto: Ryerson Press, 1965). Solange Chaput Rolland, *My Country, Canada or Quebec?* (Toronto: Macmillan, 1966) brings out some aspects of the continuing debate between the two language groups, and Ramsay Cook, *Canada and the French-Canadian Question* (Toronto: Macmillan, 1966) is a collection of penetrating essays.

Canadian Nationalism

Most of the writing on this subject has appeared in periodicals, but a few books may be mentioned. Vincent Massey, *Speaking of Canada* (Toronto: Macmillan, 1959) and *What's Past is Prologue* (Toronto: Macmillan, 1963) are by a former governor general; Walter L. Gordon,

A *Choice for Canada: Independence or Colonial Status* (Toronto: McClelland and Stewart, 1966) is by a former Canadian minister of finance; W. L. Morton, *The Candian Identity* (Madison: University of Wisconsin Press, 1961) and George Grant, *Lament for a Nation: The Defeat of Canadian Nationalism* (Toronto: McClelland and Stewart, 1965) are by professors. All these writers are apprehensive about American influences in Canada. The best single title on the subject is Peter B. Russell, ed., *Nationalism in Canada* (Toronto: McGraw-Hill, 1966), containing essays by twenty-two authors. Donald V. Smiley, *The Canadian Political Nationality* (Toronto: Methuen Publications, 1967) discusses the interactions between nationalism and federalism.

The United States and Canada—General

The standard historical accounts are now somewhat dated: Hugh L. Keenleyside and G. S. Brown, *Canada and the United States*, rev. ed. (New York: Knopf, 1952); J. M. Callahan, *American Foreign Policy in Canadian Relations* (New York: Macmillan, 1937); E. W. McInnis, *The Unguarded Frontier: A History of American-Canadian Relations* (Garden City, N.Y.: Doubleday, Doran, 1942); and the most influential of the group, J. B. Brebner, *North Atlantic Triangle: The Interplay of Canada, the United States and Great Britain* (New York: Columbia University Press, 1958, reprint of the original 1945 edition).

More recent accounts dealing with current issues are Joseph Barber, *Good Fences Make Good Neighbors: Why the United States Provokes Canadians* (Indianapolis: Bobbs-Merrill, 1958), by an American observer; John Sloan Dickey, ed., *The United States and Canada* (Englewood, N. J.: Spectrum, 1964); and Livingston T. Merchant, ed., *Neighbors Taken for Granted: Canada and the United States* (New York: Frederick A. Praeger, 1966), the last two being collections of essays. S. R. Tupper and D. L. Bailey, *Canada and the United States* (New York: Hawthorn Books Inc., 1967) also provides an American viewpoint.

United States and Canada—Various Topics

The most comprehensive treatment ever undertaken was in the series, "The Relations of Canada and the United States" sponsored by the Carnegie Endowment for International Peace, and published in the United States by Yale University Press, with James Shotwell as director. The twenty-five volumes appeared between 1936 and 1945; they are now out of print, although some have been reprinted by other publishers. Several titles remain the standard works on their subjects. On another level, the University of Windsor, Windsor, Ontario, has held an annual seminar since 1959 on Canadian-American relations, and the proceedings have been published annually, most recently by the University of Toronto Press.

On diplomatic relations, many of the standard works are in the Carnegie Series, mentioned above. An extensive collection of documents is W. R. Manning, ed., *Diplomatic Correspondence of the United States: Canadian Relations, 1784-1860*, 4 vols. (Washington: Carnegie Endowment for International Peace, 1940–1945). Some recent books on diplomatic relations, in whole or in part, are Frederick Merk, *The Oregon Question: Essays in Anglo-American Diplomacy and Politics* (Cambridge, Mass.: Harvard University Press, 1967); Robin W. Winks, *Canada and the United States: The Civil War Years* (Baltimore: The Johns Hopkins Press, 1960); J. O. McCabe, *The San Juan Boundary Question* (Toronto: University of Toronto Press, 1965).

On the west, John E. Parsons, *West on the 49th Parallel: Red River to the Rockies, 1872–1876* (New York: William Morrow & Co., 1963) narrates how the international boundary was fixed by British, Canadian, and American engineers, and Alvin C. Gluek, *Minnesota and the Manifest Destiny of the Canadian Northwest: A Study in Canadian-American Relations* (Toronto: University of Toronto Press, 1965) describes the activities of American expansionists. Annexationism in Canada is analyzed by Donald F. Warner, *The Idea of Continental Union: Agitation for the Annexation of Canada to the United States, 1849–1893* (Lexington: University of Kentucky Press, 1960). A book which deals with both political and economic relations is R. C. Brown, *Canada's National Policy, 1883–1900: A Study in Canadian-American Relations* (Princeton: Princeton University Press, 1964).

Cooperation along the boundary is treated in William R. Willoughby, *The St. Lawrence Waterway: A Study in Politics and Diplomacy* (Madison: University of Wisconsin Press, 1961); L. M. Bloomfield and G. F. Fitzgerald, *Boundary Waters Problems of Canada and the United States: The International Joint Commission, 1912-1958* (Toronto: Carswell, 1958); David R. Deener, ed., *Canada-United States Treaty Relations* (Durham: Duke University Press, 1963), and D. C. Piper, *The International Law of the Great Lakes: A Study of Canadian-United States Cooperation* (Durham: Duke University Press, 1967).

Stanley W. Dziuban, *Military Relations between the United States and Canada, 1939–1945* (Washington: G.P.O., 1959) and Stetson Conn and Byron Fairchild, *The Framework of Hemisphere Defense* (Washington: G.P.O., 1960) are two volumes in the "U.S. Army in World II" series. Among books on defense questions in recent years are Melvin Conant, *The Long Polar Watch: Canada and the Defense of North America* (New York: Harper and Brothers, 1962); Jon McLin, *Canada's Changing Defense Policy, 1957–1963* (Baltimore: The John Hopkins University Press, 1967); and Andrew Brewin, *Stand on Guard: The Search for a Canadian Defense Policy* (Toronto: McClelland and Stewart, 1965).

Alexander Smith, *The Commerce Power in Canada and the United States* (Toronto: Butterworth's, 1963) is a legal study.

Canada in World Affairs

A general history down to World War II is G. P. deT. Glazebrook, *A History of Canadian External Relations*, 2 vols. (Toronto: McClelland and Stewart, 1966, reprint).

The Canadian Institute of International Affairs, with headquarters in Toronto, provides a wide range of information. Since 1946 it has published a quarterly, *International Journal*, and it has published about a dozen volumes in the series *Canada in World Affairs*, each volume covering about two years in the post-1945 period.

One of Canada's leading students of external policy is James G. Eayrs; among his writings are *Northern Approaches: Canada and the Search for Peace* (Toronto: Macmillan, 1961); *The Art of the Possible: Government and Foreign Policy in Canada* (Toronto: University of Toronto Press, 1961); with H. L. Keenleyside and others, *The Growth of Canadian Policies in External Affairs* (Durham: Duke University Press, 1960): *In Defence of Canada*, 2 vols. (Toronto: University of Toronto Press, 1964, 1965). See also Peyton V. Lyon, *The Policy Question: A Critical Appraisal of Canada's Role in World Affairs* (Toronto: McClelland and Stewart, 1963).

James M. Minifie, *Peacemaker or Powder-Monkey: Canada's Role in a Revolutionary World* (Toronto: McClelland and Stewart, 1960) and *Open at the Top: Reflections on U.S.-Canada Relations* (Toronto: McClelland and Stewart, 1964) are by a journalist. J. King Gordon, ed., *Canada's Role as a Middle Power* (Toronto: Canadian Institute of International Affairs, 1966) is a collection of papers. See also J. K. Spicer, *A Samaritan State? External Aid in Canada's Foreign Policy* (Toronto: University of Toronto Press, 1966).

Index

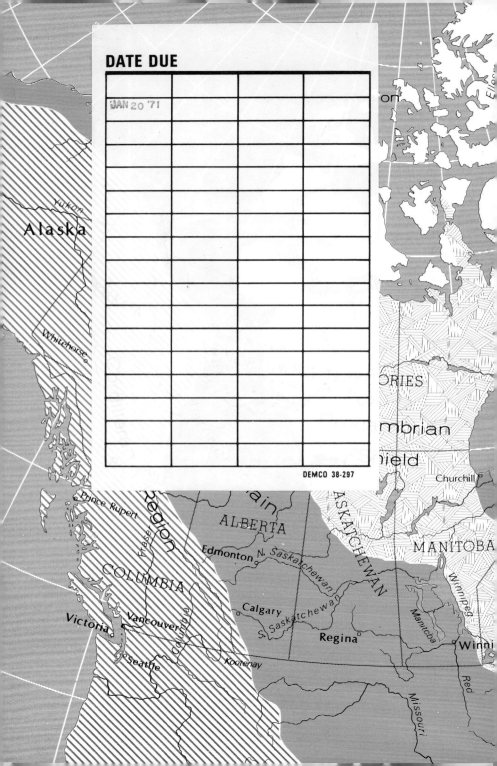